The Short Oxford History of Italy

The Nineteenth Century

The Short Oxford History of Italy

General Editor: John A. Davis

Italy in the Nineteenth Century
edited by John A. Davis

Italy since 1945
edited by Patrick McCarthy

The Short Oxford History of Italy

General Editor: John A. Davis

Italy in the Nineteenth Century 1796–1900

Edited by John A. Davis

OXFORD
UNIVERSITY PRESS

OXFORD
UNIVERSITY PRESS

Great Clarendon Street, Oxford OX2 6DP

Oxford University Press is a department of the University of Oxford.
It furthers the University's objective of excellence in research, scholarship,
and education by publishing worldwide in

Oxford New York

Athens Auckland Bangkok Bogotá Buenos Aires Calcutta
Cape Town Chennai Dar es Salaam Delhi Florence Hong Kong Istanbul
Karachi Kuala Lumpur Madrid Melbourne Mexico City Mumbai
Nairobi Paris São Paulo Shanghai Singapore Taipei Tokyo Toronto Warsaw

with associated companies in Berlin Ibadan

Oxford is a registered trade mark of Oxford University Press
in the UK and in certain other countries

Published in the United States
by Oxford University Press Inc., New York

British Library Cataloguing in Publication Data
Data available

Library of Congress Cataloging in Publication Data
Data available
ISBN 0–19–873128–0 (hbk)
ISBN 0–19–873127–2 (pbk)

10 9 8 7 6 5 4 3 2 1

Typeset in Minion
by RefineCatch Limited, Bungay, Suffolk
Printed in Great Britain by
T.J. International Ltd., Padstow, Cornwall

General Editor's Preface

Over the last three decades historians have begun to interpret Europe's past in new ways. In part this reflects changes within Europe itself, the declining importance of the individual European states in an increasingly global world, the moves towards closer political and economic integration amongst the European states, and Europe's rapidly changing relations with the non-European world. It also reflects broader intellectual changes rooted in the experience of the twentieth century that have brought new fields of historical inquiry into prominence and have radically changed the ways in which historians approach the past.

The new *Oxford Short History of Europe* series, of which this *Short History of Italy* is part, offers an important and timely opportunity to explore how the histories of the contemporary European national communities are being rewritten. Covering a chronological span from late antiquity to the present, the *Oxford Short History of Italy* is organized in seven volumes, to which over seventy specialists in different fields and periods of Italian history will contribute. Each volume will provide clear and concise accounts of how each period of Italy's history is currently being redefined, and their collective purpose is to show how an older perspective that reduced Italy's past to the quest of a nation for statehood and independence has now been displaced by different and new perspectives.

The fact that Italy's history has long been dominated by the modern nation-state and its origins simply reflects one particular variant on a pattern evident throughout Europe. When from the eighteenth century onwards Italian writers turned to the past to retrace the origins of their nation and its quest for independent nationhood, they were doing the same as their counterparts elsewhere in Europe. But their search for the nation imposed a periodization on Italy's past that has survived to the present, even if the original intent has been lost or redefined. Focusing their attention on those periods—the middle ages, the *Renaissance*, the *Risorgimento* that seemed to anticipate the modern, they carefully averted their gaze from those that did not—the Dark Ages, and the centuries of foreign occupation and conquest after the sack of Rome in 1527.

Paradoxically, this search for unity segmented Italy's past both chronologically and geographically, since those regions (notably the South) deemed to have contributed less to the quest for nationhood were also ignored. It also accentuated the discontinuities of Italian history caused by foreign conquest and invasion, so that Italy's successive rebirths—the *Renaissance* and the *Risorgimento*—came to symbolize all that was distinctive and exceptional in Italian history. Fascism then carried the cycle of triumph and disaster forward into the twentieth century, thereby adding to the conviction that Italy's history was exceptional, the belief that it was in some essential sense also deeply flawed. Post-war historians redrew Italy's past in bleaker terms, but used the same retrospective logic as before to link fascism to failings deeply rooted in Italy's recent and more distant past.

Seen from the end of the twentieth century this heavily retrospective reasoning appears anachronistic and inadequate. But although these older perspectives continue to find an afterlife in countless textbooks, they have been displaced by a more contemporary awareness that in both the present and the past the different European national communities have no single history, but instead many different histories.

The volumes in the *Short History of Italy* will show how Italy's history too is being rethought in these terms. Its new histories are being constructed around the political, cultural, religious and economic institutions from which Italy's history has drawn continuities that have outlasted changing fortunes of foreign conquest and invasion. In each period their focus is the peoples and societies that have inhabited the Italian peninsula, on the ways in which political organization, economic activity, social identities, and organization were shaped in the contexts and meanings of their own age.

These perspectives make possible a more comparative history, one that shows more clearly how Italy's history has been distinctive without being exceptional. They also enable us to write a history of Italians that is fuller and more continuous, recovering the previously 'forgotten' centuries and geographical regions while revising our understanding of those that are more familiar. In each period Italy's many different histories can also be positioned more closely in the constantly changing European and Mediterranean worlds of which Italians have always been part.

John A. Davis

Contents

List of Contributors

ANTHONY CARDOZA is Professor and Chairman of the Department of History at Loyola University of Chicago. He is the author of *Agrarian Elites and Italian Fascism* (1982) and *Aristocrats in Bourgeois Italy* (1997), for which he received the Marrarro Prize from the American Historical Association in 1998.

JOHN A. DAVIS holds the Emiliana Pasca Noether Chair in Modern Italian history at the University of Connecticut and is joint editor of the *Journal of Modern Italian Studies*. His books include *Conflict and Control: Law and Order in Nineteenth Century Italy* (1988) and *Economy and Society in Bourbon Naples 1815–1860* (1981).

CHRISTOPHER DUGGAN is Reader in Italian History at the University of Reading. His books include *Fascism and the Mafia* (1989) and *A Concise History of Italy* (1994). He is currently completing a biography of Francesco Crispi.

ALEXANDER GRAB teaches history at the University of Maine. He is the author of *La politica del pane: Le riforme annonarie in Lombardia nell'età teresiana e giuseppina* (1986), and numerous articles on Napoleonic Italy including 'Army, state and society: Conscription and desertion in Napoleonic Italy (1802–1814)', *The Journal of Modern History* (1995).

RAYMOND GREW is Professor of History Emeritus at the University of Michigan. He works primarily on French, Italian, and comparative history, publishing especially on nineteenth-century Italian history. His most recent book is an edited volume, *Food in Global History* (1999). In 2000 he received a citation for Career Achievement from the Society for Italian Historical Studies.

DAVID I. KERTZER is the Dupee University Professor of Social Science at Brown University, where he is also Professor of Anthropology and History. His most recent books include *Politics and Symbols—the Italian Communist Party and the Fall of Communism* (1996), and *The Kidnapping of Edgardo Mortara* (1997).

DAVID LAVEN is Lecturer in Modern European History at the University of Reading. He is currently completing a study on Habsburg rule of Venetia in the post-Napoleonic period, and writing a short history of Venice.

LUCY RIALL is Senior Lecturer in Modern European History at Birkbeck College, University of London. She is the author of *The Italian Risorgimento: State, Society and National Unification* (1994) and *Sicily and the Unification of Italy: Liberal Policy and Local Power, 1859–66* (1998), and is currently researching a study of family, land, and power in the Duchy of Bronte, 1799–1950.

ROLAND SARTI is Professor of History at the University of Massachusetts at Amherst. His publications include *Fascism and the Industrial Leadership in Italy, 1919–1940* (1971), *Long Live the Strong: A History of Rural Society in the Apennine Mountains* (1985), and *Mazzini: A Life for the Religion of Politics* (1997). He has served as department chair, President of the New England Historical Association and, currently, as President of the Society for Italian Historical Studies.

Introduction: Italy's difficult modernization

John A. Davis

Few political events caught the imagination of the nineteenth century more dramatically than the creation of an independent and unified state in Italy between 1859 and 1870. Yet in many respects Italy's unification was just another example of the emergence of new, and of the realignment of older, European states in the same period. Bismarck was forging the new German Reich in the same decades that Italy became a unified nation. Earlier in 1831 a new Kingdom of the Belgians had been created across the cultural and linguistic differences that divided Walloons, Flemings, and Germans, and in 1833 the Greeks had obtained independence from the Ottoman Empire. In the north, the Scandinavian rulers were inventing new national identities for their dynastic states, but so were older states like Britain and France.

Nonetheless, Italy's unification had special significance. The struggles for independence had forced an 'Italian Problem' on the reluctant attention of European statesmen from much earlier in the century, but few could have anticipated that these would result in both independence and unification. Yet Italy did not become unified because European statesmen decided to redraw political boundaries that had become anachronistic, nor had unification been imposed by one powerful state over others, as in the case of Germany. The role of the Piedmontese monarchy had been quite different from that of

Prussia, while Germany had no Mazzini and no Garibaldi either. Italy's unification, by contrast, seemed to be the result of a national revolution that had mobilized the energies of all Italians, irrespective of their political persuasions, around the goals of independence and unity. Even more impressive for contemporaries was the fact that this revolution had been accomplished without the social turmoil that had accompanied the European revolutions of 1848–49, and without political extremism. It was a revolution marked instead by heroic sacrifice, cooperation, and high-minded ideals that endorsed the validity of the principles of nationalism, liberalism, and secularism, making its heroes household names throughout Europe and beyond.

Italy's unification was symbolic of the modernity of a new Europe in another important respect. As well as reversing a history of political disunity as old as Christendom, it also brought to an end an institution that had been one of the foundations of the European political order since the earliest Middle Ages: the temporal dominions of the papacy. For that reason, many saw in Italy's unification both the close of the European *ancien régime* and the demise of Catholic Europe.

In religious and cultural terms the papacy had been one of the great unifying forces in Italian history, but geographically the Papal States separated the North from the South and cut Italy in two. The papal dominions still formed one of the largest Italian states in the nineteenth century, stretching north from Rome to the lower Po Valley, east to the Adriatic, and south to the frontiers of the Kingdom of Naples. But from the time of the Holy Roman emperors, the privilege of protecting the papacy had been contended among the leading European Catholic powers. As a result, Italy had rarely been free from foreign domination and the three-cornered contests between Spain, France, and Austria had left deep imprints on every aspect of its history.

Thanks to the protection of powerful foreign patrons the popes could afford to have the best-dressed army in Italy since it served mainly for show. This was still the case in the nineteenth century. The Papal States were invaded by French armies in 1798 and later briefly dismembered by Napoleon, but the victorious allies at the Congress of Vienna (1814–15) restored them to their fullest extent and made Austria their protector. Spain had long since dropped from contention, but France was not slow to resume the old rivalries.

Within a year of the establishment of the July Monarchy, the revolutions in central Italy in 1831 provided a pretext to station a French garrison in Ancona. French influence was further increased in March 1849 when the French Republic sent an army to crush the Roman Republic and restore Pope Pius IX. Louis Napoleon's proclamation of the Second Empire in 1852 marked the final round in France's attempts to wrest Continental hegemony from Austria, and, as had happened so many times before, this final struggle between the two great Catholic powers would be contested in Italy.

Secret alliance with France in 1859 made it possible for Piedmont to risk a second war against Austria in 1859 (the first had resulted in defeat in 1848 and again in 1849), but except for Nice and Savoy Napoleon III made no other territorial gains. This was due partly to the diplomatic agility of the Piedmontese statesman, Count Camillo Benso di Cavour, and partly also to the British who mobilized for war to prevent France regaining a foothold in Italy. Nevertheless, Austria's defeat made France the unchallenged protector of the pope and when Victor Emanuel II of Savoy, the former king of Sardinia and descendant of one of the oldest ruling dynasties in Europe, was proclaimed king of Italy in March 1861, Venetia remained under Austrian control while Rome and the remnants of the Papal State were still under French protection.

The new partition would prove unexpectedly short-lived. Germany's unification signalled a decisive shift in the fulcrum of European geo-politics, crippled the two Catholic powers that for centuries had dominated Italy's political history and finally removed the international guarantors of the integrity of the Papal State. In 1866 the Venetian territories passed to Italy following the Prussian victory over Austria, and Napoleon III's defeat at the battle of Sedan finally made it possible for Italian *bersaglieri* to enter the Eternal City on 20 September 1870.

When Pope Pius IX and his cardinals withdrew across the River Tiber to the Vatican a millennium of papal temporal rule came to an end, adding to the epic stature of Italy's struggles for independence and making the new Italy the embodiment of the secular values of a new Europe. If Italy's heroes were celebrated by nationalists everywhere, it was no accident that they found their most enthusiastic acclaim in the Protestant world where Italian unification signified the collapse of the political power of the papacy.

Representation and reality were freely interwoven in these contemporary perceptions. The bitter political and social upheavals that had accompanied the Italian struggles for independence were neatly written out of the script, while unification retrospectively became their long-standing goal. But contemporaries were right when they linked Italy's unification to the broader forces that were changing the face of European politics, shifting power to the nations that were the epicentres of the new industrial economies and transforming the political, economic, and cultural institutions of the *ancien régime* world. What was being described from as early as the 1840s as the age of Italy's *Risorgimento*, or 'rebirth', was in essence Italy's appointment with modernity.

The attempts to achieve political change within the Italian states were inseparable from the broader changes that were taking place in Italian society, and in its political, economic, and cultural institutions. But although the struggles for independence from Austria were an extension of the attempts to win political change within the existing states, opposition to Austria never offered a platform capable of reconciling the differences between moderates and radicals, monarchists and democrats, federalists and supporters of a unified Italian state. Many Italians came to accept that without independence there could be no political change in the existing states, but the form an independent Italy might take was always more vague and contentious. Mazzini's vision of a single democratic republic was not only considered dangerously subversive by moderates, but was also viewed with suspicion by many democrats. Not all republicans supported the idea that independence should lead to unification, while Carlo Cattaneo and Giuseppe Ferrari argued that the federal governments of the Swiss cantons and America's United States were models better suited to the diversity of Italy and its peoples.

These political confrontations engaged the energies of only a tiny minority of Italians, however, and were never more than one dimension of the broader crisis that resulted in Italy's unification. Popular unrest and social tensions were no less important and were driven by the chronic insecurity, unemployment, and hardship that new forces of change were bringing to rural Italy and hence to the overwhelming majority of Italians. In contrast to the reformers, who sought to accelerate the pace of those changes, much of rural Italy was engaged in desperate struggles to resist these new and threatening forces.

Popular unrest and the political discontents of the propertied and educated elites frequently crossed paths, but were separated by contradictory aims and an abyss of incomprehension. Yet both had common roots in the broader forces of modernization that were transforming the economic, cultural, and political worlds of the European *ancien régime*. The pre-unification Italian states were inevitably confronted by the same forces, but their economic and political circumstances also made it certain that Italy's encounter with modernity would occur on particularly contradictory and divisive terms.

The challenges of modernity: the eighteenth century

The contours of Italy's difficult modernization were already visible by the end of the eighteenth century. The wealthy foreign travellers who flocked to Italy on the itineraries of the Grand Tour to admire the wonders of antiquity and nature were heralds of the new forms of wealth and consumption, new cultural values and tastes that else-where were already transforming the closed and corporate world of the European *ancien régime*.

The impact of the new was felt most deeply in the rural world, and the fact that Italy was initially far removed from the heartlands of the new economic order did not make the forces of modernization less disruptive. New commercial incentives brought instability and pre-cariousness to the rural world, and as private property expanded and common lands were enclosed the slender resources on which the survival of rural communities depended came under threat. These losses were exacerbated by unprecedented rates of population growth, giving rise to the acute land-hunger that became the most persistent cause of rural discontent.

The changes taking place elsewhere in Europe also faced Italy's eighteenth-century rulers with pressing new challenges. The impetus for reform was strongest in the Austrian lands—the former Duchy of Milan covering most of Lombardy—and in the principal dynastic states: the Kingdom of Sardinia, the Grand Duchy of Tuscany, and the Kingdom of Naples and Sicily that after centuries of Spanish rule had become an independent monarchy in 1734. In each case, the rulers looked to reduce the privileges and exemptions that sheltered the wealthiest social groups and institutions from taxation, and to replace the devolved jurisdictions of the *ancien régime* with new forms of rationalized, centralized, and absolutist bureaucracy. Where dynastic imperatives did not exist—in the old republics of Venice and Genoa, in the smaller duchies and principalities, and in the temporal dominions of the Roman pontiff—incentives for reform were necessarily much weaker.

As in France and Austria, these initiatives provoked fierce resistance from the privileged orders of the *ancien régime* whose interests were most at risk: the nobility, the Church, the religious orders, the papacy, and powerful lay corporations. But the cultural and intellectual energies that had been released by the modernizing initiatives of the rulers were also signs of profound changes in Italian society. The Enlightenment was more than a chapter in intellectual history, and the lively public debates that accompanied the reform initiatives of the Italian rulers signalled the emergence of new forms of public opinion that would prove deeply subversive of the closed corporate worlds of the *ancien régime*. A new generation of philosophers, economists, and publicists rallied to the rulers' reform initiatives, presenting themselves as partners in a modernizing mission whose aim was to emancipate the forces of material and cultural development from the corporate shackles of the *ancien régime*.

The aspiration to achieve more autonomous forms of civil society was a central theme of the debates and publications that made Milan, Florence, Turin, and Naples important centres of the European Enlightenment in the 1770s and 1780s. In the following century that aspiration would also be the principal inspiration of the *Risorgimento*. But the crisis that struck the *ancien régime* states in the closing decade of the eighteenth century indicated that the realization of this project would be divisive, dangerous, and difficult.

The impact of the French Revolution and Napoleon

The French Revolution and its aftermath profoundly and irrevers-ibly changed the political and cultural contexts of modernization in Italy. The year 1789 marked the close of an unprecedented period of peace and relative political independence for the Italian states and the opening of a new era of political upheaval, foreign invasion, and occupation that would last until the fall of Napoleon's empire in 1814.

The short-lived Italian republics of 1796–99 were the gravediggers of the *ancien régime* in Italy, and in the following period of direct and indirect French rule the reforms left unfinished by the eighteenth-century rulers were completed. The *ancien régime* principalities were transformed into centralized, bureaucratic autocracies. Feudalism and all forms of independent jurisdiction were abolished, the abso-lute sovereignty of the state was asserted, fiscal and financial adminis-tration was centralized and rationalized. To finance these reforms and to refloat the debts of *ancien régime* rulers, vast tracts of former crown and Church lands were sold. Together with more energetic intervention to promote the privatization of land, to improve agri-culture, and to encourage the development of new industries and manufactures, these measures accelerated the pace of economic change but also heightened the social costs of modernization.

The Revolution also brought new political vocabularies to Italy, and the 'patriots' who rallied to the Italian republics of 1796–99 were the first to appeal to the principles of popular sovereignty and democracy. Their language contrasted with that of the eighteenth-century reformers who had entrusted the mission of modernity and progress to enlightened rulers. But these radical voices would soon be silenced in the more authoritarian climate of Napoleon's political resettlement of Italy after 1800. The modernizing features of French rule at first attracted wide support, but as the autocratic realities of the Napoleonic states became evident and the burdens imposed on Italy by the emperor's insatiable demands for taxes, men, and *matériel* to support France's imperial enterprise grew heavier, disaffection spread amongst both the poor and the propertied classes.

For the first time political discontent would focus around the demands for constitutional government which were channelled through the secret societies that multiplied in the closing years of Napoleonic rule. The call for political representation voiced the heterogeneous discontents of aristocrats resentful at the loss of former privileges, as well as the aspirations of the emergent propertied and professional classes to acquire a public voice of their own. Like the democrats, the advocates of constitutional government also spoke a European language. They took their models from the liberal opponents of Napoleonic autocracy in France, but they were especially attracted to the explicitly nationalist constitutional project that had been drafted by Spanish liberals at Cadiz in 1812.

Subordination to the French Empire for the first time linked the issues of political reform and independence and gave nationalism a new political focus. But nationalism was not new, and from much earlier times there had been a clearly defined sense of the shared cultural and historical identities derived from language and custom, from ways of dressing and eating, forms of recreation, and of religiosity that made Italians distinctive. These might vary from region to region, but they formed a cultural matrix that distinguished Italians from others.[1]

In the eighteenth century nationalism had acquired sharper political overtones, but its focus was primarily the dynastic state as historians, jurists, philosophers, and economists competed to adorn the dynastic rulers with national attributes. The 'patriots' of 1796–99 were the first to link nationalism to a more ambitious goal of political unification when they called for the creation of an independent Italian republic, 'single and indivisible' like its French sister. In doing so they established an association between unification and political extremism, however, that discredited the project in the eyes of more moderate nationalists. For them, independence continued to mean regaining the autonomy already enjoyed by the eighteenth-century Italian rulers.

---

[1] See E. Galli della Loggia, *L'identità italiana* (Bologna, 1998); A. Schiavone, *Italiani senza Italia: storia ed identità* (Einaudi, 1998) and R. Romano, *Paese Italia* (Rome, 1994).

Restoration Italy

Hopes that the fall of Napoleon might have restored the independence of the *ancien régime* rulers and introduced some new form of
power-sharing with the propertied classes were dashed when the
Congress of Vienna assigned to Austria the role recently vacated by
France. The aim was to prevent France regaining a foothold on the
peninsula, and at the same time to stamp out the ideas and political
principles that had brought revolution and turmoil to Europe for
three decades. Austria ruled directly only in the newly formed Kingdom of Lombardy-Venetia, but from the impregnable fortresses of
the Quadrilateral in the central Po Valley Austrian bayonets could
reach any part of Italy. Military might was reinforced by networks of
diplomatic and dynastic alliances that made Vienna the power
behind every Italian throne and every Italian ruler either cousin or
client of the Habsburg monarchy.

Austria was the dominant, but not the only foreign power in Italy,
and despite the intentions of the allies France recovered a foothold
following the revolutions of 1831 in the Papal States. But after 1814
Great Britain was also an important presence. The defeat of
Napoleon's fleet at the Battle of the Nile (1798) and the later
acquisition of the island of Malta had made Britain the dominant
naval power in the Mediterranean, a region that had assumed critical
strategic importance because of its position on the lines of communication with Britain's rapidly expanding empire in the east. This,
together with rapidly expanding commercial contacts, gave British
governments a close interest in Italian politics. But although by the
1840s Italian liberals and nationalists would find a strong ally in
British public opinion, down to 1860 successive British governments
continued to view Austria as the best safeguard against French
attempts to regain political influence in Italy.

The system of alliances established at the Congress of Vienna
locked the Italian states into the hold of the Habsburg monarchy, and
for so long as those alliances remained in force there was little chance
of political change. But while the terms of the Restoration settlement
made political change less likely, they also intensified the pressures
for change. The allies had restored the Italian legitimist rulers, but

had made no attempt to restore the *ancien régime.* The new absolutist bureaucracies were not only retained but also considerably enlarged. The Austrian Kingdom of Lombardy-Venetia in northern Italy included the lands of the former Republic of Venice, while the Kingdom of Sardinia was significantly extended by the inclusion of the former Republic of Genoa. The papal dominions were restored to their fullest extent, while in the South no sooner had the Bourbon monarchy regained its throne than it arbitrarily terminated Sicily's centuries-old status as a separate crown and imposed administrative union with the proclamation of a unified Kingdom of the Two Sicilies in 1816.

The enlargement and centralization of the Restoration states overrode local, regional, and municipal autonomies and was a cause of persistent conflict. The revolutionary upheavals of 1820–21, 1831, and 1848–49 would all be dominated by the rivalries that set Genoa against Turin, the Venetian cities of the Terraferma against Venice, the papal Legation cities, and especially Bologna and Ancona, against Rome, Livorno against Florence, the provincial centres of the southern mainland (Mezzogiorno), and above all Sicily, against Naples. Behind these apparently localized conflicts could be clearly heard the voices of the provincial and municipal elites whose aspirations to regain control over local administration and local affairs swelled the pressure for political representation and constitutional government.

Nothing revealed more clearly the contradictions on which the Restoration autocracies were based than the failure to find ways of accommodating these centrifugal forces. That failure would lead to the internal collapse of two of the largest states in Italy, the pope's temporal dominions and the Bourbon Kingdom of the Two Sicilies, whose rapid disintegration in the wake of Austria's defeat in 1859 were primarily responsible for bringing about Italy's political unification.

Nor could the Restoration formula offer solutions to the tensions that were bringing distress and unrest to rural Italy. Though the Restoration rulers might wish to mitigate the pace of economic modernization, they could no more opt out of modernization than could their eighteenth-century predecessors. On the contrary, the accelerating pace of change elsewhere in Europe made dynastic survival more dependent than ever on economic growth: the Restoration rulers could turn their backs on the economic development of their states only at the risk of their own dynastic self-interest. This proved a fatal contradiction, and as the rulers looked for ways to promote economic growth without making concessions to greater political or cultural freedoms their policies became increasing contradictory and confused.

These contradictions could no longer be disguised once the European economy entered a new phase of buoyant expansion in the 1830s. Events outside Italy gave new force to pressures for political reform, since both the July Monarchy of 1830 in France and the political reorganization that followed the Great Reform Act of 1832 in England now offered models of political change achieved without social revolution. In both cases change had been highly conservative, but had opened the way to new administrative responses to the pressing challenges of the age. The new public debates on pauperism and its remedies, on crime and its repression, on public health, and the role of science and medicine that had accompanied these innovations also demonstrated that effective government could only be achieved in partnership with the practical, technical, professional, and scientific resources that only an independent civil society could provide. The first terrible outbreaks of cholera that struck Italy in the 1830s were further proof that the Restoration autocracies could neither inoculate Italy from the new challenges nor provide adequate responses to them.

Within Italy the new models of material and cultural progress were taken up most enthusiastically by the generation that had grown up since the Restoration. But Europe offered many alternative political models and while both the radicals and moderates translated these into terms that fitted Italian institutions and culture more closely, the divisions between them became more polarized. The former found in Romanticism a language that gave nationalism a new mystical and populist force, while moderates looked instead to the *juste milieu* embodied by the July Monarchy in France.

Renewed pressure for political change made the issue of independence once again central. But independence was never just a matter of reducing Austria's interference in the internal affairs of the Italian states. It also meant removing the political powers exercised by the papacy and the extensive civil jurisdictions still enjoyed by the Church. For the radicals, with the exception of Mazzini, this most typically took the form of strident anticlericalism. But the idea that there could be no real independence for civil society without a radical redrawing of the boundaries between spiritual and secular authority was also at the heart of the moderate programme, and would find its clearest statement a decade later in Cavour's call for a free Church in a free state.

The contrasts between moderates and radicals became greater, however, when the economic boom gave way to the first great cyclical crisis of the European economies. The devastating unemployment, famine, bank failures, and commercial stagnation of the 'Hungry Forties' brought renewed social unrest, raising apprehensions of impending disaster among the propertied classes and creating fertile ground for the conspiracies and insurrections of the radicals.

Against this background the moderates now appealed openly to the rulers to make political concessions to forestall the threat of revolution. In contrast to the revolutionaries, they believed that independence and political change could be achieved by negotiation and without revolution by means of the moral persuasion exercised by the new force of informed public opinion—what Massimo d'Azeglio described in 1847 as a 'conspiracy in open daylight'.

This explains the enthusiasm aroused throughout Italy by the election in 1846 of Pope Pius IX, who was widely believed to be sympathetic to the cause of reform. But these expectations rapidly led to the virtual collapse of papal government, and the disorders spilled over into neighbouring Tuscany. They became more widespread when a revolt in Palermo in January 1848 panicked the Bourbon government into offering narrow constitutional concessions in the hope of staving off further upheaval.

The revolutions that followed in Paris in February and in Vienna in March extended the crisis to the whole of Italy. But if the Italian revolutions of 1848–49 were a result of the social unrest and political uncertainty that gripped the entire Continent, the political upheavals that followed again revealed the divisive impact of modernization on every aspect of Italian society. Moderates and radicals fought out their rival political programmes against a backdrop of violent social conflicts that fractured along class lines and around the centrifugal forces of local and regional separatism.

Attempts to organize collective resistance against Austria foundered on these fierce internal divisions, demonstrating that independence was a programme too vague and contentious to reconcile contradictory social and political discontents. Nonetheless, the revolutions utterly changed the political situation in Italy and the restoration of the Italian rulers in 1849 offered no new solutions to the political and social conflicts exposed by the revolutions, leaving them even more heavily dependent on Austria than before. This would prove fatal, however, since Austria's triumph in 1849 could not disguise the damage that the revolutions had caused the Habsburg monarchy, whose political decline was first revealed in the diplomatic isolation that followed the Crimean War (1854–56).

The 1850s: Piedmont's new role in Italian and European politics

Even before the weakness of the Habsburg monarchy became evident, the consolidation of a constitutional monarchy in Piedmont had transformed the political situation in Italy. The alliance between the monarchy and the Piedmontese liberals had been the result of parallel rather than convergent interests and was driven by the dynastic ambitions of Piedmontese rulers. Neither Charles Albert nor Victor Emanuel had any instinctive sympathy for liberalism; both were reluctant to surrender power, but both understood that the nationalist cause gave legitimacy to the dynasty's older expansionist ambitions. Even more important was the fact that the liberals and nationalists would support an expansionist policy, whereas the monarchy's conservative supporters opposed conflict either with Austria or with the papacy.

The liberals had been relatively weak in Piedmont before 1848, but their influence grew once Cavour's reforms made Piedmont the most dynamic economy in Italy in the 1850s. Political refugees from all over Italy flooded into Turin where their presence strengthened the liberals and nationalists and transformed the House of Savoy into a national monarchy even before the war of 1859.

No other Italian rulers could have followed the lead taken by the Piedmontese monarchy for the simple reason that the Kingdom of Sardinia was the only Italian state to enjoy a real degree of diplomatic security. The possessions of the House of Savoy had grown over the centuries because geography made it a natural buffer between Austria and France. The Congress of Vienna was only the most recent example of how the leading powers had sought to extend the Piedmontese kingdom at every successive European peace settlement in order to strengthen that buffer. The knowledge that even military defeat would not put the integrity of their kingdom at risk made it possible for the Piedmontese monarchy to pursue an independent dynastic policy. This was why Charles Albert had been able to renew the war against Austria in February 1849 even though the outcome was almost certain defeat. It was the same knowledge that enabled his son, Victor Emanuel II, to raise the standard of the House of Savoy against Austria in 1859.

The new political and economic conditions in Piedmont increased the pressures for political change in the other Italian states, but the other Italian rulers were too dependent on Austria to follow the Piedmontese lead. Lacking the dynastic security of the House of Savoy, they had no alternative but to trust in Austrian protection. They could not take up the nationalist cause against Austria, nor could they make political concessions to their own people, and the savage reprisals and purges that followed the collapse of the revolutions made any new political dialogue almost impossible. But there were deeper obstacles to political reform. In the Papal States Pius IX could not compromise temporal rule without jeopardizing the papacy's political influence in other states, while any concessions would have revived the demands for autonomy in the Legation cities. In the South, the strength of Sicilian separatism and the pressure for greater autonomy in the mainland provinces also ruled out political concessions.

The new constitutional government in Piedmont and the signs that Vienna's grip on Italy was slackening confronted the papal government and the Bourbon Kingdom of the South with an endgame. But the political outcome of Austria's defeat in 1859 was not pre-ordained and political fortunes vacillated unpredictably for eighteen months. By the spring of 1860, following the cession of Nice and Savoy to France, it seemed that the outcome would be an enlarged Piedmontese state in northern and central Italy embracing Lombardy, the central duchies, Tuscany, and the northern provinces of the Papal State. But this was thrown into question when, in May, Garibaldi's expedition triggered Sicily's third and finally successful separatist revolt against Naples and caused the break-up of the Bourbon monarchy.

If realized, Garibaldi's declared intention of invading the territories that remained under papal rule and liberating Rome risked provoking French intervention in defence of the pope that might easily have triggered a general European war. But by now the radical nationalists had no clear plan and their position was being weakened by the violent unrest that was spreading through Sicily and the Mezzogiorno after Garibaldi reneged on the promises of agrarian reform that had initially rallied the peasants to the nationalist cause. Cavour's decision in September 1860 to block Garibaldi's advance by sending an army led by Victor Emanuel through the Papal States risked civil war, which was averted only when Garibaldi loyally surrendered his command to the king. The nationalists had helped extend the process of political reorganization, but Cavour and the Piedmontese monarchy had won the ultimate political battles.

The new Italy: unity and division

Once achieved, it was easy to assume that unification had always been the goal of the preceding political and social upheavals, and the *Risorgimento* was interpreted simply as a confrontation between rival political platforms. Much of the history of liberal Italy has been written in the same confrontational terms, which were accentuated by the crisis of parliamentary government in Italy after the First World War. Under the shadow of fascism, many historians turned to the shortcomings of the *Risorgimento* to explain the roots of Mussolini's dictatorship.

The idea that unification had been a 'failed revolution' owed much to the Italian communist leader and intellectual, Antonio Gramsci, whose reflections on Italian history (written clandestinely in fascist jails before his death in 1937) were premised on the idea that Italy had never experienced a modern capitalist revolution. The *Risorgimento* bourgeoisie had been too weak to carry through a political revolution without the assistance of the reactionary Piedmontese monarchy and the pre-modern landowning classes. These compromises, Gramsci argued, resulted in a form of capitalist revolution that was incomplete and flawed in ways that prevented the development of a more open bourgeois democracy in Italy. As a result, both parliamentary liberalism and organized labour were left fatally exposed to the fascist counter-revolution in the twentieth century. Non-Marxist historians were equally insistent on the political shortcomings of unification, and argued that the governing classes of the new state had lacked the commitment to the values of political or economic liberalism needed to create a modern nation-state.

These perspectives now seem too narrow to explain either fascism or Italy's long history since fascism, since they reduce the nineteenth century to a one-way highway running unerringly from unification to Mussolini. The complex historical forces that had converged to bring about Italy's unification are stripped down to a simpler political revolution, which is judged to be a 'failure' by comparison with abstract models that have no clear historical bearings but imply that there was some fatal flaw in Italian society that prevented Italy becoming a modern state.

Unification was not a completely fresh start, despite what these interpretations suggest. Unification did give rise to a political revolution, but this was also partly the result of those broader processes of change that had transformed the pre-unification states and which would continue to shape the development of the new state. The new state offered a new political framework within which to confront the challenges of modernization, but neither the pace nor the intensity of those forces would slacken and Italy's experience of modernization would be no easier after than before unification.

The continuing challenges of economic modernization

As had occurred in Piedmont in the 1850s, the new liberal order gave fresh impetus to economic development, but as in the past economic change had at least two faces. If one was the emergence of a new industrial economy in the north-western regions by the end of the century, the other was the destructive impact of modernization on the older sectors of agrarian society, which in many cases intensified and became more devastating in the decades after unification.

The relative weakness of the Italian economy, its scarce resources, and the poverty of the vast masses of the Italian population ensured that Italy's modernization would continue to be difficult and dangerous. This was brutally revealed by the European agricultural depression of the 1880s that brought ruin to thousands of small farms and provoked the first waves of overseas emigration that in the following decade become a mass phenomenon, as hundreds and thousands of impoverished Sicilians and southerners crossed the Atlantic in search of work. At precisely the same time, the expansion of more modern and intensive capitalist farming in the lower Po Valley provoked new social conflicts as the landless rural labourers (*braccianti*) began to organize collectively and embrace revolutionary socialism. In the northern cities, where new industrial enterprises were beginning to multiply, a new and militant industrial labour force had also become a reality.

The crisis of the older sectors of the economy and the development of more modern ones were taking place just as the international economy entered a new phase of more intensive industrialization and increasingly aggressive forms of international competition as the brief era of free trade gave way to protectionism in the 1880s. These developments left the weaker economies highly exposed to the devastating and unpredictable swings of international boom and recession.

The relatively weak and disadvantaged terms on which Italy confronted the challenges of economic modernization ensured that the political life of the new state would not be tranquil. It was no accident that its most severe political crises coincided with periods of major international recession, the first starting in the 1880s with the European agricultural depression that ran through to the following decade, and the second with the pre-First World War international recession that opened 1907, bringing to an end the decade of Italy's first 'economic miracle'.

The state and the nation

The political development of the new state was made more difficult by the narrowness of the classes whose interests it most directly represented. At the time of unification barely 2% of Italians had been qualified by property or education to vote in the election of the first Italian parliament. This was not evidence that unification had been a 'failed revolution', however, but an accurate snapshot of the poverty in Italian society. Half a century later the situation was very different and although manhood suffrage was not introduced until 1911, the gap with Italy's neighbours had shrunk by 1900. The suffrage for local elections had been large from much earlier, and in 1888 was extended to all literate males.

The new political order was confronted by powerful opponents, however. Its legitimacy was challenged by democrats like Mazzini who denounced the conservative constitutional monarchy as a betrayal of the high ideals of the nationalists who had dreamed of creating a new Rome of the People in the place of the Rome of the Popes and the Caesars. In the 1870s the anarchists gave that opposition more overtly revolutionary tones, which grew stronger in the following decade when revolutionary socialism proved the most effective voice of popular political discontent, culminating in the founding of the Italian Socialist Party in 1892. But the new state was also under attack from conservatives who rejected the narrow interests of its ruling class and the modernizing and secular values it embraced. The latter were also the target of ringing denunciations from the Vatican, which refused to acknowledge the legitimacy of the new state or to call on Catholics to participate in it. By the close of the century a new generation of nationalists was also decrying Italy's spiritual and material shortcomings.

These political conflicts were not peculiar to Italy, however, and in the shadow of the Paris Commune of 1871 fears of social revolution haunted bourgeois Europe. If the governments of liberal Italy made frequent and even systematic use of measures that overrode basic constitutional liberties, neither France nor Germany hesitated to employ similar measures against those identified as enemies of the social and political order. By the end of the century, the denunciations of the anti-liberal right were certainly no more strident in Italy than in France. The conflict between the Church and state was also part of a broader European pattern, and in this respect too liberal Italy followed a similar path to the French Third Republic. For both liberals and democrats in Italy, however, the strength of clerical influence over the rural population continued to be a powerful argument against extending the popular suffrage.

Despite these conflicts the unification of the new state in many ways proved less problematic than might have been expected. In part this reflected the relative cultural homogeneity of Italian society, and in sharp contrast to many older European states Italy was virtually free of ethnic or religious differences. The small ethnic and religious minorities that did exist—the Protestant Valdensians in Piedmont, the small Jewish communities in northern and central Italy, the Greek Orthodox and Albanian communities in the Mezzogiorno and Sicily—had been amongst the most active supporters of the *Risorgimento* ideals of civil liberty and religious toleration and were strongly committed to the new order.

Cultural homogeneity also facilitated the construction of new national identities. The myth of the *Risorgimento* played an important part in this and was endlessly celebrated in art, literature, and architecture, and the strategies adopted to promote the cults of civic patriotism differed little from those of other European states. The rapidly growing middle classes were vectors for a national culture that coexisted easily with regional or municipal identities, while the expansion of schooling and literacy extended this national culture to the urban petite bourgeoisie and sections of the working classes as well. As elsewhere in Europe, military service, conscription, and veterans associations all reinforced patriotic idioms and national identity. Even the most committed enemies of the liberal order accepted the sanctity of the nation: revolutionary socialists sought to realize the ideals of the *Risorgimento* by democratizing, not destroying the nation, while even the Catholic Church came to stake a claim to be its true voice.[2]

Many Italians did indeed remain distant from the new nation: the mountain populations, Sardinia, much of Sicily, and most of rural

---

[2] The most recent survey of the literature on Italy's national identities is E. Gentile, *La Grande Italia. Ascsesa a declino del mito nazionale nel ventesimo secolo* (Milan, 1997).

Italy. But this was not unusual in an age when most French peasants had yet to think of themselves as Frenchmen.[3] For most of its citizens, by contrast, the new Italy was remarkably familiar. Its administrative institutions were inherited from the former states, and Italians continued to wait in the same offices to pay their taxes and to obtain the permits and licenses that were the indispensable record of every change in social status from birth to death, every change in residence, every legal and commercial transaction.

If these institutions were familiar, however, the relative poverty of the new state was especially evident in the functional shortcomings of public administration. Cost and the absence of a professionally trained civil service comparable to those of France, Britain, or the new German Reich were major obstacles to the modernization of public administration. This critically reduced the effectiveness of state intervention in areas like education, public health, and welfare, where the influence of the Church and local notables remained strong. The emergence of new forms of 'mass society' towards the close of the century would make these weaknesses more evident, contributing to the belief that there was a wide gap separating the state from the nation.[4]

The liberal political order and the role of the South

Effective new political sinews were being grafted onto these old bureaucracies, however. As in the French Third Republic, parliamentary politics functioned through forms of political exchange that contemporaries described as *trasformismo*, by which government ministers brokered individual or collective favours in exchange for votes. As in France, this inhibited the development of broader political parties but offered a means of communicating with a multitude

---

[3] Cf. E. Weber, *Peasants into Frenchmen: The Modernization of Rural France 1870–1914* (Stanford, 1976).

[4] See S. Cassese, *Lo Stato Introvabile. Modernità e arretratteza delle istituzioni italiane* (Donzelli, Roma, 1998). See also: P. Ginsborg, *A History of Contempory Italy: Society and Politics 1943–1988* (Penguin Books (London 1990), esp. pp. 145–7).

of different and often regionally based interest groups. Despite the highly centralized form of administration adopted at the time of unification, in practice this proved to be an effective basis for dialogue between central government and local elites.

The cohesiveness of the political system that took shape in the first decades after unification can be measured by the decline of the separatist forces that had played a major role in the collapse of the preunification states. Despite the violence in the South after unification and the best efforts of the exiled Bourbon court in Rome, social unrest on the mainland never give rise to a popular royalist Vendée, while the Palermo revolt of 1866 proved to be the last serious expression of Sicilian separatism.

The most important change came a decade later when the southern deputies emerged as the most biddable group in the Italian parliament and the surest guarantee of a government majority. The political role of the southern parliamentary deputies was inseparable from the economic and social backwardness of the southern provinces that made the small southern electorate easy to control and broker. The backwardness of the South and the absence of any popular political movements or forms of collective organization proved to be a political asset whose value increased exponentially as economic and social change made the northern electorates more independent.

This made the southern deputies indispensable political partners, and that partnership came to be the basis for a conservative strategy of modernization. The southern deputies traded their votes for political favours that strengthened their own standing, but did not oppose measures that diverted resources from the South as a whole to finance public expenditure and infrastructural developments in the North. As a result, the population of the South bore the heaviest burdens of Italy's modernization.

The discovery that there were 'Two Italies' caused growing concern, much of which was directed against southerners in general who, like the Irish in Victorian Britain, were identified as the authors of their own misfortunes. Yet the different paths of economic and social development followed by the North and South constituted the mechanism by which Italy achieved economic development and political unification. But the continuing under-development of the South perpetuated the power of the southern elites, whose costs were measured in the poverty of the southern population, the massive emigrations that began in the 1890s, and the absence of new forms of economic activity or political organization. Nor were contemporaries slow to grasp that the political power of the southern elites was a formidable obstacle for the new political forces emerging in the North as well.

The interdependence of North and South proved to be one of the most enduring features of Italian politics down to the end of the twentieth century. This, too, was only one example of a range of European conservative strategies of modernization, however, and forms of internal colonization were found in nearly all the nineteenth-century industrializing nations. What made the unequal North–South relationship in Italy unusual was not even its political dimensions, but rather its longevity, which in turn reflected the continuing narrowness of the resources on which Italy sought to sustain the imperatives of modernization well into the twentieth century.

Italy's fragile independence

The imperatives of modernization could not easily be avoided, however. In a climate of increasingly competitive and aggressive international relations, Italy's independence could not be realized without a modern industrial economy. Relations with both Austria and France were fraught with potential conflicts. In the case of Austria the problems derived from the extensive Italian-speaking territories that remained within the Austro-Hungarian monarchy. Tensions with France were even greater and came close to war when French expansion in North Africa threatened the large Italian community in Tunisia, where Italy was nurturing its own colonial ambitions.

Lacking the resources to engage in war with a major European nation, Italian governments had to pursue or defend national interests through powerful allies, and in 1882 Italy entered into the Triple Alliance with Germany, and its former enemy, Austria. But when the Italian foreign minister, Visconti Venosa, claimed that Italy's policy was to be 'independent, but never isolated', he captured the fragility of the new state's independence, which would prove perhaps the most dangerous legacy of unification and nationhood. The developments that by the end of the century had brought Italian society and culture in most other respects in line with the most powerful European states made Italy's limited independence the more apparent. The defeat at Adua, which brought Crispi's colonial enterprise to a disastrous close in 1896, only heightened the contrast with the great powers and fuelled an aggressive new nationalist rhetoric that ignored economic realities and laid the blame for Italy's uncertain independence on materialism and liberalism.

In an age when colonial expansion was the measure of national power, Italy's weakness in the international arena was a dangerous focus for internal political discontent. Giolitti would resist pressures for expansion until 1911, but in 1915 they brought Italy into a war for which it was poorly equipped and prepared. Italy's 'mutilated peace' in 1919 again exposed her limited independence, and the outrage this provoked played an important part in the collapse of parliamentary government in the crisis that followed. But Mussolini's imperialism of the 1930s, which was an explicit attempt to assert Italian autonomy, left the Duce a prisoner of Hitler's Germany even before the start of the Second World War. That war brought renewed foreign invasions and occupation, leaving the new Italian Republic of 1946 dependent for virtually everything on its American invader then liberator and ally. The incubus of Italy's ambiguous independence would not finally disappear until the Cold War ended and the new European Union offered a different source of security, although ironically one that may, in the twenty-first century, make the nineteenth-century nation-state an anachronism.

Italy's twentieth century was not predetermined by the nineteenth, however. The grave crisis with which the century closed was in many senses the terminal crisis of the old Italy, inherited from the *Risorgimento* and the beginning of a new phase of economic expansion, and political and cultural change. This would not remove the disadvantaged and difficult terms on which Italian society had to confront the challenges of modernization, but after 1900 Italian society, economy, politics, and culture were already very different from what they had been half a century earlier.

Liberal Italy was an imperfect democracy, but not one that was noticeably more imperfect, illiberal, or divided than its nineteenth-century neighbours. The political instincts of the classes most powerfully represented in the new state were deeply conservative, but so, too, were those of the dominant classes of the French Third Republic, late Victorian Britain, and the United States. But paradoxically, the desire for independence that had inspired the struggles of the *Risorgimento* would prove more difficult to realize than Italy's unexpected political unity.

From the French Revolution to Napoleon

Alexander Grab

Italy and the revolution in France

'In the beginning was Napoleon. His influence upon the history of
the German people, their lives and experiences was overwhelming'.[1]
This statement by Thomas Nipperdey on Germany applies also to
Italy. The Napoleonic invasion into northern Italy in 1796 laid the
foundations of the modern Italian state and society and launched the
long march toward the peninsula's unification. No other country
except Germany was so affected by Napoleonic rule. Before 1796, Italy
was divided into ten states: the Kingdom of Sardinia (Piedmont); the
Duchy of Milan, belonging to the Habsburg Empire; the republics of
Venice, Genoa, and Lucca; the Papal State; the Duchies of Modena
and Parma; the Grand Duchy of Tuscany; and the Kingdom of
Naples, which included Sicily. Those Italian states varied considerably. Different dynasties and social elites ruled over them, and they
possessed diverse legal codes, economic structures, administrative
institutions, currencies, and spoken dialects. Provincial and municipal rivalries, and competition between city and country, intensified
the diversity. In the second half of the eighteenth century, the gap

---

[1] Thomas Nipperdey, *Germany from Napoleon to Bismarck, 1800–1860* (Princeton,
1996), p. 1.

widened between states like Lombardy and Tuscany, which experienced broad reform policies launched by enlightened absolutists, and states like the Kingdom of Naples where reform programmes largely failed.

During the two decades of French rule (1796–1814), Napoleon brought the French Revolution to the peninsula. He deposed old dynasties, abolished aristocratic and ecclesiastic privileges, and united regions, gradually establishing uniform legal, administrative, fiscal, and conscription systems. The French invasion also inspired Italian 'Jacobins' to articulate plans of unity and independence, thereby inaugurating Italian nationalism. The Napoleonic transformations notwithstanding, it is important to emphasize their limits and diverse impact on various regions. The distinct pre-Napoleonic structures and old regime legacies, along with varying degrees of opposition to Napoleon, and the unequal durations of French rule, resulted in a different extent and depth of change in various parts of the peninsula.

The French Revolution stimulated interest and support in the Italian states that were undergoing social and political crises. Enlightenment intellectuals, disillusioned with the limited scope of reforms, viewed the French developments as evidence that reforms must expand. The Milanese economist Pietro Verri saw the revolution as a safeguard against tyranny, and proposed a constitutional project, as did the Piedmontese Dalmazzo Francesco Vasco. The revolution also found popular support in the Italian countryside, where agricultural commercialization had increased poverty and social tension. In the early 1790s, discontented peasants in Piedmont and the Kingdom of Naples who protested the loss of communal rights expressed a wish to imitate the French reforms.

In several Italian cities, political dissenters, mostly members of the middle classes, established secret societies that endorsed radical French ideas. The most prominent Italian revolutionary was Filippo Buonarroti, who participated in Babeuf's Conspiracy in Paris in 1796. In several states, the radical societies conspired to topple their governments. In Turin, a group of revolutionaries, including the future historian Carlo Botta, planned to proclaim a republic. In Palermo, a group led by Enlightenment thinker Francesco Paolo Di Biasi planned an uprising. In Bologna, law student Luigi Zamboni plotted to free his city from the papacy.

Italian governments, on the other hand, were hostile to the French Revolution. The papacy had broken relations with France in 1791, while Piedmont and the Kingdom of Naples joined the anti-French coalition. France quickly conquered Savoy and Nice. Internally, the governments launched repressive policies, ceasing reform programmes and tightening censorship. Upon uncovering the conspiracies, they executed, jailed, or deported their leaders. Clearly, the Italian revolutionaries were too weak and too few to effect changes.

Conditions in Italy changed considerably after Napoleon Bonaparte crossed the Alps in April 1796. The French Directory viewed the Italian campaign as primarily 'a financial operation'.[2] Napoleon imposed heavy taxes on the Italian population, while the French army lived off the occupied lands, thereby alienating the population. Militarily, the Directory had assigned the Napoleonic army a diversionary role in support of the French armies in Germany, but Napoleon's rapid victories over the Austrians transformed Italy into the main front. After defeating the Piedmontese, he overcame the Austrians at Lodi and entered Milan on 15 May 1796. Soon, the French also occupied the Papal Legations of Bologna and Ferrara, and the Duchy of Modena. In April 1797, Napoleon and the Austrians signed the Truce of Leoben, and in October both sides agreed to the Peace of Campo Formio, ending the War of the First Coalition. Austria recognized the French occupation of Belgium and Lombardy, and in return received Venice.

The Italian republics 1796–99

Napoleon's victories marked the start of the Revolutionary Triennium (1796–99) in Italy, the first stage of French domination and a period of important change and lively debate. Republican governments replaced the old regimes and experimented with democratic systems, while Italian 'Jacobins', calling themselves 'patriots', advocated national independence and social reforms. The French, however, closely controlled those 'sister' republics by exerting fiscal pressure and intervening in their internal affairs. Along with the

---

[2] Carlo Zaghi, *L'Italia di Napoleone dalla Cisalpina al Regno* (Turin, 1986), p. 37.

fact that the new laws benefited primarily the propertied and educated classes, the French taxes and levies provoked popular resentment and uprisings. When the anti-French offensive resumed, this opposition would lead to the demise of the republics.

Milan, the first major city to be occupied by the French, constituted the most important centre of political activity and debate. Patriots formed popular societies and published numerous newspapers, such as *Termometro politico* and *Giornale dei patrioti d'Italia*. Many exiles, like the Piedmontese Giovanni Antonio Ranza, the Roman Enrico Michele L'Aurora, and the Neapolitan Matteo Galdi, flocked to Milan. The patriots originated mainly from the middle class, although they included nobles and clergy as well. In September 1796, the Lombard administration proclaimed an essay competition on the theme, 'Which form of the free governments is best suited for the happiness of Italy?'[3] The winner, Melchiorre Gioia, voiced the opinion of most patriots by insisting on the formation of an independent Italian republic, 'one and indivisible'. Only in a republic, argued Gioia, could liberty flourish. Others, like Ranza and Botta, advocated a federation of Italian republics reflecting regional differences.

The patriots viewed an independent united republic as a precondition to the creation of a modern state and a democratic society. When it came to how far reforms should go, however, they were divided between moderates and radicals. The former emphasized legal equality and the right of private property. They supported opening public positions to merit, free commerce, and freedom of religion. Most patriots advocated the adoption of the 1795 French constitution. Unlike France, this signified a revolutionary step for the Italian states, which had never proclaimed a constitution.

Radical patriots like L'Aurora, Giuseppe Abbamonti, Vincenzo Russo, and Galdi, who can truly be called Jacobins, supported the French constitution of 1793. Gaining the support of the popular classes was crucial for them. While accepting the principle of private property, they wished 'to realize . . . an equality of opportunity, and establish limits on concentration of wealth; (and secondly) to create instruments of political participation for all citizens, and exercise

---

[3] Armando Saitta (ed.), *Alle origini del Risorgimento. I testi di un 'celebre' concorso (1796)*, 3 vols (Rome, 1964).

continuous and conscious control over government activity.'[4] Radical patriots believed that free public education, designed to teach the popular classes the new revolutionary principles, would encourage them to embrace the new order. 'Without well-run public education, the government will change only in name but not in substance', stressed Galdi.[5] To close the social gap and provide for the needy, they advanced various reforms, including the distribution of Church land, a progressive tax, and the creation of a welfare system. They believed such programmes would generate enthusiasm among the people for the new republic, thereby strengthening it and building a democratic society.

The patriots' aspirations for national liberation clearly contradicted the objectives of the French. Napoleon's aim was to consolidate French domination over the peninsula, to exploit its resources, and to use it as a lever in his negotiations with Austria. Initially, Napoleon used the patriots to bolster his position and stimulate anti-Austrian sentiments. Yet after his victories Napoleon became suspicious of the radicals, who 'were carefully kept on the margins of the meagre powers (entirely executive) which the French delegated to the Italians'.[6] In sum, Napoleon and the Directory prevented the patriots from implementing their national and social programmes. But Napoleon also shunned conservative nobles who favoured the old regimes and chose to rely on 'the more moderate elements, the only ones who seemed to him equipped with experience, prestige and the necessary docility to assure operation of the governments, check the counter-revolutionary tendencies manifested among the masses, and at the same time maintain with the Grand Nation a link of political and financial subjection.'[7] The moderates who represented the propertied classes included reformers like Francesco Melzi (Milan), Giovanni Paradisi (Reggio Emilia), and Lodovico Ricci (Modena), who also feared the patriotic movement and cooperated with the French to avert radical changes.

The first republic Napoleon created was the Cispadane republic, situated south of the Po and including Bologna, Ferrara, Modena,

---

[4] Anna Maria Rao, *La repubblica napoletana del 1799* (Rome, 1997), p. 45.
[5] Delio Cantimori (ed.), *Giacobini italiani*, Vol. I (Bari, 1956), p. 223.
[6] Renzo de Felice, *Italia Giacobina* (Naples, 1965), p. 30.
[7] Carlo Capra, *L'età rivoluzionaria e napoleonica in Italia 1796–1815* (Turin, 1978), pp. 25–6.

and Reggio Emilia. It began functioning in April 1797, but in July 1797 Napoleon merged the Cispadane with the Cisalpine republic that had been formed in Milan. Soon the Cisalpine expanded to include Brescia, Bergamo, and the Valtelline. The Cisalpine was the most important republic of the 'Triennium'. It lasted for 22 months and possessed a flag, an army, and a population of 3½ million inhabitants. Unique among the Italian republics, the Cisalpine consisted of regions previously belonging to five different states. Its constitution, modelled after the French constitution of 1795, established a Directory and a bi-cameral legislature. The authorities abolished entails, and established military conscription, free internal trade, and equality between male and female heirs. They formed a uniform administration, dividing the state into 20 departments, districts, and *comuni*. The government also reduced the power of the Church by abolishing religious orders, requiring priests to swear loyalty to the state, and establishing freedom of religion. The authorities confiscated Church land and sold most of this national property (*beni nazionali*) to the wealthy. The legislature debated many issues that it never enacted, due to lack of time, resources, or their radical nature. Those issues included progressive tax, public education, judicial reorganization, a minimum wage, and price control.

The independence of the Cisalpinian republic was largely nominal, however, and ultimately the French were in control. They imposed territorial limits and prevented the Cisalpine from having access to the sea. In June 1797, a separate Ligurian republic was established at Genoa. At Campo Formio, Napoleon delivered the former Republic of Venice to the Austrians, ignoring requests by the new democratic Venetian government to join the Cisalpine, and infuriating Italian patriots. Later, the Directory refused to add Ancona and Piedmont to the Cisalpine. Clearly, neither Napoleon nor the Directory wished to see a powerful Italian state.

The French continuously intervened in the Cisalpine's internal affairs. Napoleon nominated the Directors and the legislators to ensure that the moderates retained control. The Cisalpine was forced to maintain a costly army and pay for the upkeep of 25,000 French troops, but opposition induced the Directory to dismiss nine legislators and two Directors (April 1798). Three more French coups reduced the power of the democrats in the legislature. In August, French ambassador Trouve proclaimed a new, less democratic constitution that increased the authority of the Directory and decreased the legislature's power. Journals and popular societies were suppressed and several patriots were arrested. In sum, the French intervention established a more authoritarian system. Financially the Cisalpine was in dire straits, and under such unstable fiscal and political conditions the authorities were unable to consolidate the new republic.

Two more republics, the Roman and the Neapolitan, were created after Napoleon left Italy (November 1797). The French occupied Rome, and on 15 February 1798 local patriots proclaimed the Roman republic. Pius VI left Rome, and in August 1799 he died in exile. The Roman republic was essentially a French protectorate during its eighteen-month existence. A French commission proclaimed a constitution modelled after the 1795 French constitution. The French commander nominated government officials and issued laws. Support for the republic came from professionals, some aristocrats, and Roman Jews who, for the first time, received equal rights. The Roman legislature abolished the entails and imposed limits on bishops' income. Roman patriots and Neapolitan exiles created popular societies and published the *Monitore di Roma*, but had no influence over the government. Heavy French taxes forced authorities to sell Church land; and those impositions, coupled with Church incitement and plunder by troops, provoked popular revolts throughout central Italy which the French suppressed.

In late November 1798, the Neapolitan Bourbons sent an army to occupy Rome, thereby initiating conflict with France. They clearly blundered. Their army was unprepared, their treasury was empty, and their rule was weak. A French army led by General Championnet soon expelled the Neapolitans from Rome and marched on Naples. Ferdinand IV fled to Sicily, and the French occupied Naples. On 22 January 1799, Neapolitan patriots proclaimed a republic. Championnet nominated a provisional government that included patriots, but whose action had to be approved by the French commander.

Faced from the start with serious fiscal difficulties and popular opposition, the Neapolitan republic lasted for less than five months. The Directory, whose main concern was to raise cash indemnities, was hostile to the republic's formation and soon recalled its supporter, Championnet, to Paris and replaced him with the more malleable Macdonald. The only effective law of the Neapolitan government was the abolition of entails. In practice, the administrative reorganization changed only the provinces' names, and plans to restructure the judiciary never materialized. The authorities' greatest failure, however, proved to be their inability to quickly and decisively abolish feudalism. While all agreed on the need to abolish personal feudal rights, such as labour services, tolls, and monopolies, the government was divided over feudal jurisdiction and land held as feudal title. In early March, the authorities abolished feudal jurisdiction payments, tolls, and monopolies; awarded part of the feudal land to the rural villages; and allocated the rest to the barons as private property. The French approved the law only at the end of April, too late to prevent a peasant uprising. The moderates' hesitation and the nobles' pressure on Macdonald to delay signing the feudal law played a role in preventing an earlier end to feudalism, thereby alienating the country's masses. Neapolitan patriots played an active part in the brief life of the republic. Exiles like Pagano, Russo, Lauberg, and Abbamonti returned to Naples and served in the government. Eleonora de Fonseca Pimentel published the *Monitore napoletano*. Radical patriots set up an Instruction Hall where they voiced their concerns and met the lower classes.

In December 1798 the French also occupied the Kingdom of Sardinia, forcing its monarch, Charles Emanuel IV, to abdicate. That monarchy was in deep crisis following the defeat by France in 1796. Economic hardships caused peasant revolts and brigandage. French financial pressure and military plunder hampered the provisional government's stability and increased discontent. The authorities uncovered a conspiracy by patriots who supported an independent republic, and the French ruthlessly suppressed a peasant revolt in Monferrato.

1799: the end of the Italian republics

The formation of the Second Coalition in 1799 marked the beginning of a new counter-revolutionary offensive in various parts of Europe. Nowhere was that offensive more comprehensive and successful than in the Italian peninsula. Between February and September 1799, foreign armies and popular insurgents expelled the French from Italy and overthrew the 'sister' republics, except for Genoa, which would resist until June 1800.

Resistance to the French troops had started soon after their invasion in 1796. The insurgents, who were frequently incited by hostile clergy, were comprised primarily of peasants and the urban poor, who reacted against French looting. The Lombard towns of Pavia and Binasco rose up in May 1796, and in June towns in Romagna revolted. In April 1797, Verona rose up, leading to the bloody 'Pasque Veronesi'. In 1797 and 1798, uprisings also erupted in Piedmont, Liguria, Umbria, and Lazio.

Opposition to the French and their republican allies culminated in 1799. The Cisalpine was the first republic to fall, following a victory over the French at Cassano d'Adda (April 1799) by General Suvorov, commander of the Austrian and Russian armies. The Austrians established a new government in Milan, and in May, Suvorov defeated Macdonald and occupied Piedmont. Those victories provoked popular uprisings in northern and central Italy. Piedmontese peasants joined the Austrian army. In Tuscany, inhabitants of Arezzo chanted 'Viva Maria' as they destroyed republican symbols and attacked 'Jacobins.' In Siena, insurgents killed many Jews. Revolts spread also to Lazio, Umbria, and the Marche.

'Yet nowhere was the scale of violence of the counter-revolution greater than in the South.'[8] The Neapolitan republic faced royalist uprisings in Puglia and Abruzzi. In February 1799, Cardinal Fabrizio Ruffo disembarked in Calabria, where he soon led an anti-republican army of thousands of peasants who opposed the French plunder and were disillusioned by the republic's failure to abolish feudalism. On 13 June, Ruffo's SanFedist army entered Naples, which had been abandoned by the French, and killings of republicans ensued. The republican leaders capitulated after Ruffo promised to allow them to leave for France. Ferdinand IV and Admiral Nelson, whose ships had supported the assault on Naples, reneged on this agreement, however, and 120 republican leaders, including most of the members of the provisional government, were executed. On 30 September, following the French withdrawal, the Roman republic collapsed as well. The Revolutionary Triennium was over.

[8] John Davis, '1799: The 'Sanfede' and the crisis of the 'ancien regime' in Southern Italy'. In John Davis and Paul Ginsborg (eds), *Society and Politics in the Age of the Risorgimento. Essays in Honour of Denis Mack Smith* (Cambridge, 1991), p. 1.

In his famous book, entitled *Saggio storico sulla Rivoluzione napoletana del 1799* (1801),[9] provisional government official Vincenzo Cuoco reacted to the failure of the Neapolitan revolution by trying to explain the quick collapse of the republic. Cuoco argued that the Neapolitan revolution had been a 'passive revolution' in two ways: first, the ideas that guided the revolution had been imported from France and were not applicable to the Neapolitan reality; and secondly, the patriotic leaders, who were inspired by those abstract principles, were unable to communicate with the masses. Cuoco's thesis stimulated a conservative–nationalistic interpretation that viewed the Revolutionary Triennium as an interruption of the reforms begun in the eighteenth century, and saw the Italian '*giacobini*' as demagogues and utopians who served foreign rulers and were estranged from the Italian people. However, more recent research on the Italian Jacobins, and the publication of their writings by historians like Delio Cantimori, Armando Saitta, and Renzo De Felice, largely revised those anti-Jacobin views. The absence of ties with the masses owed less to the abstract nature of the Jacobins' beliefs than to French opposition to any radical reform.

The Napoleonic revolution in Italy 1800–14

After the coup of Brumaire and the reorganization of power in France, Napoleon returned to Italy. On 14 June 1800, he defeated the Austrians at Marengo, thereby restoring French domination over much of northern Italy. The Austrians recognized this at the Peace of Luneville (February 1801). Marengo initiated the second phase of Napoleonic rule over Italy, which lasted until Napoleon's fall in 1814.

During those years, Napoleon reshaped the peninsula's map at will, changing borders, deposing rulers, annexing territories, and establishing new states. By 1810 he dominated the entire peninsula, and only Sicily and Sardinia remained under the old monarchs. This reorganization was aimed at strengthening Napoleon's control over the peninsula and assuring the success of the Continental blockade.

---

[9] Vincenzo Cuoco, *Saggio storico sulla Rivoluzione napoletana de 1799*, Pasquale Villani (ed.) (Bari, 1976).

Ultimately, Napoleon consolidated the peninsula into three parts: the northern Italian republic, later transformed into the Kingdom of Italy; the Kingdom of Naples; and areas annexed to imperial France.

The formation of centralized states constituted a second important feature of Napoleonic Italy. To achieve that goal, the authorities launched the rationalization and centralization of the administrative, financial, judicial, and military structures, in harmony with the French system. Strengthening the state's machinery enabled Napoleon to more efficiently draft Italian troops and increase public revenues, his two main interests in the peninsula. The Napoleonic reforms signified the establishment of unifying legal and institutional structures, which would lay the groundwork for the political unity of the peninsula. Indeed, the reform policies of Napoleon reflected the regime's Janus-faced character that combined subordination and exploitation, innovation and progress.

The alliance between the Napoleonic state and the new elite of notables represented the third important feature of Napoleonic Italy. The notables represented an *amalgame* between the nobility and the wealthy bourgeoisie. Landowners were the most significant element in this elite, since 'At the start of the century, an elite could not imagine itself without landed property. It was still the possession of the land that determined the hierarchy.'[10] The commercial, professional, and educated classes also belonged to the notability. Napoleon carried out the *ralliement*, a policy designed to secure the notables' support and recruit former enemies of the revolution; he appointed them to high positions, sanctioned their purchase of *beni nazionali* and the right of private property, and guaranteed law and order. Naturally, a part of the nobility opposed or remained lukewarm to Napoleon, resenting the loss of traditional privileges, the tax burden, and the assault on the Church.

From the Republic to the Kingdom of Italy

In January 1802, Napoleon established the Republic of Italy, and an assembly of notables gathered in Lyons elected him as the republic's president. In March 1805, after becoming emperor, Napoleon

---

[10] Jean Tulard, *Napoléon ou le myth du sauveur* (Paris, 1987), p. 243.

transformed the republic into the Kingdom of Italy (1805–14), and became its king. The republic and kingdom constituted a Napoleonic satellite state that maintained French troops on its territory, provided Napoleon with soldiers, and enforced the Continental blockade. Based upon the French model, Napoleon's transformation of the Republic and Kingdom of Italy surpassed that of any other part of the peninsula, perhaps even of Europe, because French domination there lasted longer than in other parts of Italy. The active cooperation of the Lombard elites contributed to this, as did the earlier reforms of the Habsburg rulers. Napoleon expanded the kingdom's territory three times, joining Lombardy with the Novarese and most of Emilia Romagna, the Veneto (1806), the Marche (1808), and Alto Adige (1810). At its peak, the kingdom covered an area of 35,000 square miles and possessed 6.7 million inhabitants, about one-third of the peninsula's population.

Napoleon's main accomplishment in northern Italy was the unification in a single central state of regions that were previously part of five different states, and the formation of uniform and increasingly effective legal and administrative structures. The republican constitution began the centralization process by establishing a very powerful executive. Napoleon and his vice-president, Francesco Melzi d'Eril, had the ultimate say on all internal policies, nominated top officials, and ran foreign policy. Seven ministers (respectively for war, finance, treasury, interior, religion, justice, and foreign relations) reported to them. In contrast, the legislature was divided into three bodies and had very limited power. The Legislative Body voted without discussion on laws prepared by a Legislative Council. An electoral body, consisting of three colleges of landowners, merchants, and the intelligentsia, elected the members of the Legislative Body. Political participation was reserved for the propertied and educated classes.

The vice-president, Melzi d'Eril, a Milanese patrician, played a key role in running the republic. He was an excellent representative of the propertied classes, a staunch believer in the right of private property, held moderate liberal views, and was intensely hostile to any form of Jacobinism. Melzi's ultimate goal was an independent northern Italian state ruled by a constitutional monarchy, and this aspiration, along with his demands for more autonomy, led to tension with Napoleon. When the emperor established the kingdom in 1805, he appointed his submissive stepson, Eugène de Beauharnais, as his vice-roy in Milan, and moved Melzi to a ceremonial post.

Napoleonic rule was highly authoritarian. In July 1805 Eugène was ordered: 'If Milan is in flames, you must ask for orders to extinguish it; you must let Milan burn and wait for orders.' As the king, Napoleon constituted the executive and originated much legislation. The viceroy and the seven ministers executed Napoleon's orders and ran the daily business of the government. In July 1805, Napoleon dissolved the Legislative Body after it had opposed a new tax. He created a Council of State and later a Senate. The Council consulted him and discussed legislative projects, while the Senate voted on those projects. Neither body posed any challenge to Napoleon.

In 1802, Melzi d'Eril had laid the foundations of the central administration. He divided the republic into departments, districts, and *comuni*. The 12 departments, which increased to 24 with the kingdom's expansion, varied in size and population but possessed a uniform bureaucratic structure. The linchpin of the entire system was the prefect, a department head nominated by and responsible to the executive.[11] The prefect was responsible for enforcing the laws, main-taining public order, supervising the military draft, and managing the department's finances. In sum, the prefect was the indispensable link between the centre and the periphery. The vice-prefects governed the districts while *podestà* and *sindaci* ran the *comuni*. Under the king-dom, the prefects' powers expanded while the *comuni* lost all auton-omy. As centralization took root, the administration became fairly efficient and reliable. Bureaucrats were chosen increasingly on the basis of their skills and were gaining in experience and professional-ism.[12] Yet administrative efficiency varied among departments, depending upon the duration of French rule, the accessibility of the department's terrain to officials, the tradition of resistance, and the results of earlier reforms. On the *comuni* level, there was a shortage of qualified officials; often, local administrators fulfilled their duties inadequately, due to favouritism and intimidation.

All but one of the top officials in the republic and kingdom were Italian citizens. Melzi d'Eril had nominated officials of moderate views while the authorities of the kingdom showed more openness,

---

[11] Livio Antonielli, *I prefetti dell'Italia napoleonica* (Bologna, 1983).
[12] Capra, *L'età rivoluzionaria*, p. 242.

and appointed some officials who had a radical past. Most ministers, prefects, vice-prefects, and municipal officials came from the landed classes, the rest came from the ranks of merchants, professionals, and the intelligentsia. A number of ministers came from the nobility: of 52 prefects who served in the republic and kingdom, 30 were nobles and 22 came from the bourgeoisie.[13]

The state's centralization and uniformity was strengthened through the introduction of the French legal system. Napoleon ordered the French codes translated into Italian, and they became the law of the land between 1806 and 1810. The Civil Code reinforced legal equality and the right of private property, and legalized civil marriage. The kingdom also imitated the French court system: a justice of the peace in every canton, a civil and criminal tribunal in every department, a Court of Cassation in Milan, and courts of appeal in Milan, Venice, Bologna, Brescia, and Ancona.

To maintain public order, the authorities instituted a regular, salaried police force. The prefects were responsible for policing in their departments, and a director-general of police coordinated police activities throughout the state. Police commissioners in the cities inspected public and private activities. In addition, the *gendarmerie* constituted an elite corps of close to 2000 men who fought against smugglers, deserters, and brigands. In times of emergency the authorities also used regular troops and the National Guard.

The success of the state's administration was epitomized in the financial and military areas. With increasing efficiency, the government extracted growing amounts of money and annually drafted thousands of men. The largest annual expenditure, normally comprising 50% of the budget, went to support a growing Italian army and the maintenance of 25,000 French troops in northern Italy. Other major expenses included the construction of waterways and highways, and paying interest on the public debt. The authorities liquidated the public debt by issuing creditors two types of bonds, one (*iscrizioni*) carrying 3.5% interest, and the other (*rescrizioni*) acceptable as payment for *beni nazionali*. Most of the state's revenues derived from direct and indirect taxes supplemented by customs, the lottery, and the sale of *beni nazionali*. To pay for increasing

Napoleonic demands, finance minister Giuseppe Prina launched reforms aimed at augmenting and improving tax collection. Napoleon clearly appreciated Prina's efforts, and wrote to Eugène in 1805, 'There is no person who is more essential than the finance minister; he is a hard worker who knows his profession.' To gain the support of the landowners, Prina kept property tax, the main source of the state's income, at a relatively modest level. To offset the reduced property tax, he established a personal tax and increased indirect taxes, such as the salt gabelle and tobacco and consumption duties, that fell more heavily on the poor. In 1807, Prina launched a property survey (*catasto*), thereby eliminating differences among taxpayers and increasing state control over taxation. The survey progressed rapidly but would be concluded only during the Restoration. In order to establish a timely and accurate levy, Prina reorganized tax collection in March 1804, creating a new hierarchy and establishing new guidelines for tax collectors. Tax exaction became centralized, more efficient, and less expensive. The new financial policies, along with an increase in the number of taxpayers, almost doubled state revenues between 1802 and 1811. Despite these increases, Napoleon's growing fiscal demands were the cause of deficits in the later years of the kingdom.

In August 1802, the republic proclaimed mandatory military conscription, annually drafting thousands of recruits between the ages of 20 and 25 for four years' service. Priests and the handicapped were exempt, and conscripts could pay for a substitute. The peasantry carried the main burden of the draft, and many resisted through desertion, draft dodging, and even uprisings. To combat this opposition, the government tightened the draft apparatus, dispatched the *gendarmerie*, and set up special tribunals and harsher penalties. The conscription system enabled state officials to penetrate remote towns, compelling their citizens to acknowledge the state and obey its laws. Those measures reinforced the power of the state, which, despite the resistance, drafted 155,000 men during 1802–14 and expanded the Italian army to 70,000 men in 1812. Italians fought in Spain, Russia, and Germany, where they suffered huge casualties. Finally, military service inspired national consciousness. By bringing together citizens from different parts of Italy to serve in Italian units, conscription encouraged the rank and file and some of the officers to start thinking of themselves as belonging to the Italian nation.

Following the French Concordat (1801), Napoleon ordered Melzi d'Eril to try to reach a similar agreement with the pope. The negotiations were long and difficult. While Melzi believed in the supremacy of the state over the Church, the pope opposed any reduction of Church power and the annexation of papal territories to the republic. The two sides finally signed a concordat on 16 September 1803. Patterned after the French Concordat, it proclaimed Catholicism as a state religion, confirmed freedom of religion, and authorized the republic to nominate bishops and the pope to consecrate them. It also ratified the new owners of the *beni nazionali*. Melzi was dissatisfied with the concessions made to the Church and issued an organic decree designed to limit the implementation of those concessions. Napoleon abolished Melzi's decree, yet he himself disregarded the concordat and persisted in strengthening the state vis-à-vis the Church. The emperor confiscated and sold Church land, reorganized parishes, and introduced civil marriage and divorce. Many priests refused to collaborate with the authorities, and some incited disobedience.

In the field of the economy, the authorities of the kingdom created a national market through the elimination of internal tariffs and the promulgation of a uniform commercial code, a single currency, the lira, and unified weights and measures. Communications were improved through extensive construction of roads and waterways, most notably the transalpine Simplon Pass, completed in 1805. While military expenses burdened the treasury, local industry in the kingdom was stimulated through the production of much of the army's equipment.

French imperial policy did have some negative impact on the kingdom, however; because customs duties between the two countries were halved, textile imports from France increased, damaging the Italian silk industry in particular. Ports like Venice were paralysed by the Continental blockade, which harmed maritime commerce, caused a shortage of colonial goods, and encouraged smuggling. Even so, the elimination of English competition boosted the wool and cotton industries. Moreover, the decline in commerce helped shift resources to the agrarian sector, thus encouraging agricultural growth. Landowners also benefited from the creation of a larger market, a rise in the prices of grain, rice, and wine, and the continuing sale of *beni nazionali*, most of which were purchased by the wealthy.

While the propertied classes benefited from many of the economic changes, the conditions of the lower classes deteriorated in some important ways. They carried the main burden of conscription, saw a rise in indirect taxes, and suffered the consequences of the ongoing agricultural commercialization. Nonetheless, the Napoleonic authorities never faced the lasting massive popular revolt that they confronted in the South. Popular resistance was limited mostly to desertion and brigandage in mountainous and wooded areas, neither of which threatened Napoleonic rule. In the summer of 1809, however, a widespread, brigand-led, rural revolt broke out in several departments to protest a new milling tax. The rebels attacked numerous towns, destroyed government property, and briefly threatened Bologna and Vicenza. Although the authorities suppressed the revolt quickly, inflicting heavy casualties on the rural population, Prina also repealed the tax.

The Napoleonic Kingdom in the South

In southern Italy, the six and a half years between the collapse of the Neapolitan republic and the Napoleonic occupation (1799–1806) had been a period of deep crisis. The weakness of the Bourbon monarchy persisted, and the fiscal crisis deepened. Ferdinand IV also alienated the rural masses by failing to abolish the feudal system and alleviate the tax burden. In 1805, Naples signed a treaty of neutrality with France but at the same time joined the Third Coalition. After Napoleon's victory at Austerlitz he declared Bourbon rule in Naples to be at an end, and in February 1806 French forces led by General Massena occupied Naples, forcing the royal family to flee to Sicily where they remained under British protection until Napoleon's fall. French rule in the *Mezzogiorno* lasted until 1815. The population of the southern mainland amounted to 5 million inhabitants. Napoleon's older brother, Joseph, ruled over the Kingdom of Naples for the first two years; but when he moved to Spain in May 1808, Napoleon's brother-in-law Joachim Murat replaced him.

By occupying southern Italy, Napoleon intended to consolidate his domination over Italy and assure the success of the Continental blockade. After easily defeating the Bourbon army, the French faced fierce popular resistance, the strongest such opposition except by Spain. In July 1806, British forces landed in Calabria and defeated the French at Maida. The defeat encouraged widespread revolt that drove the French out of Calabria. When the French launched a campaign to reoccupy the region, a ruthless war ensued. Brigands played a leading role in the revolt while clergymen incited the rebels. By February 1808, the French had regained control of Calabria, but brigandage persisted, fuelled largely by military conscription and persistent rural misery. As a result, the authorities needed three more years to pacify the country.

The Kingdom of Naples also took the form of a Napoleonic satellite state, on conditions that were made explicit in the Treaty of Bayonne when Murat became king (July 1808). The treaty obliged the kingdom to maintain the French army in Naples, provide the emperor with troops and ships, and enforce the Continental blockade. Napoleon also demanded that Naples favour French imports. Yet Joseph, and more so Murat, exerted efforts to become autonomous of the emperor. To achieve that goal, they nominated the propertied and educated classes to high posts, trying to rally them in support of their rule. Joseph appointed Frenchmen like Saliceti, Roederer, and Dumas as ministers of police, finance, and war; but under Murat, the Neapolitans Zurlo (interior), Ricciardi (justice), and Di Gallo (foreign), wielded the greatest influence. A State Council served as the consulting body, comprised mainly of Neapolitan nobles and bourgeois. In 1811, Murat even tried unsuccessfully to require French officials in his government to assume Neapolitan citizenship or face dismissal.

Reforms designed to strengthen the central government constituted another way of gaining independence. Indeed, the French period 'was one of intensive administrative and juridical reforms and the speed with which the French administration set about dismantling the *Ancien Regime* state was remarkable.'[14] Yet the authorities had only limited success with their reform policy, due to limited resources, a shortage of competent personnel, and strong resistance by the landed elite.

Those limitations were clear in the case of the abolition of feudalism, the most significant Neapolitan reform. On 2 August 1806, the

---

[14] John Davis, 'The Napoleonic era in southern Italy: An ambiguous legacy?' In *Proceedings of the British Academy* (Oxford University Press), Vol. 80: *1991 Lectures and Memoirs*, p. 134.

government suppressed, without compensation, feudal jurisdiction, declared feudal fees on land redeemable, and transformed baronial land into private property, free of feudal restrictions. On 1 September 1806, the authorities decreed the division of common lands between landlords and *comuni*, ordering the latter to divide their share among local peasants. Two other reforms affecting the land regime stipulated the termination of entails and the sale of confiscated Church property.

The abolition of feudal jurisdiction was aimed at strengthening the central state. Moreover, it was designed to encourage land movement, stimulate agricultural development, and create a substantial class of small and middle landowners, thereby generating a solid tax base and a reduction in social tension. In 1810, Murat wrote Zurlo, 'Without doubt, the greatest benefit of my reign will be the total abolition of feudalism.'[15] Yet much in the Neapolitan countryside remained unchanged. Property division and the redemption of feudal fees aroused numerous disputes between feudatories and *comuni*, requiring a lengthy examination of titles and deeds.

A special Feudal Commission, set up in November 1807, operated until August 1810 and settled all the litigations that were submitted. However, the barons prevented a prompt implementation of the decisions, and many were still outstanding in the early twentieth century. The Feudal Commission had no time to execute the complex operation of partitioning the common lands, and the reform remained incomplete due to the landlords' hostility. In cases where small peasants received land, they frequently lost it to the large landlords because they lacked the means to cultivate it. In sum, while the barons lost their jurisdictional rights and tax prerogatives, they gained full ownership over their property and remained the dominant group. The landed bourgeoisie benefited by becoming free of feudal jurisdiction and appropriating part of the common lands. Both the former feudatories and the bourgeoisie also increased their possessions by purchasing much of the *beni nazionali*. Yet the bourgeois property holders changed little in the way they farmed. The peasants, on the other hand, had few gains. While free of feudal duties, most remained property-less and also lost their communal

---

[15] Angela Valente, *Gioacchino Murat e l'Italia meridionale* (Reprint, Turin, 1976), p. 278.

rights. Their misery remained a major problem in the South throughout the nineteenth century.

The abolition of feudalism provided the premiss for a uniform administration. It eliminated the difference between the communities subject to the state and to the *feudi*, and established legal equality. Joseph established a uniform central administration modelled on France, and divided his kingdom into 14 provinces, run by intendants. On the communal level, the authorities set up a uniform structure in which councils of *decurioni*, comprised of proprietors and professionals, elected *sindaci*. Incompetence at this level, however, meant that 'the objective of establishing efficient communal administrations and expeditiously enforcing laws, regulations, and instructions issued by the ministers . . . was never reached'.[16] Personnel problems also arose in the judicial sphere, where the authorities instituted a court hierarchy based on the French model, but were unable to find judges for the new positions. Murat proclaimed the Napoleonic codes, yet the abolition of entails and the introduction of divorce had little effect in Naples and was ignored by the local elite.

The abolition of feudalism also paved the way for financial reforms. Hoping to stimulate agrarian growth, the authorities abolished tax privileges, thereby creating a solid tax base. The government had inherited a huge public debt of more than 130 million *ducati* from the Bourbons. The cost of the French army, and the national army and navy, amounted to 69% of the 1812 budget.[17]

Reorganization of the tax system constituted an important part of the fiscal reforms. In August 1806, the government replaced the numerous Bourbon direct taxes with a uniform property tax on all real estate and investments in industry and commerce. In August 1809, Murat initiated a modern land assessment, but this had hardly begun by the end of his reign. The authorities abolished some of the indirect taxes but preserved state monopolies over salt and tobacco. Lottery, property registration, and customs supplemented state revenues. Confiscated Church land—the state suppressed 1300 monasteries—constituted another important source of income. Creditors received 5% interest (3% under Murat) or could be paid

---

[16] Pasquale Villani, 'Il decennio francese'. In G. Galasso (ed.), *Storia del Mezzogiorno* (Rome, 1986), p. 599.

[17] Ibid., p. 630.

through the *beni nazionali*. As in other parts of the peninsula, the wealthy classes were the main beneficiaries from the sale of the *beni nazionali*. The increase in state revenues enabled Murat to reduce the deficit and balance the budget in 1813.[18] Yet to accomplish that and cover military expenses, he had to curtail various reform programmes.

The Continental blockade hurt Naples' economy, particularly the agricultural sector that relied on exports. Since the war interrupted sea-borne trade, Murat was reluctant to enforce the Continental blockade effectively. This reluctance was part of his efforts to assert Naples' independence vis-à-vis the emperor and caused tension with Napoleon, who demanded strict implementation of his anti-British policy. Other factors also strained relations between the two. Murat was very protective of his own sovereignty, while Napoleon viewed the Kingdom of Naples as a vassal state. Napoleon criticized Murat for delays in introducing Code Napoleon. Murat also wanted to develop Naples' economy and refused to grant exemption from customs to French products.

Developing a national army was important, since it constituted another way of bolstering the Neapolitan state and its independence. Joseph introduced annual conscription in 1806, exempting married men and single children, and allowing replacements. Recruitment met with difficulties due to the Calabrian revolt and was not enforced. By the time Joseph left for Spain, the army numbered 11,000 men, only 2000 of whom were Neapolitans. Joseph took part of the troops to Spain, leaving his successor a small army. Murat exerted great effort in enforcing conscription to build a national army. Eventually his army stood at 32,000 men. Murat viewed the army as more than a military tool, and 'from the outset intended to turn the army into his principal political base in the Kingdom and sought to use it as an instrument by which to forge an *amalgame* between his own dynastic ambitions and the Neapolitan national-ism.'[19] He succeeded in gaining the loyalty of many civilian and mili-tary supporters, yet the army never provided an adequate basis to make possible a transition to a new political system.

The Neapolitan army fought in various Napoleonic campaigns,

[18] Valente, *Giaocchino Murat*, p. 295.
[19] John Davis, 'The Neapolitan army during the *decennio francese*'. *Rivista italiana di studi napoleonici*, 25 (1988), p. 169.

including Russia, and suffered high casualties. In 1808, it had captured Capri from the British. Building the Neapolitan army, however, caused two main problems for the southern state; first, conscription provoked much discontent, which fed brigandage; secondly, the high military costs drained Naples' limited resources, hampering the implementation of various reforms.

The annexed territories

The third part of the peninsula consisted of northern and central regions that Napoleon annexed to imperial France: Piedmont (annexed in 1802); Liguria (1805); Tuscany (1808); Parma and Piacenza (1808); and Umbria and Lazio, including Rome (1809). The Napoleonic authorities introduced the French administrative, fiscal, and judicial systems to those lands to integrate them with France. They divided them into departments headed largely by French prefects, established Code Napoleon, imposed French taxation, and conscripted their men into the *Grande Armée*. Napoleon faced no major revolts, although his taxation and conscription provoked popular hostility. Opposition came also from the clergy. The propertied classes largely supported the Napoleonic regime and were rewarded with government positions and integration into a larger market.

The Kingdom of Sardinia had the longest experience of French rule. Following Marengo, Napoleon reoccupied Piedmont; in September 1802 he annexed it to France, inflicting a blow on the Italian nationalists. In neighbouring Genoa, Napoleon restored the Ligurian republic, but in June 1805 he annexed it to France to gain close control of the port of Genoa. Napoleon divided Piedmont into six departments, headed mostly by French prefects, and established the French legal and tax structures. The *gendarmerie*, police, and army eliminated many brigand bands. Subsequently, 'There can be little doubt that the French had restored civil order in Piedmont by 1809, nor is it contestable that they made their rule effective.'[20] Achieving internal peace was crucial to rally the Piedmontese propertied classes

---

[20] Michael Broers, *Napoleonic Imperialism and the Savoyard Monarchy, 1773–1821: State Building in Piedmont* (Lewiston, NY, 1997), p. 404.

to the government, many of whom also benefited from the opportunities to pursue military and administrative careers and from the sale of *beni nazionali*. Yet some aristocrats and many intellectuals resented the loss of autonomy and the government's introduction of the French language into the administration. Many aristocrats remained loyal to the House of Savoy while the Continental blockade and French competition caused heavy losses and great dissatisfaction among silk producers. To this was added the discontent of the lower classes, which was provoked by taxes and conscription.

Central Italy came under Napoleon's rule within a few months in 1808. Tuscany, which in 1801 became the Kingdom of Etruria, was annexed to the French Empire in March 1808. The old Duchy of Parma and Piacenza, administered since 1805 by Napoleon's sister, Paolina Borghese, was officially annexed to France in May 1808. More significantly, Napoleon gradually dismembered the Papal States. Relations with Pius VII deteriorated after the imperial coronation. The pope never approved of the loss of Bologna and Ferrara. He opposed the organic articles in the Italian Concordat, Napoleon's reorganization of the Church in the Kingdom of Italy, and he objected to the introduction of divorce into that state. Pius VII's neutrality during the Third Coalition, along with his refusal to stop trading with Britain, induced Napoleon to chip away at the papal territory. After occupying Ancona in October 1805, and Civitavecchia in May 1806, Napoleon ordered General Miollis to occupy Rome in February 1808. In April 1808, he annexed Urbino, Ancona, and Macerata to the Kingdom of Italy. Finally, on 17 May 1809, Napoleon officially annexed the rest of the Papal States to the French Empire, thereby terminating the pope's temporal authority. In response, Pius VII excommunicated Napoleon and in June the emperor exiled the pope to Savona.

Miollis served as the governor, and Roman aristocrats assumed various administrative positions. The government imposed conscription, introduced Code Napoleon, and initiated public works. The authorities dispersed convents and sold Church land. Not surprisingly, the clergy refused to swear allegiance to the new ruler. The rural population was hostile to conscription, which, along with poverty, encouraged widespread brigandage.

The end of Napoleonic Italy, 1812–15

The debacle in Russia made it clear that Napoleon's rule was nearing its end. Throughout the peninsula, hostility toward Napoleon increased due to the high number of Italian casualties, escalating financial pressure, the negative effects of the Continental blockade, and the banishment of the pope. Advocates of independence and a liberal constitution formed secret societies. The *Adelfia* in northern Italy had its origins in Jacobin elements and the Society of the Rays, which had dissolved in 1802. In the South, the *carbonari* (charcoal burners) formed the largest secret society, consisting mainly of army officers, soldiers, and the small provincial bourgeoisie. These secret sects posed no concrete threat to the Napoleonic regime, however, nor could they establish Italian unity and independence.

The two rulers of the Kingdoms of Italy and Naples would not succeed in accomplishing those goals either. In October 1813, the Austrians invaded the Kingdom of Italy, forcing Eugène de Beauharnais to retreat. Upon Melzi's urging, and following Napoleon's abdication, Eugène proclaimed the kingdom's independence in April 1814. This was opposed by certain prominent citizens in the Senate in Milan, however. Some supported the Austrians, while a second group, known as 'Pure Italians', and led by Count Federico Confalonieri, were advocates of an independent state. Anti-French sentiment culminated on 20 April 1814 when a Milanese crowd, agitated by a group of nobles, lynched Prina, the hated minister of finance. Eugène left Italy shortly thereafter, and the Austrians entered Milan and restored their domination over Lombardy. Later that year, Victor Emanuel I and Pius VII returned to Turin and Rome, respectively, and the Austrians restored the old dynasties in central Italy.

With the collapse of the Kingdom of Italy, Murat remained the only surviving Napoleonic ruler in Italy. In January 1813, he joined the Austrians and the English in an attempt to save his throne. His position became precarious, however, at the Congress of Vienna, as the European powers were inclined to restore the Bourbons in Naples. Following Napoleon's flight from Elba, Murat declared war on the Austrians and led an army into central Italy. In Rimini he issued a proclamation urging Italians to join his fight for Italian independence and unity, but was defeated in Tolentino on 2 May 1815 and left for exile in Corsica. The Bourbons returned to Naples. In October 1815, Murat landed in Calabria, aiming to reoccupy his kingdom, but was captured by Bourbon forces and executed.

With the defeats of Eugène and Murat, the Napoleonic political–territorial structure collapsed. The crisis of the Napoleonic regime, and the growing discontent and opposition during the final years, demonstrated the limits of the Napoleonic system. Exploitation and intervention from Paris had weakened the ability of the northern and southern states to expand and solidify their reform programmes. This was particularly true in the Kingdom of Naples, where the success of the Napoleonic reforms in strengthening state power was much more limited than in the Kingdom of Italy, and where the state's ability to enforce its new laws remained rather weak.

These limitations notwithstanding, the experience of the two decades of French rule left significant legacies in the Italian peninsula. The Napoleonic period laid the political, institutional, and ideological foundations of Italy's unification and independence. By consolidating the ten pre-Napoleonic states into three parts, toppling the old dynasties, and inspiring patriots to develop new programmes of unity and independence, Napoleon advanced the cause of national unity. While Italy remained territorially and politically divided, and major differences still existed among its regions, particularly between North and South, the entire peninsula, for the first time in many centuries, came under a united code of law, one administrative organization, a single system of conscription, and a uniform tax system.

These innovations accelerated the modernization of society and the Italian states, two other Napoleonic legacies in Italy. The amalgam between the old landed nobility and the wealthy bourgeoisie created a new elite that would remain in power throughout the nineteenth century. Napoleon also introduced the indispensable foundations for the formation of a central and powerful government, including a national army, a central bureaucracy, unified legal and fiscal systems, a national market, and state control over the Church. Indeed, the Restoration governments adopted and continued to develop many of the Napoleonic financial, administrative, and judicial systems. They also employed many Napoleonic administrators and army officers. Likewise, the Napoleonic central state would serve as a model for the rulers of united Italy, while the Code Napoleon would constitute the basis for its legal system.

The age of Restoration

David Laven

The territorial settlement and Habsburg hegemony

The defeat of Napoleon in Italy, and the subsequent imposition of Austrian hegemony at the Congress of Vienna, was more than a mere continuation of what Metternich called 'the three-hundred-year-long struggle for domination in Italy'. The priority given by the Habsburgs in 1814–15 to establishing mastery over the peninsula reflected the way in which this struggle had radically altered since French revolutionary armies first crossed the Alps. Traditionally, Habsburgs and French had fought over Italy for its own sake; from 1797, Napoleon had also used Italy as a base from which to launch attacks deep into the heartland of the Habsburg Empire. After 1815 the rulers of the Habsburg Empire would see control of Italy as an essential bastion against French aggression.

The Austrian hegemony in Restoration Italy differed considerably from that imposed by the French. Unlike Napoleon, Metternich and Francis I were not overtly expansionist. Despite demands in military circles that parts of Piedmont and the Papal States be annexed, the Austrians sought with few exceptions to secure only lands with a strong precedent for Habsburg rule. Essentially this meant Lombardy (first acquired in 1713) and Venetia (held briefly from 1798 to 1806). These were incorporated into the empire as a single kingdom. In addition, four other states received rulers from the House of

Habsburg: Tuscany went to the emperor's brother, Ferdinand III (1814–24) and thereafter to his descendants; Parma to Francis I's daughter—Napoleon's second wife—Marie Louise for life, and both Modena and the tiny state of Massa and Carrara were given to members of the cadet d'Este branch of the family. The rest of the Italian peninsula, and the islands of Sardinia and Sicily—that had both escaped French conquest—had no direct dynastic link with Austria. Two states received Bourbon rulers: the small Duchy of Lucca was given for life to a Bourbon princess, and the Neapolitan branch of the family was restored to its mainland territories, administratively united from 1816 with Sicily as the Kingdom of the Two Sicilies. Similarly, Victor Emanuel I was able to return from Sardinia to his Piedmontese lands, swollen by the acquisition of Liguria. (As with Venice and Lucca, there was no thought that Genoa should have its *ancien régime* status as an independent republic revived.) Pius VII also regained full temporal control of the Papal States.

It was Metternich's hope that the non-Habsburg lands of Italy could be subjected to some form of Austrian authority. To this end in 1814 he proposed an Italian confederation under Habsburg presidency. This scheme proved stillborn in the face of opposition from both Victor Emanuel, hostile to any one power exercising too much power in the peninsula, and the papal secretary of state, Cardinal Ercole Consalvi (1757–1824), who argued that the pope could not be placed under any temporal authority. Metternich was reluctant to antagonize either. Piedmont constituted a valuable buffer state on the borders of France, like Prussia in Germany, a useful friend and an awkward foe. It was even more important not to alienate the pope, risking the wrath of the Catholic hierarchy, or worse still, driving the papacy into the embrace of France.

The absence of a confederation did not prevent the Austrians from exercising enormous influence beyond their frontiers. Where the rulers were Habsburgs they depended ultimately on the Austrian army for protection. Even when they were not, ties of marriage, strong diplomatic links, and military vulnerability left them with little choice but close cooperation. In the immediate aftermath of Napoleon's defeat, Austrian armies of occupation remained throughout Italy. Even when these withdrew, the Vienna Settlement allowed Habsburg troops to occupy key papal fortresses. Moreover, a military convention and defensive treaty with the Two Sicilies placed the

Neapolitan army under de facto Austrian control. When rebellions broke out in 1820–21 in both Sardinia–Piedmont and the Two Sicilies, the Austrians had abundant excuse for armed intervention— sanctioned by the powers through the so-called Troppau Protocol of November 1820—that established the precedent for interference in the internal affairs of other states to an extent that even a confederation would not have guaranteed.

Although high standards of government were usually enjoyed in the states under Habsburg rule, the rigorous resistance to revolution that characterized Metternich's Italian policy made Austrian domination of the peninsula appear fundamentally reactionary. This generated widespread resentment among more progressive Italian opinion and contributed to a growing nationalist rhetoric within reformist circles. However, it should be stressed that the main cause of unrest in Restoration Italy was not 'foreign' domination. Instead it was the fact that the territorial reorganization of the peninsula not only failed to address historic local and regional rivalries, but also generated new ones. The Sardinians and Sicilians, for example, both resented the return of royal courts to mainland capitals, while the Sicilians also found that the 1816 fusion with Naples, and the accompanying administrative and legal integration, curtailed many old privileges and led to the adoption of practices (most notably conscription) that were alien to the island's traditions and interests. Likewise, the return of Bologna to papal rule was unwelcome among the local elites who, having grown used to the modernizing government of Napoleon's Kingdom of Italy, would have preferred incorporation into the Habsburg Empire. Among the Genoese, simmering discontent would remain at their transfer to the House of Savoy. In contrast, one reason why Venice remained so notoriously passive during the Restoration was that the Habsburgs elevated the former *Dominante* to the same status as Milan. What these examples help demonstrate is that for the vast majority of Italians the concept of a national political identity had little significance: to rid oneself of 'foreign' rule could just as well mean casting off the unwanted control of another Italian city or region, as driving out the Austrians.

Napoleon's legacy and Restoration administration

Whatever their dynasty, Italy's rulers after 1815 had much in common. All were essentially absolutist in nature, and all were faced with the same overwhelming question of what to keep and what to reject of the Napoleonic system of 'administrative monarchy' (*monarchia amministrativa*). At the crux of this problem was the remarkable efficiency of the Napoleonic state, which far surpassed even the most progressive of Italy's *ancien régime* governments. Napoleon's enormous success in reforming legal codes and fiscal procedures, as well as the police and armed forces, had been achieved at the expense of traditional rights and privileges—of the nobility, Church, and provinces. For many of the restored dynasties—who had themselves often sought to curb the power of privileged estates in the eighteenth century—there were good practical reasons to retain much of the French system. In short, the modern *stato amministrativo* introduced by the French was recognized as an impressive foundation for the construction of an absolutist system.

Yet there were also sound reasons to discard Napoleon's legacy. In the popular imagination French domination was associated closely with heavy taxation, conscription, and anticlericalism born of Jacobinism. Despite some nostalgia amongst those who had profited from the career opportunities offered in the Napoleonic administration and army, few ordinary Italians mourned the fall of the Corsican's empire. For the restored rulers, too, Napoleon was a figure of hatred—albeit tinged with admiration—who had humiliated them on the battlefield, stolen their lands, and driven them into exile. The rulers' position was further complicated by problems that stemmed from the dramatic and fundamental changes effected during the Napoleonic era in the relations between civil society and the state. First, while uniform laws and centralization brought obvious bureaucratic benefits, applied too rigorously they created sharp tensions between periphery and centre, aggravating the already noted regional jealousies and municipal rivalries. Second, Napoleonic rule had plunged relations with the Church and nobility into confusion. Under the *ancien régime* these two powerful groups had often blocked princely attempts to rationalize and centralize the adminis-tration. Thus, on one hand, restored rulers often welcomed limita-tions imposed by Napoleon; on the other, aristocratic and clerical support was important for the legitimacy of the restored rulers, beg-ging the question of how far to restore former rights and privileges. And further, the years of French domination had witnessed the emer-gence of a class of men, drawn from both noble and bourgeois ranks, that had served its French masters with great ability and become attached to the new ways introduced from beyond the Alps. These men generally resented attempts to jettison Napoleonic practices and institutions, and were potentially dangerous enemies if slighted, purged, or simply denied the opportunities for advancement they had, until recently, enjoyed.

All the Restoration regimes opted to keep the fiscal structures they inherited largely intact. Their response to other elements of the Napoleonic heritage varied greatly. At the most reactionary end of the spectrum stood Francesco IV of Modena (1815–46) and Victor Emanuel I of Sardinia–Piedmont (1802–21). The former was a maverick who entertained absurd expansionist fantasies that led him eventually into a bizarre flirtation with the liberal revolutionary Enrico Misley (1801–63). In general, however, Francesco IV was fiercely opposed to reform or innovation of any kind, and worked to return Modena to the pre-revolutionary era. Victor Emanuel shared this obsessive desire to turn back the clock to the *ancien régime*. The danger inherent in this position was immediately recog-nized by Metternich, who forced the rehabilitation of two key figures who had served under the French: San Marzano and Prospero Balbo. Even such talented ministers, however, could not prevent purges and demotions in the army and civil service. Instead, Victor Emanuel's true colours were revealed in the prominence afforded the Jesuits in education and censorship, and a host of petty measures such as the closure of the botanical gardens opened by Napoleon. This style of government made Sardinia–Piedmont fertile breeding ground for discontent: in 1821 insurrection erupted, centred on discontented army officers (many with experience in Napoleon's armies) and secret societies of both democratic and moderate ambitions. The attempted rising was short-lived, but highlighted the dangers implicit in adopting polices of intransigent reaction. Significantly, Charles Felix (1821–31), who came to the throne on Victor Emanuel's abdication, heeded the warning, and, throughout the 1820s, pushed through moderate conservative reforms.

The success of the Papal States in avoiding revolt during the early years of the Restoration stands in sharp contrast with Piedmont. Despite the opposition of ultra-conservative cardinals, the so-called *zelanti*, Cardinal Consalvi managed to retain the best features of Napoleon's centralized system (including the French-style *gendarmerie*), and refused to countenance the reintroduction of aristocratic feudal rights. Denounced as a cassocked Jacobin by the *zelanti* and feudal lords with a vested interest in a return to the old ways, Consalvi enabled the Papal States to escape 1820–21 without serious disorder. Unfortunately, Pius VII's successor, Leo XII (1823–29), dismantled much of the bureaucratic and police apparatus established by Consalvi, while reintroducing feudal rights and a whole host of minor but vexatious regulations designed to safeguard the moral welfare of his subjects. These policies generated administrative chaos, contributed to a breakdown in law and order, and aroused popular disdain. During the 1820s discontent in the Papal States mounted; by the early 1830s some areas were in a state of endemic revolt. Of course, it cannot be known whether loyalty to Consalvi's brand of *monarchia amministrativa* would have permanently forestalled discontent—after all, there had been many risings in Italy under French rule. However, at least Consalvi's system would have provided the necessary machinery to address problems as they arose, unlike the ill-run, poorly policed state that emerged later in the 1820s.

As the experiences of the Papal States and Piedmont demonstrate, attempts to reconcile traditions of *ancien régime* government, in which privileged groups wielded enormous powers of jurisdiction, with the legacy of Napoleonic, centralized bureaucracy were always problematic. Indeed, many rulers became vulnerable because of their tendency to oscillate, attempting both to satisfy supporters of the *stato amministrativo* and to appease reactionaries anxious to purge collaborators, monopolize high office, defend the power of the Church, and regain lost privileges. Such attempts at accommodation allowed jealousies and tensions to fester throughout society, from peasants anxious to regain common land rights up to competition for the highest government offices. Usually, rather than effecting a compromise, all groups were dissatisfied. In Naples, for example, the police minister, Antonio Canosa, who energetically persecuted anyone associated with the Muratist regime, became locked in conflict with the more moderate minister of the interior, Luigi De' Medici. So provocative was Canosa's position that the British and Austrians bullied the king into sacking him. However, Medici's bridge-building policy of 'amalgamation'—an attempt to reconcile the Bourbon loyalists with the servants of the defunct Muratist regime—proved no better at preventing revolt. Admittedly, the disastrous economic and fiscal situation resulting from the recent wars made Medici's task extremely difficult, but through his tolerance of the liberal-orientated secret society, the *carboneria*, and the concessions made in the concordat with the Church in 1818, he managed to antagonize reactionaries and alienate moderates, respectively. In Sicily separatism played a vital part in the outbreak of revolution in 1820, but the revolution on the mainland above all represented the failure of Medici's middle path. The wide support that the Neapolitan insurrection won from peasantry, army, middle-class landowners, and urban bourgeoisie shows the breadth of opposition to Bourbon rule. Yet divisions within the revolutionary ranks also hampered any effective resistance to the Habsburg forces sent to restore the rule of Ferdinand I.

The most stable parts of the peninsula in the earliest years of the Restoration were the lands controlled directly from Vienna, or ruled by immediate members of Francis I's family. Francis's daughter, Marie Louise of Parma (1814–47), seemed to succeed where Medici failed in Naples. On the one hand, she retained most of her husband's machinery of government, and even introduced a progressive law code, widely held to be an improvement on his Code Napoleon; on the other, she compensated the aristocracy and clergy for loss of privileges, by affording them high office and personal favour. However, it is important to beware a myth of good government: in 1831 revolution spilled over from neighbouring Modena; Marie Louise refused concessions, choosing instead to flee to the safety of Austrian Mantua. Indeed, pivotal for the stability of all the Habsburg territories was the fact that, even more than other states, they fell within the protective sphere of Metternich's 'forest of bayonets'. The Grand Duchy of Tuscany, however, did become a byword for good government. Perhaps this was because its Habsburg rulers were able to look to reforming traditions less likely to generate conservative hostility than the Napoleonic legacy. In the Grand Duchy, it was not the *monarchia amministrativa* of French domination that served as a model, but the enlightened Leopoldine government of the late eighteenth century.

Had Francis I followed his younger brother's lead and similarly adapted the eighteenth-century model of rule for Lombardy, he would certainly have won the gratitude of the Milanese aristocracy. Largely excluded from power by the French, this group looked back nostalgically on the golden era of autonomy and local power that they had enjoyed under Maria Theresia. However, when Francis I charged a special commission with the reincorporation of Lombardy and Venetia into the Habsburg Empire, it soon became evident that some version of his son-in-law's machinery of government offered attractive opportunities for control and exploitation, and fitted more comfortably with the emperor's penchant for centralization. The refusal to countenance a restoration of privilege and regional autonomy certainly played a pivotal part in turning many Lombard aristocrats towards an anti-Austrian position, and fostered a peculiar alliance with progressive elements of the bourgeoisie. Among the latter there was widespread resentment at the loss of career opportunities that resulted from the dismantling of the Kingdom of Italy, the relocation of authority elsewhere (whether vertically to Vienna or horizontally to Venice), and the employment of officials from the Hereditary Lands of the Habsburg Empire. Paradoxically, bourgeois Lombards who regretted the fall of the Napoleonic regime, and aristocrats who had helped bring it about, became allies, developing a national and liberal critique of Austrian rule.

Yet there was much to recommend Austrian government. We have already seen how the Venetians welcomed the end of control from Lombardy. Moreover, although the Napoleonic model was retained primarily because of the advantages it afforded the empire, there is no doubt that such continuity provided efficient administration, and in Lombardy—where the *gendarmerie* was retained—efficient policing. There were other benefits, too. If the relative wealth of Lombardy–Venetia did sometimes encourage Vienna to treat it as a 'milch cow', there is no question that exactions of conscripts and cash were far less burdensome than under the French. Censorship, though irksome, was less oppressive than in most Italian states, and the bureaucracy, while notoriously slow—in large part because of the emperor's own obsession with detail and tendency to procrastinate—

was neither marred by corruption nor unsympathetic to the conditions of the local population; the judicial system was characterized by remarkable even-handedness. Indeed, the 'black legend' of oppressive Austrian rule was the invention of patriotic propagandists who paid scant regard to reality. Genuine grievances existed, of course, but the relative quiescence of Lombardy and, especially, Venetia during the reign of Francis I must in large part be attributed to good government. This would not last under his son.

The growth of opposition

After the risings of 1820–21, the 1820s proved a relatively untroubled decade. By the early 1830s, however, discontent was widespread throughout the peninsula and revolutionary activity repeatedly threatened the status quo. What led to these changes?

To begin with, the discontent of the early 1830s, which particularly threatened the Papal States and the smaller duchies, can be attributed to the complacency of rulers in the 1820s. Secure in the knowledge that the Austrians were prepared to crush insurrection wherever it occurred, some rulers made relatively little effort to improve the quality of their administration—or to bolster their forces—to pre-empt unrest. When, therefore, the economic crisis of the late 1820s hit the peninsula, there was already a good deal of brooding hostility to the status quo. Problems, were further aggravated by the international situation. The July 1830 revolution in France stimulated ill-founded optimism that the new French government would prevent foreign (i.e. Austrian) interference in Italy. Consequently, those who had long been cowed through fear of the Habsburg army were now prepared to risk revolt. Secret societies and sects seized the moment to demand change, often under the banner of patriotism. Taking inspiration from the Greek struggle to overthrow Ottoman rule in the 1820s, the idea of national resurgence and independence gained increasing favour. After 1830–31 it could also draw on the example of the brave, if doomed, Polish resistance to the tsar. Above all, Belgian independence from The Netherlands demonstrated that the Vienna Settlement was not written in stone.

It would be misleading to suggest, however, that the revolts of the early 1830s were primarily nationalist in their goals. Take, for example, the most systematically rebellious region in mainland Italy, the so-called Papal Legations surrounding Bologna. Here the origins of the revolt of 1831 lay largely with the frustration of the local elites at the inability of the government to maintain law and order in a time of economic crisis. This situation was aggravated by the administrative confusion that developed after the death of Pius VIII in December 1830. While sects eager to overthrow the temporal rule of the pope had been plotting for some time, what made revolution possible in 1831 was the alienation of significant sectors of the propertied classes. Years of bad government had combined with unrest among the poor to such a degree that the leading citizens of Bologna were prepared to embrace revolution rather than risk slipping into anarchy. That the Bolognese provisional government appealed to the Lombards to cast off Austrian rule should not be interpreted as a demonstration of nationalist intent, simply a recognition that some common stance needed to be adopted to prevent Austrian intervention. Needless to say, the Lombards, used to good Austrian government and facing sterner military opposition, failed to respond. Indeed, although there was some collaboration between conspirators in Bologna and other central Italian cities (Modena, Parma, Reggio), the provisional revolutionary governments failed to offer each other tangible support: civic particularism was still stronger than any common nationalist or anti-Austrian agenda.

Given the divided and often half-hearted nature of the insurrections of 1831 it is not surprising that Austrian intervention rapidly restored the old order. However, it is also significant that the Austrians, together with the other major powers (including Protestant Prussia and Britain), tried to force the new pope, Gregory XVI (1831–46), into measures that would have entirely transformed the administrative and judicial machinery of the Papal States. Although the pope briefly agreed to introduce some of the recommendations, he soon reverted to a policy of bitter reaction, backed up by the *centurioni*, a newly formed militia recruited among the poorest and most brutal elements of society. Gregory's openly reactionary stance forced the Austrians to maintain a military presence in the Papal States for years to come, rather than risk renewed disorders. That French troops were also stationed in the papal port of Ancona was less a reflection of the new

Orleanist regime's desire to maintain order than of its desire for a higher international profile.

Elsewhere, revolts and conspiracy in Italy during the 1830s and early 1840s tended either to be separatist in nature (for example, the Sicilian risings in 1837 and 1841) or the work of individuals with high ideals but little or no popular backing. In this category must be placed the failed insurrection in Viterbo in 1837, and Mazzini's two futile bids to overthrow the Piedmontese monarchy in 1833 and 1834. Planned uprisings in Naples, the Romagna, and Tuscany in 1843 proved equally futile, while perhaps the most ill-supported and ill-conceived of all was the Bandiera brothers' attempted mutiny in the Austrian fleet at Venice. After their disastrous failure to win support in their native city or in their subsequent travels around the Mediterranean, they were eventually captured and shot after landing in Calabria.

Failed conspiracies and revolutions notwithstanding, the 1830s and 1840s saw both mounting dissatisfaction and the development of ideological alternatives that were to find dramatic articulation in the events of 1848. A number of elements combined to create an increasingly unstable situation. While the change in regime in France did not bring the challenge to Habsburg hegemony in the peninsula for which some had hoped, it did open possibilities for undermining Austria's position. More significant was the death in 1835 of the Austrian emperor, Francis I. Under his successor, the good-natured imbecile, Ferdinand I (1835–48), Austrian policy lost what little direction it had enjoyed in the previous two decades. Francis I had been reluctant to introduce the reforms advocated by Metternich, but he had not been entirely inflexible (despite his vaunted enmity for change). His son, by contrast, was completely incapable of government. During Ferdinand's reign the empire fell into ever greater debt, and complete immobilism, characterized by the perpetual squabbling of Metternich and his rival Kolowrat. Austria, therefore, while retaining its position of dominance within Italy, appeared more and more vulnerable. Resentment was fuelled by the lurid propaganda of men such as Misley and Giuseppe Mazzini (1805–72), who forgot (or chose to ignore) that the Austrians had often championed progressive policies. Meanwhile, anger grew within Lombardy–Venetia over the burden of taxes and conscription, vexatious censorship, and the unresponsive nature of the central administration.

The succession of new rulers in a number of Italian states after 1830 also contributed to the volatility of the situation. As we have already seen, in the Papal States Gregory XVI's profoundly conservative position meant that many laymen became even more aggrieved at the iniquities of clerical rule. It was not just that they were excluded from high office and pestered by police and *centurioni*. The pope's refusal, for example, to permit railway construction hampered economic development, while his fiscal policy was a disaster. Gregory's rule embodied all that was worst about the government of Restoration Italy. Even loyal subjects began to call for reform. In contrast the succession to the throne of Ferdinand II (1830–59) in the Two Sicilies, and of Charles Albert (1831–49) in Sardinia–Piedmont, dramatically altered the peninsula's position vis-à-vis Austria. Ferdinand II was far less biddable than his predecessors and was determined to govern unconstrained by the Habsburgs. Similarly Charles Albert, although married to a Habsburg princess, was anxious to free himself from any outside restrictions. Charles Albert's independent—even confrontational—foreign policy made him the focus for the patriotic aspirations of many Italian moderates. His domestic policy also attracted admiration. Reforms such as the new law code introduced in 1837, reductions in clerical privileges, the reorganization of the army, the pursuit of trade agreements with other Italian and European states, helped lay the basis for Piedmont's rise as the most dynamic state in the peninsula in the 1850s. It is little surprise that already by the 1840s Piedmontese moderates—most notably Cesare Balbo (1789–1853) and Massimo D'Azeglio (1798–1866)—received a wide audience for their argument that Piedmont should assume the leading role in the regeneration of Italy.

Not all ideological challenges to the existing order ascribed a prominent a role for Piedmont. Many moderate thinkers believed that the major need was not for any radical political restructuring of the peninsula but for economic and social reform. The brilliant Milanese polymath Carlo Cattaneo (1801–69), for example, while eager for greater Lombard autonomy, was much more interested in developments in education, manufacturing, agriculture, and infrastructure than any struggle for national independence. Cattaneo's two journals—the *Annali universali di statistica* and the *Politecnico*—echoed the original intentions of the *Antologia*, a progressive journal set up in Florence by a businessman and reformer of Swiss extraction,

Gian Pietro Vieusseux (1779–1863). Nevertheless, Cattaneo's journalism did help foment opposition to Habsburg rule, contributing to the growing critique of rigid and reactionary government. Similarly *Of Italy's railways* (1845) by the Piedmontese aristocrat Illarione Petitti (1790–1850) and Camillo Cavour's (1810–61) (supposed) review of it for a French journal the following year, while not overtly political in their goals were part of a peninsula-wide movement for reform that went beyond modernization in an attempt to break down municipal and regional rivalries. This increasing readiness to question the assumptions of the established order—however timidly—found echo among the participants in the scientific congresses held in major Italian cities after 1839.

Opposition took many different forms. Giuseppe Mazzini's *Giovane Italia*, established in 1831, urged mass popular revolution to establish a democratic, united Italian republic. Both Mazzini himself and the increasingly paranoid police of the Italian states probably overestimated the actual support for his movement. Still, it cannot be denied that Mazzini's skilful propaganda won over increasing numbers to the idea of a united Italy, including a growing body of foreign sympathizers. More significant than the Mazzinians or other radical, republican groups, was the development of a patriotic, liberal Catholic movement, centred on the Piedmontese cleric, Vincenzo Gioberti (1801–52). This was not because Gioberti's views, put forward in his long, rambling, and often bizarre *Of the moral and civil primacy of Italians* (1843) were necessarily more popular, but because they seemed to appeal to one very important convert: the future Pope Pius IX (1846–78).

Gioberti's book called for the establishment of an Italian confederation as the first step towards greater unity. Believing strongly that a powerful papacy was the key to all human progress, he held that the leadership of such a future confederation had to rest with the pope. The *Primacy* was dedicated to Gregory XVI, who had no time for the ideas of Gioberti, a former republican and political exile from Piedmont. His successor, Pius IX, was more sympathetic. After his election in 1846 various reforms were introduced, including an amnesty for political prisoners, the relaxation of censorship, public works schemes, and proposals to introduce a new legal code and permit the construction of railways. Papal subjects were even permitted to attend scientific congresses for the first time. These measures made many educated Italians feel that Pius IX was the 'patriot pope' heralded by Gioberti. Moreover, Pius's apparently reformist stance began to find echo at a local level in the pulpits of churches across the peninsula, so threatening to mobilize much greater support than had ever been achieved by the worthy tomes and pamphlets of the moderates, or the radical propaganda of Giovane Italia. Pius IX, of course, was not a liberal and certainly never meant his reforms to destabilize the peninsula. Nevertheless, the clerical impulse was to play a significant role in the politicizing of all levels of Italy's population in the months before the outbreak of revolution in 1848.

New ideologies and criticism of the established order do not of their own make revolutions. The actual outbreak of revolts in 1848 would not have occurred had it not been for the sharp deterioration in economic conditions that took place in Italy (and most of the rest of Europe) in the period 1845–47. Repeated harvest failures, which saw the price of staples such as maize and wheat more than double, devastated the economy and triggered a recession, undermining faith in governments that proved unable or unwilling to respond adequately to the crisis. The Habsburg authorities in Lombardy–Venetia, who had dealt with the famine of 1816–18 with great efficiency, were particularly culpable, slow to put a ban on cereal exports and continuing to levy taxes without remission. Where once the Habsburg provinces had been among the most stable in Italy, they now became a centre of agitation. During 1847 demands for self-government, civil liberties, and an end to censorship received wide public support among the educated and popular classes alike. A boycott of cigars and snuff in protest at the state-controlled tobacco monopoly (and Habsburg fiscal exactions in general) led to bloodshed when Milanese clashed in January 1848 with members of the city's Austrian garrison. In the university town of Padua, the longstanding—previously apolitical—animosity between students and soldiers took on a more overtly political aspect and ended in butchery in February 1848.

The tensions evident in 1847 were not limited to Lombardy–Venetia. In almost all Italian states 1846 and 1847 witnessed mounting unrest. In Tuscany a loose coalition of patriots, disgruntled artisans, radicals, and moderates successfully campaigned for reforms often mirroring those introduced by the pope. By early autumn 1847 greater freedom of the press, an enlarged constituent assembly, and a national guard had all been granted to forestall more serious threats to public order. In Piedmont, too, Charles Albert tried to distract criticisms of his rule by cultivating his anti-Austrian stance, and dismissing unpopular ministers. When this proved inadequate he responded with a range of reforms limiting police powers, introducing the principle of consultation at local level, strengthening the Council of State, and granting greater Sardinian autonomy. Such concessions, however, carried with them dangers, for although the popularity of Charles Albert, Pius IX, and Leopold II of Tuscany (1824–59) rose in many quarters, their reforms also encouraged more extreme demands, further threatening the Restoration order.

The revolutions of 1848–49

In January 1848 separatist revolt erupted in Sicily. Shortly afterwards a peasant rising broke out on the mainland. By the end of the month Ferdinand II had granted a limited constitution in the hope of appeasing at least the more moderate critics of his rule. Similar concessions were soon forthcoming elsewhere, granted by rulers made uneasy by public unrest during the preceding months. Leopold of Tuscany granted a constitution on 11 February; Charles Albert of Piedmont followed suit on 5 March; on 14 March Pius IX did the same, as did Charles II (1847–49) of Parma on 29 March. All of these constitutions were very moderate, maintaining vast powers in the hands of the ruling princes, and reflecting their 'determination to give way as little as possible to democratic pressure'.[1] In each state the grant of these constitutions was accompanied by the appointment of new ministers usually drawn from the more conservative ranks of the moderates.

The concessions made late in 1847 and early 1848 would probably have gone a long way towards ending unrest in Italy. While discontent certainly persisted, constitutional gains would have attached most moderates to the status quo, while the amelioration in economic conditions would have pacified the poor. Where unrest still persisted rulers might have been expected to deflect it through compromise or

---

[1] Stuart Woolf, *A History of Italy 1700–1860* (London, 1979), p. 372.

to respond with troops, as in 1820–21 and 1831–32. However, the outbreak of revolution to the north of the Alps prevented such a solution to unrest in the peninsula.

The Parisian revolution of 22–24 February 1848 not only overthrew the Orleanist monarchy with remarkable ease, but also caused panic among the crowned heads of Europe, adding impetus to the pattern of pre-emptive reform already emerging in many German and Italian states. In the latter, despite the bitter experience of 1830, many radicals were sanguine that a republican government in France would protect the peninsula from Austrian intervention. Events in the Habsburg Empire also gave grounds for optimism. By early March, popular demonstrations had broken out in Vienna and Hungarian nationalists had demanded autonomy. The emperor's response was to dismiss Metternich on 13 March and, shortly afterwards, to grant a constitution and freedom of the press. The fall of Metternich was pivotal to the gathering pace of revolution in Lombardy and Venetia because, his reforming instincts notwithstanding, the ageing statesman had always been happy to deploy force to crush revolt. His dismissal was seen as a sign that Vienna had lost its nerve.

When the news of Metternich's flight reached Venice, crowds gathered in St Mark's Square. In an attempt to placate them, the Habsburg governor, Aloys Palffy, released Daniele Manin (1804–57), the Venetian patriot and republican whose brief imprisonment by the authorities had transformed him into both popular hero and revolutionary. By 23 March mutinies had taken place among the Italian troops in the Habsburg garrison, and Manin, backed by all classes, but above all by the workers from the arsenal, drove the Austrian troops from Venice with scarcely a shot fired. Within days the Austrians had deserted most of the Venetian mainland, and Manin had declared a Republic. News of Metternich's fall also sparked revolt in Milan. Here the fighting was bitter. The famous 'five days' of 18–22 March saw a vicious battle for the Lombard capital until the Habsburg commander, Josef Radetzky (1766–1858), finally retreated to the safety of the four great fortified cities of the so-called 'Quadrilateral'. Without the security of Habsburg protection, the rulers of Parma and Modena also fled.

By the end of March 1848 it appeared that Italy had a new order. The Austrians had been driven from most of Lombardy–Venetia, and every state now possessed some form of constitutional or republican government. Yet within months this new order was under threat, and by the late summer of 1849 it had completely disintegrated. What brought about this collapse? To understand the ephemeral nature of revolutionary victory it is essential to recognize two key points.

The first is that the defeat of the Habsburg forces in Lombardy–Venetia was illusory. Although shaken by the events of Milan, Radetzky never relinquished the Quadrilateral, a near impregnable bridgehead within easy access of the Brenner Pass. Experience had demonstrated that, for a new order to survive, the Austrians had to be conclusively vanquished. Indeed, it was probably this realization as much as any genuine nationalist sentiment that made a war against the 'barbarians' so popular in the spring of 1848. Since it soon became clear that the newly established republic in France was unwilling and probably incapable of providing assistance, it became equally evident that the necessary war of liberation against the Habsburgs would have to be fought by Italians alone. As we shall see, the military resources available were far from adequate. Moreover, disagreements over how to wage war soon highlighted the enormous divisions— regional, ideological, tactical, and social—that existed within Italy. It is this combination of military weakness and internal division that must be stressed as the second major reason for defeat.

In the earliest stages of the war, a remarkable united front emerged among the rulers of the Italian states. Bowing to popular pressure, both Ferdinand II and Pius IX offered military support for an anti-Austrian campaign. More surprisingly, Leopold II jettisoned family loyalty and agreed to send an army against his cousin. The most significant military support came from Charles Albert, whose forces crossed into Lombardy on 23 March 1848. However, within weeks of the outbreak of fighting sharp divisions had emerged within the anti-Austrian camp. Reluctant to move into an area where radical popular revolt had so recently demonstrated its power, Charles Albert hesitated in his advance, giving Radetzky time to summon reinforcements. Meanwhile Pius IX, worried by the Piedmontese king's reluctance to adopt proposals for a federal Italy, forbade his troops, commanded by Giovanni Durando (1804–69), to cross into Austrian territory. When Durando disobeyed, Pius realized that the situation was slipping from his control. His response, the papal allocution of 29 April, rejected war against a fellow Catholic state, so dealing a hard blow to the legitimacy of the anti-Austrian struggle. On 18 May, following successful military action against an attempted republican coup, Ferdinand II also withdrew his troops. Like Durando, their commanding officer, the Neapolitan Guglielmo Pepe (1783–1855), veteran revolutionary of 1820, disobeyed orders and proceeded to Venice, where he was subsequently put in charge of organizing the city's resistance. Yet, despite Durando and Pepe, by the summer of 1848 the outcome of the military struggle had become almost entirely dependent on Piedmont.

Such heavy reliance on Piedmont was not without its critics. Cattaneo, the reluctant revolutionary, who emerged as the dominant figure in Milan during the 'five days', warned against trusting Charles Albert, the conservative, expansionist dynast. However, moderate aristocrats led by the mayor, Gabrio Casati, soon seized control of Milan. Frightened lest popular insurrection develop a more radical, republican slant, Casati pursued fusion with Piedmont as the best defence against both Radetzky and revolution. Significantly, even Mazzini, who arrived in Milan early in April, was prepared to appeal to Charles Albert, at least until the Austrians were defeated. Cattaneo's reservations were soon justified by Charles Albert's hesitation in pressing home early victories, and by his treatment of Lombardy as a conquered province.

Like Cattaneo, Manin was wary of Charles Albert's motives. Yet because he 'refused to envisage the possibility of a peasant army',[2] Manin was obliged to look for foreign aid. Eventually this contributed to his conversion to a pro-Piedmontese position, but other factors also constrained him to support fusion. Concerned above all with defending Venice itself, Manin left the terraferma largely to the mercy of the Austrians. By the end of May, Habsburg forces had been able to re-establish control over many of the mainland cities. Those that remained free, felt betrayed by the Venetian republic. Although there were several cases of brave resistance, most believed that only Piedmontese intervention could save them. By early June the mainland had overwhelmingly demanded fusion with Lombardy under the House of Savoy. With Venice now isolated, opinion in the capital also began to move towards annexation, and on 4 July Manin himself

---

[2] Paul Ginsborg, *Daniele Manin and the Venetian Revolution of 1848–49* (Cambridge, 1979), pp. 369–70.

reluctantly added his influential voice to the pro-Piedmontese camp.

The adoption of fusionist policies by Lombards and Venetians alike proved futile. On 24 July 1848 Charles Albert's army was crushed in battle at Custoza. By the Salasco armistice of 7 August, the House of Savoy abandoned Lombardy and Venetia. Bar a handful of fortresses, only Venice remained outside Habsburg control. Piedmontese commissars sent to Venice by Charles Albert were almost immediately withdrawn, and Manin assumed dictatorial powers. His leadership was soon challenged by non-Venetian democrats who had arrived in the city hoping to make it the seat of a pan-Italian, republican movement. Manin was obliged to expel these disruptive 'foreigners', revealing both the stark internal divisions of the revolutionaries, and their essentially municipal agenda.

In the spring of 1849, Charles Albert once again went to war, seeking to profit from the heavy commitment of Habsburg forces in the struggle against the Hungarians. Charles Albert's second campaign was again widely supported by patriots who recognized Austrian defeat as a precondition for lasting change. However, once again the Piedmontese monarch's main motive was personal aggrandizement, and his intention was to fight a limited dynastic war. On 23 March, less than a fortnight after Charles Albert's denunciation of the Salasco armistice, Radetzky humiliated the main body of the Piedmontese army at Novara, conclusively demonstrating Austria's military superiority. Charles Albert abdicated in favour of his son, Victor Emanuel II (1849–78), who was left to negotiate a peace with Radetzky. Although Piedmont received remarkably generous terms from Austria and retained its constitution, any hope that the House of Savoy might free Italy evaporated with the Vignale armistice of 24 March 1849. This was further emphasized by the fiercely repressive measures adopted by General Alfonso La Marmora (1804–78) when insurrection broke out in Genoa in response to peace with Austria. Indeed, when the parliament in Turin proved reluctant to ratify the peace terms with Austria, Victor Emanuel twice called fresh elections and on 20 November 1849 issued the so-called 'Proclamation of Moncalieri' in which he made it quite clear that, unless the electorate proved more biddable, he would suspend the 'Statuto'. With Piedmont defeated, Venice alone held out in the north of Italy, besieged by Habsburg troops, and hoping vainly for foreign aid. It was the last of all the revolutionary regimes to capitulate: worn down by cholera, food shortages, bombardment, and feuding among its leaders, it surrendered in August 1849.

In the south of Italy the struggle against Austria had assumed rather less significance. We have already seen how, in Naples, Ferdinand II had virtually restored his authority as early as May 1848, despite not suspending parliament permanently until the following year. In Sicily the revolution proved more durable. However, internal divisions had emerged within the Sicilian insurrection from the outset. Although the traditional rivalry between Messina and Palermo was initially concealed by common relief at overthrowing Neapolitan rule, social tensions rapidly intensified in a period of continued economic crisis. Peasants occupied common lands, cleared forest, butchered livestock, and burned hayricks and land registers, terrifying the owners of the island's *latifundi*. Banditry flourished too, fed by the short-sighted opening of the prisons. Soon the newly established National Guard had become not an instrument of revolution, so much as a class-based militia for the defence of property: its commander, Baron Riso, saw it primarily as a weapon against peasant unrest. Meanwhile, little was done to address the new government's atrocious fiscal position, or to organize adequate defence. Indeed, the suggestion put forward by Francesco Crispi (1818–1901) that conscription be introduced was met with a mixture of derision, among those who recognized the dangers of arming the plebeians, and fury, among the poor who resented such an encroachment on their freedoms.

Given the weakness of Sicily's defences it is little surprise that when Ferdinand II sent troops to Messina in September 1848, they met no sustained opposition. When the city fell after a brief but brutal struggle, Palermo significantly did not rush to provide assistance. British pressure temporarily delayed the restoration of Neapolitan control throughout the island, but with a bridgehead established, Ferdinand knew that he had only to wait for the revolution to crumble. Although there was popular resistance, on 15 May 1849 Palermo surrendered. Among the propertied classes many were delighted to see the end of anarchy.

In the other two major states, Tuscany and the papal territories, the dominant position of the moderates was increasingly eroded during the summer of 1848. In the Grand Duchy worker and artisan demands for 'the right to work' were a constant source of anxiety for the aristocratic and bourgeois landowners who were the basis for the

moderate regime. In the port of Leghorn especially, Francesco Guerrazzi (1804–73) used his local power base to campaign for a radical
extension of the franchise from the very outset of 1848. Throughout
the summer of 1848 republican 'circles' were established to mobilize
opposition to the moderate government and to foment popular
unrest. Late in July popular demonstrations resulted in the resignation of Cosimo Ridolfi (1794–1865), deemed insufficiently keen on a
continued struggle against Austria. On 12 October Ridolfi's successor,
Gino Capponi, was also forced from office following violent demonstrations in a number of provincial towns. Giuseppe Montanelli
(1813–62), who took over as chief minister in the Tuscan government
on 27 October 1848, was the first genuine democrat to lead one of the
monarchical states. His priority was to organize a national constituent assembly that would seek first to coordinate war against the
Austrians, and only later to lay the basis for a unitary Italian state.
Montanelli and Guerrazzi recognized the need to avoid alienating
moderate opinion, but still found themselves criticized on all sides.
From Piedmont, Gioberti—prime minister from December—still
called for a confederation with a nominated assembly, and Charles
Albert harboured plans for dynastic expansion under the cover of
patriotism. At home Leopold II grew steadily less enthusiastic about
war. Meanwhile the most radical democrats, led by Mazzini, fostered
republican and democratic agitation for a constituent assembly,
based in Rome and elected by universal suffrage. Fearing that Mazzinian republicans were taking over Tuscany, and faced with a real threat
of revolution, Leopold fled the duchy on 8 February 1849. However, it
was not long before the peasantry—instinctively hostile to urban
radicals, profoundly Catholic, and encouraged by moderate
landowners—had started to resist the new order. Guerrazzi, who had
substantially usurped Montanelli's authority after the democratic
elections in Tuscany in November 1848, had already shown a preoccupation with maintaining order. He now abortively sought
accommodation with the Tuscan moderates and Leopold. The grand
duke returned in April 1849, welcomed both as a representative of
order and as a Habsburg whose restoration would prevent the worst
excesses of an Austrian invasion.

In the Papal States, the summer months of 1848 also saw growing
militancy among the lower classes, led in Rome by the charismatic
popular leader, Ciceruacchio. Combined with Mazzinian agitation,

such popular unrest increasingly threatened the moderates' control of government. Pius IX sought an answer to the problem in his appointment in September as minister of the interior the academic theologian, Pellegrino Rossi (1787–1848), a brilliant administrator. Despite a number of thoughtful reforms, Rossi's aloof manner and his refusal to countenance war with Austria made him unpopular. On 15 November 1848, Rossi was savagely stabbed to death by one of Ciceruacchio's sons. Faced by a hostile mob, Pius IX fled Rome on 24 November to Gaeta where, under the protection of the king of Naples, he condemned the revolution in the Holy City. Rome in the meantime had fallen entirely into the hands of the republicans. During the course of the next few months it witnessed the most radical experiment in republican government undertaken in any Italian state during the revolutionary years.

After the flight of the pope, Rome became a magnet for radicals and republicans from all over Italy. In January the elections for the Roman representatives for a proposed Italian constituent assembly produced massive support for Mazzini. Backed by the adventurer, Giuseppe Garibaldi (1807–82), the Mazzinians pressed for the creation of a Roman republic. Proclaimed on 8 February 1849, the Roman republic offered an interesting example of Mazzinian policies in action. Even before its declaration, measures had been taken to improve the conditions of the poor (most notably the abolition of the hated grist tax). Once Mazzini assumed control of the government, a widespread programme of reform was initiated, including the seizure of Church lands and their distribution among the peasantry. The republic must be credited with considerable success in both maintaining law and order, and addressing some of the worst social and economic injustices that had characterized papal rule. The experiment was to be short-lived.

The most obvious reason for the collapse of the Roman republic was the foreign intervention of the Catholic powers. Even before Louis Napoleon Bonaparte (who ironically had himself been involved in conspiracy against the pope as a young man) became president in December 1848, Catholic opinion in France had been outraged by the republicans' ill-treatment of Pius IX. The new president, needing domestic Catholic support, and keen that Austria alone should not dictate the course of events in Italy, rapidly endorsed a policy of military intervention. On 25 April 1849 around 10,000 French troops under the command of Marshal Nicolas Oudinot landed at Civitavecchia. In a remarkable action on 30 April Garibaldi, who had been entrusted with the defence of the republic, repulsed Oudinot's first attack on Rome. He then marched south, defeating the Neapolitan army twice on 9 and 15 May. Despite these victories, Rome was not safe. Mazzini had not allowed Garibaldi to press home his advantage against the French, and, early in June, Oudinot, strengthened by reinforcements, again advanced on the city. As the month progressed, the number of men under Oudinot's command was systematically increased. A Spanish contingent also joined the besieging army. Meanwhile, the Austrians, having defeated Charles Albert for a second time, had seized Bologna, and advanced deep into Roman territory. Despite the bravery of Garibaldi, the republic was unable to resist such overwhelming odds. On 3 July Rome surrendered. Garibaldi himself had left the city with a small force the previous night, hoping to march northward to relieve Venice. Although the stuff of romantic legend, Garibaldi's mission was foolhardy and useless. Venice stood no more chance of resisting the Austrians than Rome had the French.

With the collapse of the two republics, Italy's revolutionary parenthesis came to a conclusive end. The legacy of the revolutions, however, was to endure. In the Two Sicilies the restored Bourbons returned to policies of reaction that discredited them both at home and abroad. Much the same was true of Rome, where Pius IX reverted to the policies of his traditionalist predecessor. Meanwhile, Louis Napoleon's decision to leave a garrison in Rome to protect the pope had mixed consequences, since their presence signalled that Austria was no longer the sole European power with an Italian interest. In Piedmont the retention of a constitution, and the patriotic myth that grew up around the twice defeated House of Savoy, made Turin increasingly the focus of patriot aspirations; moreover, its more liberal atmosphere encouraged many exiles from other Italian states to settle there giving it a much stronger 'Italian' identity. Finally, the ease with which the revolutionary republics had been crushed, combined with the propertied classes' fear of the social direction that many of the revolutions had taken, encouraged many former republicans and democrats to reject the very idea of revolution and to adopt the sort of principles that found articulation in the 1850s in the propaganda of the National Society and in the policies of Cavour.

Giuseppe Mazzini and his opponents

Roland Sarti

For Mazzini, the cause of Italian unity was part of the larger struggle for the emancipation of all oppressed nationalities and groups, particularly women, serfs, and slaves. Patriot and democrat at one and the same time, Mazzini lived at a time when it was still possible to imagine that free nations would not infringe on one another's rights or on the rights of individuals. The optimism of such an outlook is perhaps surprising in one who belonged to the generation of romanticism which was more likely to despair at the hopelessness of the human condition than to accept the idea of progress. Therein lies a preliminary observation appropriate to any discussion of Mazzini, whose thinking seldom conforms to ready-made classifications and whose salient trait in life was to go his own way.

Another preliminary observation is that in Mazzini the person cannot be separated from the message. Those who responded to Mazzini were drawn less by the power of his ideas than by his moral authority, a moral authority based on his image of selfless dedication to the cause of revolution. Failure to take the role of that image into account can be a major stumbling block. It presents a problem for historians who look for originality of ideas, systematic thinking, or evidence of concrete achievements, and who consequently wonder what to make of a figure whose ideas seem to lack rigour and whose work was marked by disappointments and failures. Poets have had an easier time with Mazzini than historians. George Meredith's evocation of Mazzini as the soul of modern Italy is rightly famous. It conveys the spiritual aura that surrounded Mazzini and that was, indeed, the essential component of his power.

Thus, it should come as no surprise that Mazzini remains a somewhat elusive figure, certainly the most elusive among the major figures of the *Risorgimento*. The contributions of Garibaldi can be judged in terms of battles won or lost, numbers of volunteers gathered, and territories liberated; Cavour's work reveals itself in parliamentary majorities, diplomatic agreements, and miles of railways constructed. Mazzini's role is more complicated, for while his moral exhortations suggest the figure of the prophet, his talents for conspiracy, journalism, and political infighting point to a more worldly figure. In Mazzini, patriot and democrat, prophet and politician, are different faces of the same figure.

The vision and the controversy

Views of Mazzini tend to be extreme. The admiring view prevails in England where he spent most of his adult life, found friendship, and inspired unlimited devotion among a few. It is in Anglo-Saxon scholarship that one is still likely to find the most appreciative and sympathetic accounts of his work. Reactions elsewhere have been more mixed. In Italy, rivals, opponents, and enemies may well have outnumbered supporters. Mazzini's transformation into a sainted icon was part of a deliberate campaign of national reconciliation that began after his death. While he lived, his intransigent republicanism was both inspirational and divisive. So was his personality. *Verba, verba, pretereaque nihil* (All talk, no action) was the comment of Giovanni Ruffini, his intimate for many years. Mazzini was *Pestalacqua nel mortaio* (Beat the air), quipped Gustavo Modena, the celebrated actor who was often at Mazzini's side. Another thought that Mazzini's motto should be *Io e Popolo* (I and the People) rather than *Dio e Popolo* (God and the People). He was even more controversial in the European democratic movement where his aspirations to leadership encountered opposition from the likes of Louis Blanc, Pierre Proudhon, and Karl Marx. Marx dubbed him Theopompus; as far as he was concerned, Mazzinianism was mostly religious humbug.

Recapturing the controversial Mazzini is the difficult task of scholarship. He does not fit easily into the familiar classifications of contemporary politics. To describe Mazzini as a liberal nationalist, as is often done in textbook accounts of his work, is to ignore his explicit rejection of liberalism and nationalism. Liberalism he found too concerned with individual rights and seemingly indifferent to society's need for cohesive bonding. Nationalism he found too exclusive, and incompatible with the international cooperation that was his ideal. He identified with the radical current of liberalism that was called democratic, but that does not mean that he believed in majorities. It was his misfortune to live at the dawn of the democratic age, when the people seldom responded to the call of those who claimed to speak for them. Mazzini understood perfectly well that the majority was not with him, a tragic situation for someone who had to maintain faith in the people at all costs. So, when the people did not listen, or when they turned against their would-be benefactors, Mazzini invoked God and his conscience as the sole authorities to which he felt responsible. Until such time as the people achieved political maturity, he would have to speak for them, and he seldom hesitated to do so. Whether from political necessity or personal inclination, Mazzini was often an autocratic democrat.

His relationship with the social movements of his time raises other problems. He believed in revolution, and in gradual reform; he believed in education, and in action; he believed in distributive justice, and in renunciation. He was the first to insist that movements of national independence incorporate demands for social justice, but he excluded no group or class from just treatment. Cultivating the spirit and fostering 'love' across class lines was his formula for dealing with the inadequacies of capitalism and socialism, which he saw as kindred expressions of the detested philosophy of materialism. His vision was 'associationist' rather than socialist, voluntarist rather than coercive, for private property and free enterprise, but against big business. Going by how little he dealt with economics in his writings, it seems clear that economic concerns were not central to his vision. His language was essentially religious, yet the creed itself conformed to no known theology. Christianity, he believed, spoke only to the need for personal salvation, and its bleak view of human nature was incompatible with the idea of progress. Progress, for Mazzini, was the law of God.

Failure dogged him but did not deter him. Better to try and fail than not to try at all, was his response to those who accused him of rashness and irresponsibility. His journalistic talent and seductive way with words sometimes enabled him to blur the line between success and failure. The importance of words was something he understood instinctively. From the moment he started out on his own, he had to have a newspaper at his disposal for the literate public that was growing rapidly in his time. The 106 volumes of his writings are the best evidence of the importance he attached to the written word, whether meant for the public or for private correspondence. But never seeing himself as a pallid prophet unarmed, Mazzini was not content to play the role of pen-pusher. Ideas expressed in words had to be tested in action. His frequent failures as a man of action were a secret torment. 'In the *actual* time,' he confided in charmingly stilted English, 'the great man is the *succeeding* man. So many elements are at work, that there *must* be some vital deficiency in a man who cannot organize them so as to conquer.'[1] Conquering meant winning people's minds and leading them in matters of this world. The latter mission is what stands in the way of seeing Mazzini as a spiritual force. If the record of his life shows anything, it is that Mazzini employed both the worldly arts of politics and violence, not the indiscriminate violence of twentieth-century terrorism, but certainly the violence of the barricades and of conspiracy. Thought and Action is the most Mazzinian exhortation of all. The notion that true believers had an obligation to act on their beliefs was at the heart of Young Italy (*Giovine Italia*). Its goal was to unify Italy as a republic by education and insurrection.

The upbringing and self-image

That was Mazzini's call to fellow Italians. It is not without significance that it issued from Marseilles in July 1831, rather than from some stretch of Italian soil at some other date. What brought him to France was political persecution in Italy, but what kept him going was something that went much deeper. When, much later in life, he sought to explain himself to his contemporaries, he went back to first

---

[1] Letter to Emilie Ashurst, 4 March 1850, in *Edizione Nazionale. Scritti editi ed inediti di Giuseppe Mazzini.* (Imola, 1906–90), Vol. XLII, p. 124. Hereafter cited as *EN*.

principles. Few and simple were those principles, he said, and attributable solely to his upbringing: 'The democratic habits of my two parents and the identical ways with which they treated both patricians and commoners had unconsciously educated me to the cult of equality. In the individual they looked only for character and honesty.'[2] The family loomed large in Mazzini's outlook. Born in Genoa on 22 June 1805, the third of four children and the only male, he faced a world of change, filled with new and disturbing ideas. A few weeks before his birth Genoa had become part of Napoleon's empire, making Mazzini a citizen of France. The relationship with France would always be problematic. Fluent in French, Mazzini chose Italian as his language of expression; constantly influenced by French ideas and developments, he insisted, adamantly, that everything he did was Italian to the core. With Mazzini, then and later, the more ambiguous the contours, the more intransigent the response.

In a world in flux, Mazzini remembered his childhood as a period of warmth and security, and the family as a shielding and nurturing environment. Indeed, he enjoyed a secure and privileged position in his family, in part because he was the only male, but also because of the warm, effusive personality that endeared him to all, and most of all to his mother who established with him an exclusive relationship. The experience of love in the family, he would reflect as an adult, had made him aware of the possibilities of love beyond the family. Through love, the individual could stretch out to family, country, humanity, and God, developing with each step a greater capacity to empathize with others and, finally, with goodness and truth. The hierarchy of values at the core of the Mazzinian creed was rooted in an idealized experience of family life. The concepts of individual, family, country, humanity, and God would find concrete applications in the politics of the mature Mazzini.

Maria Mazzini Drago was a well-educated woman who took a strong interest in her son, in religion, and in public affairs, definitely in that order. Probably influenced by the Jansenist notion that good Christians make good citizens, she was earnest and outspoken. In family life, her approach might be described today as one of tough love. There was no catering to childish whims, no self-indulgence,

---

[2] From Mazzini's *Ricordi autobiografici*, in *EN*, LXXVII, p. 6.

and what diversions were allowed had to be for self-improvement. Mazzini never doubted his mother's love, but he also remembered that he was not allowed to have animal pets, that meals were nourishing but spare, that mother usually managed to get her way. His childhood pastimes were playing chess, reading music, and playing the guitar. The ethic of work 'took' on the child and the adult: 'There is, therefore, no rest', he said. 'Rest is immoral.'[3] The revolutionary ascetic was formed in the household.

That teenage rebellion is not a recent phenomenon is borne out by the evidence that Mazzini experienced it when he entered the University of Genoa at age 14 in 1819. It was then that his behaviour underwent a marked change that points to the person behind the image. The image of a precocious youngster caught up in his studies is contradicted by substantiated reports that he wavered between studying medicine or law, frequented cafes and billiard rooms, made fun of professors, and got into scrapes with university administrators and the police. Before the end of his freshman year, in June 1820, Mazzini was already in trouble for having led a student demonstration. Pressure from parents and police may have kept him out of trouble a year later when the revolution of 1821 reached Genoa. That event, in which Mazzini played no visible role, assumed importance when Mazzini, looking back on his life, saw it as a wake-up call. It was the sight of the defeated revolutionists begging in the streets of Genoa, he claimed, that linked in his mind the ideals of *patria* and *libertà*, intimating 'that one could, and therefore one *should*, fight for the liberty of the homeland.'[4]

Like many others of his generation, Mazzini found solace in literature as he discovered that not even the most authoritarian governments could forbid the study of authors who worked on the imagination. Consequently, literature became a way of doing politics by other means. He received his law degree in 1827, but the study and brief practice of law never absorbed him as did literature. It was love of literature that bound him to Jacopo Ruffini, who became his closest friend and political collaborator. Jacopo's brothers, Agostino and Giovanni, would be his companions in France, Switzerland, and England. They all felt the spell of Ugo Foscolo's novel *Last Letters of*

---

[3] *EN*, LXXXIV, p. 244.   [4] *EN*, LXXVII, p. 6.

Jacopo Ortis. That tale of a young man driven to suicide by unrequited love for woman and country embodied for them the ideal of the politically engaged artist victimized by an unfeeling society. Romantic angst brought together love, patriotism, and suffering. And so, at age 20, Mazzini saw himself 'cursing chance, or whatever power exists, which has flung us down here, with this unrequited longing in our hearts, with this immense love for a country that is denied to us, giving us tyrants instead. I have often thought of escaping from them, and denying them the pleasure of seeing me suffer.'[5] That temptation was momentary. Mazzini decided upon reflection that, rather than doing away with himself, he would become a plague to his tormentors.

After a brief stint as a literary critic in the columns of *L'Indicatore Genovese* on the side of the romanticists against classicists, he found his way into the secret society of the *carbonari* to conspire and agitate for government reform. Most members of the brotherhood were content to demand constitutions, political representation, and civil liberties from governing monarchs, but there were others who envisaged more radical changes. Anticlericalism, republicanism, and even redistribution of property were ideas shared by the most committed. Mazzini's place in the spectrum of opinions present among the *carbonari* is hard to ascertain for lack of coeval evidence. We cannot assume that he was a convinced republican at this stage of his development. What we do know is that as a *carbonaro* Mazzini pursued politics with that moral earnestness and sense of rectitude that he had imbibed with mother's milk. Starting with his closest friends, then reaching out to acquaintances, and finally toward complete strangers as far away as Tuscany, he became a zealous recruiter. It was then that he learned the painful lesson that in undercover activities the most dangerous enemies often lurk among one's friends. It was a fellow *carbonaro*, one Raimondo Doria, who claimed descent from that noble Genoese family, and who may have seen the younger man as a rival and an upstart, who informed on him. Arrested, then formally exonerated for lack of evidence, but still under suspicion, Mazzini was given the choice of going abroad or being confined to some remote locality. He left for France in early February 1831, not as one condemned to political exile as legend would have it, but as a

[5] *EN, Zibaldone giovanile,* III, pp. 274–5.

voluntary expatriate, free to go and do according to his means and inclinations.

Mazzini may have expected a quick return to Italy in the wake of triumphant revolution, but instead he found himself part of the great political migration. France during the July Monarchy became home to thousands of political exiles, mostly Poles and Italians stranded there by the failure of revolution in their countries. None could know that large-scale revolution would not break out again for another 17 years. In France, Mazzini discovered the heady pleasures of free intellectual discourse, gaining familiarity with the most advanced and exciting theories of social change, while distancing himself from Italy. Far from the realities of Italian life, Italy for him became a country of the imagination where ordinary people were patriots ready to die for freedom. Perhaps paradoxically, this lack of realism was also a source of strength. As his father liked to remind him, no one familiar with Italy could entertain such wrongheaded notions and go on fighting for a hopeless cause. The son paid no attention: 'This fixation with Italy is a command from God.'[6]

Mazzini's debt to French radical thought is well documented. Gaetano Salvemini first drew attention to the influence of Henri de Saint-Simon, whose view of a future society based on the principle of association, religious faith, and faith in progress became an essential part of the Mazzinian creed. Saint-Simon's *Dieu et l'humanité* became Mazzini's God and the People. The god that Mazzini and Saint-Simon envisaged bore little resemblance to the god of traditional Christianity. In part it was a logical construct based on the need for an ultimate source of authority, but also an answer to the psychological craving for certainty that marked Mazzini's generation. Moral certainty was all the more important for being involved in conspiracies that carried risks of life and death. Such risks called for the god of Martin Luther, who spoke directly to individuals and lifted the burden of responsibility from youngsters looking for a higher authority in their rebellion against the powers of this world. More than once, when cornered by his critics, Mazzini would voice Luther's appeal: 'Here I stand, so help me God!'

[6] *EN*, XIX, p. 10.

Young Italy

In Marseilles Mazzini found a large concentration of Italian exiles. Their presence, and the city's geographical proximity to Italy, with its regular maritime contacts, made it a logical base for his operations. But an additional reason was that Marseilles was not Paris, where he would have faced the competition of older and more prestigious figures with stronger claims to leadership. Young Italy was to be his creation. His later account traced the decision to establish a new type of revolutionary organization to the days of his imprisonment in Savona. It was to be an organization radically different from that of the secret societies of his day, one committed to publicizing its revolutionary programme for all to see and reaching out to the people whose cause it would defend. That account may explain the genesis of the idea, but the organizational structure and operational mode of Young Italy owed much to its French context. Its commitment to open proselytizing and open dissemination of ideas through the printed word was conceivable only in the relatively liberal atmosphere that prevailed in the early days of the July Monarchy. It resembled in many ways the secret societies working around it, which it rejected in principle. Members took secret oaths, shared secret passwords and symbols, vowed vengeance against tyrants and traitors, and conspired in the familiar ways. The novelty was in Mazzini's understanding of the importance of the printed word. Young Italy published its own journal, *La Giovine Italia*, which Mazzini ran with an iron hand. 'The press is today the arbiter of nations,' he wrote, 'the ink of the wise is a match for the sword of the strong.'[7]

Young Italy spoke to the 'wise', not to the masses, and the wise were expected to act. Inspired by Carlo Bianco's *Of National Insurrectionary Warfare by Bands Applied to Italy* (1830), Mazzini enthused over the possibilities of irregular warfare. *Insurrezione per bande*, he wrote, was the 'war of all nations striving to emancipate themselves from foreign rule.' Irregular warfare made up for scarcity of weapons, enabled the few to mobilize the many, taught the people to bear arms, and could not be defeated by regular armies. There was to be no more

---

[7] *La Giovine Italia* (Rome, 1902–25), I, pp. 129–30.

reliance on the goodwill of traitorous monarchs like Louis Philippe or Charles Albert who pretended to sympathize with reformers only to betray them in the end. That was the mistake of the *carbonari*, who expected change from above. Under Young Italy's leadership, the people would take matters in their own hands: 'Multitudes and weapons! There is the secret of future revolutions.'[8]

Frequent references to *il popolo* (the people) show the democratic slant of Mazzini's thinking, but a close reading reveals that in his mind only those who possessed a national awareness deserved to be called *popolo*. The rest, no matter how many, were merely *gente* (ordinary folks), not to be despised, but not to be honoured or heeded, either. The distinction between *popolo* and *gente* was necessary to preserve the myth that revolutions were 'popular', given that the majority showed little inclination to mount the barricades. Young Italy talked popular revolution, but addressed itself to a minority of educated Italians. The adjective 'young' underlined Mazzini's intention to address those who were born in his century and who were therefore presumably unaffected by earlier ideologies that were obsolete. In practice, Young Italy recruited among all age groups. The recruits, of whatever age, were to think of themselves as 'apostles' of a new faith that would eventually move the masses. In the meantime, the apostles represented 'the invisible Italy, the underground Italy, the chain that binds the past to the future in a secret unity of beliefs, hopes, works, a brotherhood of the strong who sharpen the sword of vengeance on their own chains.'[9]

Such heady language evoked a strong response among political refugees who were indeed sharpening the sword of vengeance on their own suffering. But Young Italy also addressed Italians in Italy, where the risks of joining were higher. Sailors smuggled copies of *Giovine Italia* into Italy through a distribution network centred in Genoa. As cells sprung up in various parts of Italy, governments took countermeasures. Mazzini took on assumed names, but the police caught on, intercepted his correspondence, and uncovered parts of the secret network. What they found caused alarm in several chancelleries. Some estimates placed Young Italy's membership in 1833 at 140,000. Even the perhaps more realistic figure of 50–60,000 would

---

[8] *EN*, II, pp. 53–4, 221.
[9] *EN*, I, p. 387. See also Roland Sarti, *Mazzini: A Life for the Religion of Politics* (Westport, CT, 1997), pp. 52–8.

have been an achievement remarkable enough to justify Metternich's reference to Mazzini as the most dangerous man in Europe .

Young Italy's strength was not just in numbers. Its network covered the regions of Lombardy, Piedmont, Liguria, Tuscany, the Romagna, and extended south to the city of Naples. The Austrian, Piedmontese, Tuscan, papal, and Neapolitan governments perceived it as a serious threat. Its mostly urban network placed it close to the seats of power. Unable to eradicate it in Italy, these governments pressured the French to arrest or expel Mazzini. The order to leave was issued in August 1832, while Mazzini was conspiring with elements in the Piedmontese army. It came at a personally difficult time because of the secret pregnancy of Giuditta Sidoli, a fellow exile with whom he was in love and whose child he almost certainly fathered at that time. Unwilling to leave Marseilles, Mazzini kept a step ahead of the police by moving from one hiding place to the next while the conspiracy developed.

Not all the trouble came from the government. Filippo Buonarroti was an older conspirator who enjoyed almost mythical status in radical circles. An old Jacobin who had left Italy to support Robespierre and Babeuf, he believed that France was the natural home of revolution. He did not take kindly to the brash young man who claimed the revolutionary initiative for Italy. Buonarroti's materialism and economic egalitarianism in turn offended Mazzini, who looked upon private property and modest accumulations of wealth as attributes of liberty. Buonarroti would not grant Mazzini's claim that Young Italy spoke for the Italian revolutionary movement, and sponsored a rival secret society, the *Veri Italiani* (True Italians), which Mazzini tried to incorporate into his network. Young Italy's message was directed as much against Buonarroti as to the people: 'Inscribe on one side of your flag EQUALITY and LIBERTY, and on the other GOD IS WITH YOU.'[10]

The Swiss years and Young Europe

The Piedmontese police cracked down on Mazzini's organization in June 1833 and wiped it out in Genoa and in the army. Jacopo Ruffini, the ringleader, committed suicide in gaol; others escaped abroad or

---

[10] *La Giovine Italia*, II, p. 88.

dropped out in fear. Mazzini was beyond the reach of the police, but renewed police pressure forced him to leave Marseilles. He crossed the border into the Swiss canton of Geneva in July 1833, disappointed and angered by what had happened in Italy, but confident that enough of his network had survived to strike back at the monarch who had ordered the crackdown. An uncontainable desire for revenge against Charles Albert, who had come to the throne in 1831, undoubtedly played a role in an ensuing plot to assassinate the king. Political passion and personal animosity also played a role in the plan to send a force of volunteers into the region of Savoy to stir up insurrection in that part of Charles Albert's Kingdom of Sardinia. The pathetic tale of that unfortunate venture need not be related in detail. Part tragedy and part *opera buffa*, the 'invasion of Savoy' began and ended quickly in the early part of February 1834. It revealed Mazzini's tendency to mix reality with wishful thinking, and the disastrous consequences of doing so. The expected peasant revolts never materialized and volunteers defected. Gerolamo Ramorino, the officer in charge, may have deliberately sabotaged the operation. Mazzini suffered a mental breakdown and had to be carried off the field unconscious.

Mazzini's behaviour after the fiasco conformed to a pattern that would be repeated in the wake of other setbacks. The manifestations were mental depression, symptoms of physical illness, public silence, and private agonizing. But there was a method to it all, for the outcome of these crises was to preserve the necessary myth of popular support for the revolution. As long as failure could be ascribed to errors by individuals, whether his own or others', one could look forward to success the next time around: individuals learned from their mistakes, defeats were only temporary setbacks, the sacrifice of the few insured the victory of the many, and the blood of martyrs watered the tree of liberty. Mazzini borrowed the idea of the martyred nation from the Polish patriot and poet Adam Mickiewicz, and made it an integral part of his creed. If Christianity had thrived on martyrs, so would the revolution; if Italians were the *cristo popolo*, he was the *cristo uomo*. And had not Christ risen from the grave to ultimate victory?[11]

What better way to overcome defeat than to take the offensive? It

---

[11] *EN*, XI, pp. 313–14.

came in the form of Young Europe, an association which Mazzini launched in the wake of the Savoy debacle, to link revolutionary movements throughout the Continent. Mazzini's conception of Europe was based on his earlier literary studies in which he had hypothesized a cultural unity that transcended national diversities. In Switzerland, he extended the concept of cultural unity to the politics of revolution. Already he had concluded that Europe was the locomotive of history: 'Europe is the lever of the world; Europe is the land of liberty; Europe controls the universe. Hers is the mission of progressive development that encompasses humanity.'[12] Therefore, Young Europe could be the lever that changed the world. The Pact of Young Europe was signed in Bern on 15 April 1834 by 17 founding members representing Young Italy, Young Germany, and Young Poland, each claiming to speak for a national movement, a conceit made plausible by the absence of freedom of expression in the regions in question. Young Europe was meant to be the instrument of revolution, not of European unity as we understand it today. Some form of political unity might come from it eventually, but its immediate purpose was to promote revolutions for national independence among oppressed nationalities. In its short and troubled life, Young Europe drew support from political exiles in Europe, Asia Minor, North Africa, and the New World. Its call was heard in South America by Giuseppe Garibaldi. He was there to escape the death penalty meted out to him by the Piedmontese government for his earlier involvement in Mazzinian conspiracies. Stranded there by the reaction, he practised in South America the art of guerrilla warfare that would make him the 'sword' of the *Risorgimento*. Young Europe refurbished Mazzini's reputation after a setback that could have put an early end to the career of a less determined and resourceful agitator.

Switzerland made a lasting impression on Mazzini. He liked the alpine scenery, the people, and the institutions. As the only sizeable republic in Europe, he looked upon it as a laboratory in which he could test his political theories. He imagined Switzerland as the fulcrum of a revolutionary axis having Germany and Italy as its wings. 'The flag that waves over our heads is a republican flag;' he wrote, 'it stands for all insurrections, guides the efforts of all Europeans who

---

[12] *EN*, II, p. 256.

believe in progress and want to wage a war of principles.'[13] If the Swiss could be persuaded to sponsor revolution beyond their borders, republicanism would surely triumph. To that end, he launched another newspaper and plunged into Swiss politics on the side of radicals who wanted to strengthen the central government. The fact that most centralizers were Protestants and that their opponents were mostly Catholics confirmed his preference for democratic Protestantism. He penned his highly personal view of religion in the essay *Fede e avvenire* (1835), which remained his most comprehensive treatment of the religious question until the very last years of his life, when he revisited the issue in his *Dal Concilio a Dio* (1870). Mazzini never embraced Protestantism because he felt that its individualistic theology precluded lasting religious and social bonds, but his experience in Swiss politics reinforced his belief in the unity of religious and political belief. He was neither Catholic nor Protestant, nor anything else, but a *believer* nonetheless: 'No one believes more ardently or deeply than me; no one more than me is convinced that the spirit of religion must dominate the new Italy and the new Young Europe.'[14]

It did not take long for the Swiss authorities to decide that he was not a welcome guest, and they made his life difficult. Mazzini looked back on the last weeks of his stay in Switzerland as the most harrowing period of his life. As the Swiss stepped up efforts to expel him, and Mazzini barely coped with mounting personal and financial difficulties, he experienced a 'tempest of doubt'. But, after teetering at the edge of the precipice, he woke up one morning feeling miraculously restored. By that account, his own, he was indeed the *cristo uomo*, risen from the grave. But a letter written when he was supposedly in the grip of despair, shows him more angry than despairing: 'As I withdraw,' he wrote referring to his impending departure from Switzerland, 'I feel compelled to declare that I yield to necessity and nothing else, that I would go on if I had the means to do so . . . I will devote the first available penny to conspiring once again, perhaps differently and on my own, but certainly to conspiring; in withdrawing, I will tell the Italian people that they have an obligation to conspire, and that if they fail to do so they are guilty of treason, that they have failed in their hearts and minds, that they betray their country,

---

[13] *EN*, VI, p. 390. Also, Sarti, *Mazzini*, pp. 83–9.
[14] *EN, Appendice epistolare*, I, p. 159. For his more general reflections on religion, see his essay of 1835, 'Fede e avvenire,' in *EN*, VI, pp. 293–358.

the legacy of our martyrs, and their duty toward Italy and toward Humanity.'[15]

Mazzini in England and his rivals

Mazzini arrived in England on 12 January 1837. In London, he joined other political exiles, but decided early on not to let himself be consumed by the sterile feuds and factions of exile politics, to reach out instead to prominent English men and women, who were quickly captivated by the slim, darkly handsome, romantic exile. Thomas and Jane Carlyle welcomed him to their drawing room, where he met other prominent Londoners. In this new environment he conceived a new role for himself as spokesman for the Italian nation of his dreams. He would be the voice of the new Italy, until the time came for conspiring once again. Prospects for revolution were dim in 1837. Memories of the failures of 1830–31 were still fresh, agitators were on the run, and with the threat of revolution receding, governments felt free to experiment with reforms. Even Mazzini's nemesis, the once ultra-conservative Charles Albert, promoted economic and administrative reforms that appealed to moderates. Young firebrands must bide their time.

As if it were not galling enough to see his declared enemies in the ascendance, there were those in his own camp who tried to cash in on his name and reputation. In Naples, one Benedetto Musolino, formerly a member of Young Italy, formed the Sons of Young Italy, with a programme that faulted Mazzini's for not paying enough attention to the material needs of the people. Nicola Fabrizi was another former follower branching out on his own. From Malta, where the British allowed him to recruit, Fabrizi claimed autonomy for his Italic Legion. Both Fabrizi and Musolino believed in the southern initiative, which Mazzini regarded with great scepticism. Fabrizi was willing to let Mazzini run theory and propaganda, but insisted on operational autonomy for himself and his paramilitary group. Mazzini wanted unity of command. He did not claim it for himself, but by this time those who knew him well seldom doubted that he intended to run everything.

[15] *EN, Appendice epistolario*, VI, p. 443.

In May 1839 Mazzini wrote to a former collaborator that his strategy for the following decade would be to organize abroad for action in Italy, banking on support from a new generation that was not demoralized by earlier failures. His intent in starting over was 'to do according to our beliefs if possible, and to prevent others from doing differently.'[16] Thus was Young Italy reborn in April 1840, in a revised version that is sometimes referred to as the second Young Italy. It called on the generation of 1820 this time, and also on workers and women, anticipating for all a long period of education and propaganda. There was little new, strictly speaking, in the new Young Italy, except in what it emphasized. Compared to the original, the revised version showed a stronger commitment to workers, who were organized in a separate *Unione degli Operai Italiani*, and had their own publication, the *Apostolato Popolare*. Mazzini told workers that 'if the revolution is to succeed, it must be carried out *for you* and *with you*, while all the previous revolutions have been attempted *not for you* and *without you*.'[17] Mazzini never went so far as to see in workers the totality of the people, but he did envisage for them a prominent place in the revolutionary coalition. Workers and women must first develop the skills that they needed to stand on their own; teaching them those skills was the duty of the better educated. He set an example by opening a school for the children of Italian workers living in London. It was an experiment which, Mazzini hoped, would show students and teachers the value of collaboration across class lines. Someday the workers would remember, he hoped, that they owed their education to Italians of the middle classes. Who could then predict, he asked, 'the ties of love and reciprocal trust that will be formed between the two classes in Italy?'[18]

The second Young Italy served as a school for the country's future elite. Younger, more ambitious, and more worldly than the conspirators of the previous decade, many of his new followers would rise in politics, business, the military, and the professions. These second-generation Mazzinians were on the whole less ideological than the first, more inclined to pursue worldly success, and more likely to challenge the decisions of the man whom they nevertheless acknowledged as their moral guide. They were also probably fewer,

---

[16] *EN*, XVIII, pp. 53–4; XIX, p. 117.   [17] *EN*, XXV, pp. 14, 53–7.   [18] *EN*, XXV, p. 84.

for governments were more vigilant and there was competition from other democrats and moderates. In any case, the strength of the new Young Italy was not in numbers. Its strongest asset was Mazzini himself, whose reputation grew even as the organization struggled. His determination to run things from London created dissent in Paris, where Mazzini wanted Young Italy to compete with socialist groups, and in Italy where his organizers ran into difficulties that Mazzini seemed unable to appreciate from the security of London. In 1843, Vincenzo Gioberti's book *The Moral and Civil Primacy of the Italians* called on the papacy to lead the movement for national independence. This Neo-Guelph movement appealed to Catholics who considered the pope a more legitimate leader than Mazzini. The following year another moderate, the Piedmontese nobleman Cesare Balbo, published *On the Hopes of Italy*, a book that held out the prospect of a diplomatic solution to the Italian question under Piedmontese leadership. Mazzini was particularly caustic toward Gioberti, a one-time collaborator, whose pitch for papal leadership worried him because he feared the spiritual ascendancy of the pope. By claiming that Italians could exert their primacy in world affairs through their special relationship with the papacy, Mazzini argued, Gioberti had perverted the idea of Italian primacy, 'the most beautiful theme that I know', filling it 'with ultra-Roman Catholicism, praise for Charles Albert, and all possible stupidities.'[19]

How could he refrain from conspiring when others spread dangerous illusions? Mazzini's deals in the early 1840s to smuggle bibles into Italy in return for American dollars, with which he could buy weapons, were part of a larger plan to counteract the activities of moderates. The other part was to prepare people to use those weapons. He was enormously pleased to discover that there were Italians trained to fight in South America, led by one Giuseppe Garibaldi, a self-proclaimed Mazzinian, whose daring deeds in admittedly obscure causes honoured the name of Italy. The publicity blitz that Mazzini orchestrated made Garibaldi's name familiar in Europe long before his return from South America. Garibaldi would be his secret weapon, 'useful to the country when it [was] time to act.'[20]

Eagerness to act could easily overrule Mazzini's better judgement.

[19] *EN*, XXIV, p. 160; XXVI, p. 193.

[20] *EN*, XXIV, p. 316, and *Protocollo della Giovine Italia (Congrega di Francia), 1840–1848* (Imola, 1916–22), II, p. 114.

The most clamorous case of misjudgement involved the brothers Attilio and Emilio Bandiera, Venetian officers in the Austrian navy, where their father was an admiral. In pursuit of Italian independence, the brothers formed a secret society called *Esperia* and planned to lead an armed raid into southern Italy. Mazzini promised them his help, thinking that he could turn a local uprising into a European event with the contacts he had among Hungarian, Polish, and Russian exiles. Political differences were to be set aside for the sake of concerted action. Political neutrality among allies in war, and the settling of differences later, would always be Mazzini's watchword. That was a concession that the mature Mazzini would always extend to his rivals. It convinced him, but seldom anyone else, that he was practical enough to set aside principles for the sake of unity.

When the Bandiera brothers and their few followers went ahead with their plan, and were captured and executed in Calabria in July 1844, Mazzini railed privately against everyone for letting him down. Publicly, he praised the brothers for their heroism and mourned their sacrifice, charging that they were the victims of treachery. That charge was based on his discovery that British government officials had intercepted his correspondence and passed on information about the conspiracy to the Austrians. The ensuing 'mail scandal' made Mazzini the most visible political exile in England, giving him a new appreciation of British freedoms: 'In any other country,' he confided, 'they would call me a ball-breaker (*seccacoglioni*), but not here. The Saxon race is hard, obstinate, insistent; they should know that Italians can be worse ball-breakers than the Saxons.'[21]

The publicity surrounding the mail scandal raised Mazzini's standing in England, but the opening he was looking for came from Italy. That was the election of Pope Pius IX in June 1846, which set in motion a series of developments that galvanized political activists throughout the peninsula. The election of a reputedly liberal pope suddenly made Gioberti's Neo-Guelph movement popular. At the same time, Charles Albert's growing reputation as a reforming monarch raised the hopes of Italians looking for political reforms by royal initiative. Mazzini saw the danger that the growing appeal of moderate programmes posed for the democratic camp. In his essay 'Thoughts upon democracy in Europe' he called on democrats to

---

[21] *EN*, XXVIII, p. 50.

unite, arguing that the progress of democracy required the success of movements for national independence everywhere, questioning the viability of rival democratic theories. Benthamites and utilitarians he attacked for their materialism, liberals for their fixation on individual rights, socialists and communists for their materialism, collectivism, and economic egalitarianism. The essay made the case for Mazzini's own brand of republican democracy, implying that he was the logical leader of the entire European movement.[22]

The revolutions of 1848–49

Mazzini's intent was to unite democrats for one concerted attack against the conservative powers on the eve of an expected revolutionary upheaval. In September 1847 he wrote an open letter to the pope, warning him of the grave danger that the papal policy of alliance with tyrants posed for the future of Catholicism. He urged the pope to 'be a believer' and unify Italy. If he refused, Italy would be unified without him, 'for such was the will of God'.[23] For all the anticipation, when revolution actually broke out Mazzini seemed taken by surprise. News of an uprising in Palermo in January 1848 cheered him for it showed Italians taking the initiative, but the much more visible Paris revolt of February depressed him because nothing good could come from that quarter. News that the Milanese had evicted Austrian troops from their city after five days of street fighting (the Five Days of Milan) restored his confidence. It also encouraged Charles Albert to declare war on Austria on 23 March. The Piedmontese army crossed the border into Lombardy, promising to bring 'the help that a brother expects from a brother'. That posed a dilemma for Mazzini, who welcomed the revolution but had decidedly negative feelings about a dynastic war waged by a king, especially when that king was the detested Charles Albert.

The enthusiasm that greeted Mazzini upon his arrival in Milan on

---

[22] The English text and an Italian translation of Mazzini's essay appear in *EN*, XXXIV, pp. 91–246. There is also a recent translation by Salvo Mastellone, *Pensieri sulla democrazia in Europa* (Milan, 1997). According to Mastellone, Karl Marx's Communist Manifesto was a reply to Mazzini's attack on socialists.

[23] *EN*, XXXVI, pp. 225–33.

8 April was short-lived. Political authority was in the hands of a provisional government, which included a number of prominent republicans. But republicanism had changed in the 17 years that Mazzini had spent in England, and republicans were not necessarily Mazzinians. That was true of Carlo Cattaneo, the dominant figure in the provisional government. Trained as an economist, Cattaneo was as empirical and concrete as Mazzini was idealistic and rhetorical. Cattaneo did not share Mazzini's faith in national unity, and he did not welcome the prospect of union with Piedmont, which he regarded as possibly the most clerical and backward state in Italy, and a likely drag on the progressive Lombard economy. Mazzini did not care for the Piedmontese either, but was willing to set that aside for the sake of unity against Austria. Cattaneo found support from another republican, the economist Giuseppe Ferrari, whom Mazzini regarded as too socialist and too pro-French. Matters came to a head over the issue of union with Piedmont, which none of the republicans favoured, but which Mazzini felt was a decision best postponed until hostilities ceased. That effort by Mazzini to straddle the two sides was a political disaster for him, as republicans accused him of selling out, and monarchists of playing a double game. Faced with the realities of power for the first time in his life, Mazzini showed more readiness to compromise than the reputedly more practical Cattaneo, who did not see the common sense of Mazzini's position. Mazzini's first foray into government policy ended in personal defeat, but the defeat was attributable to his political sense, not to his utopianism. Throughout the events of 1848–49, Mazzini would juggle the roles of politician and prophet, often to the detriment of his image as a principled figure.

Union with Piedmont became a moot issue when the Austrians forced the Piedmontese out of Lombardy. Angry demonstrators denounced Charles Albert for abandoning the people when the Piedmontese agreed to an armistice on 5 August. Mazzini could now revert to his role of radical agitator, and did so by proposing an all-out defence of the city against the Austrians. He may have thought that he had his secret weapon, for Garibaldi had returned from America and was in the city, after having been spurned by the Piedmontese to whom he had first offered his services. Given the rank of general and a few troops by the provisional government, Garibaldi left Milan to fight the Austrians. Mazzini followed him, giving speeches along the way to recruit volunteers, then left the ranks to go into Switzerland, where he hoped to regroup for another foray into Lombardy. Although Garibaldi fought on for a few more weeks, the revolution in Lombardy was over. Garibaldi and Mazzini had met, with mixed results. Later, Garibaldi remembered Mazzini's departure as a defection and their subsequent encounter in Switzerland as less than friendly. Mazzini had a different recollection, but he knew that Garibaldi was not the docile instrument that he had expected.

Defeated in Lombardy, the revolution sputtered on in Venice, Tuscany, Rome, and Sicily. Mazzini looked to Rome where, to his relief, Pius IX had lost favour with liberals after refusing to condone the war against Austria. When Pius left the city following the assassination of his chief government minister Pellegrino Rossi on 15 November, republicans seized the initiative, established popular clubs, and took over the streets. A quarter of a million voters elected a constituent assembly dominated by republicans. Garibaldi and Mazzini were among the elected. The assembly proclaimed Rome a republic, and Goffredo Mameli, a young Genoese patriot who penned the verses that would become the Italian national anthem, summoned Mazzini to Rome: *Roma, repubblica, venite.*

Mazzini would always remember his arrival in Rome on 5 March 1849 as an epiphany. Dismounting from his carriage so that he could approach it on foot like a pilgrim, he saw in the backwater that was Rome in 1849 the epicentre of world revolution: 'Rome was the dream of my youth, the mother of all my ideas, the religion of my soul. I entered it on foot that evening in early March, trembling, almost in adoration.'[24] He reminded the assembly that 'After the Rome of the Emperors, after the Rome of the Popes, comes the Rome of the People.'[25] The delegates had it in their power to change the course of history, provided they found the courage not to be hampered by legal scruples because, he informed them, 'those who lead a revolution are responsible only to the people, to God, and to their own consciences. Revolutionary legality consists of interrogating, divining, and then applying the will of the people.'[26] That was a harsh prescription for an assembly dominated by respectable notables who more than anything

[24] *EN*, LXXVII, p. 341. For an account of Mazzini's role in Rome, see Ivanoe Bonomi, *Mazzini triumviro della Repubblica Romana* (Turin, 1940).

[25] *Le assemblee del Risorgimento* (Rome, 1911), *Roma*, III, p. 573.

[26] *Roma*, III, p. 590.

else wanted an orderly transition of government. The pope, still popular in his self-imposed absence, refused to recognize the republic: the republic represented only the minority that had voted in the elections, and the bureaucracy and army that served the republic had been appointed by the pope. The executive power was vested in a triumvirate that was even more moderate than the assembly. Mazzini enjoyed personal prestige because he had long championed the cause of Rome, worked with obvious zeal on its behalf, and was readily accessible. Even after he moved into quarters in the pope's former residence at the Quirinal Palace, visitors came and went with little ceremony. He had on his side the 'foreigners' (most republicans came from other parts of the peninsula) who had paved his way to Rome, and the workers and retainers who answered to the *capopolo* Angelo Brunetti, better known as Ciceruacchio, a popular wine merchant from Trastevere who helped bridge the gap between ordinary people and the patriotic minority. A political reshuffling at the end of March resulted in Mazzini's appointment as triumvir. His partners were Carlo Armellini and Aurelio Saffi, both self-effacing enough to let Mazzini take the lead.

The Roman republic is remembered largely for the struggle that it waged to survive. That it survived for almost five months was something of a miracle, attributable in good measure to Mazzini's resourcefulness and obstinacy. By the time Mazzini became triumvir the republic faced a bleak future: Piedmont had suffered a second and decisive defeat at the battle of Novara, and an international military force was assembling to restore Rome to the pope. Only Venice still held out against the Austrians, and only the United States of America extended diplomatic recognition to the republic. Mazzini expected support from European democrats, especially from French democrats who were well represented in their national assembly. Alexandre Ledru-Rollin, leader of the radical republican faction, and a fellow political exile in London, was an ally on whom Mazzini felt he could count. He was not alarmed by a declaration that France would intervene militarily in Italy to check Austrian power. The assembly's declaration gave Louis Napoleon cover for his own designs, which aimed at making himself popular with both republicans and conservative Catholics at home, the latter favouring French intervention to restore Rome to the pope. A force commanded by General Nicolas Oudinot landed unopposed in Civitavecchia on 25 April 1849. While the

French paused, within a day's march of Rome, Mazzini assured the Roman assembly that they came with friendly intentions.

Mazzini's hopes were boosted by Garibaldi's spirited resistance when the French troops moved in on the city. Garibaldi's defence of the Roman republic has been superbly described by George Trevelyan and need not be discussed here. In two months of fighting, from the end of April to early July 1849, the exploits of Garibaldi's Red Shirts gave the *Risorgimento* most of its martyrs. Later, Mazzini claimed that credit for the republican cause, but his priority at the time was to save the republic. To that end, he summoned all his diplomatic skills, restraining anticlerical extremists who wanted to go after the clergy, to convince public opinion that republicans could be trusted to govern responsibly. The republic did expropriate ecclesiastical properties, but Mazzini was sincere in his assurances that property would be respected and unlawful acts punished. He turned radical only in the last days of the republic when he called on the people to fight to the finish, instituted state payment of clerical salaries, and allowed members of religious orders to renounce their vows. The intent of the religious measures was to loosen the ties of discipline within the clergy, curtail papal prerogatives, empower an elected Church council of the faithful, and democratize the government of the Roman Catholic Church.

Aftermath of revolution

The fall of the Roman republic ended Mazzini's role as a head of government, but not his prestige as a leader of the radical opposition. In the short run, his performance in Rome actually heightened his stature as a democratic leader. The republic had adopted universal suffrage, founded popular clubs, and introduced rituals that encouraged popular participation in public life. That brave experiment in applied democracy, and the heroism of its defenders, impressed friends and foes alike. *La Civiltà Cattolica*, the Jesuits' paper founded in 1850, paid Mazzini the compliment of depicting him as the most dangerous enemy of morality. Mazzinian propaganda credited all victories to republicans and blamed all defeats on monarchists. In the years of renewed exile, he was sustained by the hope that the forces of democracy would reawaken and recover: 'Publicly or secretly according to place, let us regroup, understand one another, and prepare. The day when, like the first Christians, we will be able to say we are one in the name of God and the People, the new pagans will be powerless; we will defeat the old order; God will guide us toward the future.'[27]

There was hope, and there were new enemies. After 1849, Mazzini clearly staked out his ground in the political terrain between the old order of monarchy in all its forms, including constitutional monarchy, and the socialists (the 'new pagans'), who were mostly French, and therefore doubly objectionable on grounds of ideology and nationality. He made his case for his own brand of democracy based on voluntary association, the break-up of banking and other monopolies, government loans to small businesses, a progressive income tax, tax credits for the poor, free education, and universal suffrage.[28] Louis Napoleon replaced Charles Albert, who died in 1849 after abdicating the throne in favour of his son, as the object of Mazzini's deadly hatred. Both were enigmatic, Hamlet-like figures who offended Mazzini on political and moral grounds. As he said, he abhorred the ambiguous more than the downright evil. He did reserve judgement on the personal qualities of Charles Albert's successor, the young King Victor Emmanuel II, who was already being hailed as a true patriot. But he would have preferred Victor Emanuel as president of a Mazzinian republic rather than as a king.

A tragedy that was more than personal struck Mazzini when his mother died in 1852. It was a political loss because Maria had been his confidante and collaborator. Her death isolated him from people and events in Italy, making him more dependent on his English friends for personal and political support. With his English supporters he formed the Friends of Italy Society as the voice of the Italian national movement abroad and as his personal pressure group in British politics. His fear that British policy would favour Piedmont now that it was a constitutional monarchy was quite justified. The fear of new rivals in Italy increased after Cavour became prime minister in November 1852. Mazzini found in Cavour an antagonist who was more than a match. Cavour detested republicanism, popular initiatives, and all political agitation that he could not control. In other

---

[27] From Mazzini's essay 'The holy alliance of the people', in *EN*, XXXIX, pp. 203–21.
[28] From 'The duty of democracy', in *EN*, XLVI, pp. 207–14.

words, he was anti-Mazzinian to the core. As prime minister he had a programme that appealed to moderate opinion because it promised change without revolution and an orderly transition to a new national order. Cavour defended parliament against royal power, challenged clerical privileges, promoted economic development, courted dissidents, and believed in Piedmont's Italian mission. Such a programme put the stamp of respectability on the national movement; it proved irresistibly attractive for patriots who might otherwise have gravitated toward Mazzini.

To make matters worse, democrats were quarrelling among themselves. Prominent figures like Enrico Cosenz, Giacomo Medici, and Antonio Mordini favoured Piedmont from the early 1850s; Cattaneo and Alberto Mario wanted a federal republic; on the fringe, Ferrari, Musolino, and Carlo Pisacane found Mazzini's social programme too moderate. London was friendlier. It was there that Mazzini set up an Italian National Committee and a European Democratic Committee. Calling itself the government in exile of the defunct Roman republic, the Italian National Committee claimed to speak for the entire Italian national movement. In that capacity, it floated a 'national loan' whose disappointing yield confirmed Mazzini's doubts about the patriotism of Italians. The European Democratic Committee served largely to disguise various undercover projects against Austria. A plan hatched with Louis Kossuth sought to incite mutinies among Hungarian troops stationed in Italy; another involved the Lombard priest Enrico Tazzoli, whom Mazzini admired as the kind of patriotic priest that he seldom saw. The most controversial and risky operation developed in Milan, where Mazzini discovered an organization of militant workers plotting street revolts. Mazzini tried to coordinate the activities of the Milanese workers with those of Kossuth and Tazzoli, with tragic results. The Hungarians did not stir, Tazzoli and his followers were arrested. Several, including Tazzoli, were hanged, while others were condemned to long prison terms and public floggings. The Milanese uprising of 6 February 1853, quickly repressed, provoked mass arrests and harsh retaliatory measures. The debacle exhausted the patience of Mazzini's 'respectable' followers among the well-to-do, who permanently closed their purse strings to him. Mazzini's charges that the middle classes had failed to support the workers only made matters worse; from then on, his following in Italy would dwindle to a small corps of true believers who operated on the fringes of the national movement.

The Party of Action and the National Society

With more enemies and fewer resources, Mazzini set out to rebuild his organization. He formed the Party of Action in the spring of 1853 to deal with the crisis of the democratic movement and provide an alternative to the politics of Cavour. The Party of Action, conceived as the 'militant Church of the national movement', issued another call to the young to take up the revolution. Like earlier Mazzinian organizations, it was democratic in principle and autocratic in practice. Mazzini's determination to control it from London created resistance in Italy where members were most vulnerable to retaliation. But the party's call to action did attract some. One who now rallied to Mazzini was Felice Orsini; he had not cared much for Mazzini as a diplomat in Rome, but found the militant Mazzini more to his liking, and joined him in London to hatch new plots and insurrections. The insurrections that they concocted in 1853 and 1854 were trivial, in and of themselves. They are indicative, however, of Mazzini's state of mind when he sensed that the democratic movement was losing momentum. His response was to commit himself more deeply to action and to refuse any compromise either with Cavour or with the 'new pagans'. The politics of exclusion that he practised after 1853 appealed to a retinue of activists who believed in action regardless of consequences.

The Party of Action pursued what Mazzini called the 'triumphant fact', meaning a spectacularly successful deed that would restore the fortunes of the democratic movement. Unfortunately for Mazzini, Cavour was in a better position to achieve such a feat for the moderates. Piedmont's intervention in the Crimean War on the side of France and Great Britain was not the great triumph of Cavour's diplomacy that patriotic propaganda made it out to be, but it did provide opportunities that Cavour would exploit later on. Mazzini, who welcomed popular wars, deplored Piedmontese intervention in the Crimean conflict because he saw it as a 'royal war', and feared that it might lead to an alliance of monarchs against the forces of democracy. The possibility of Austrian intervention on the side of France, Great Britain, and Piedmont also raised the unwelcome prospect of an understanding between Piedmont and Austria. Such an unnatural alliance could not possibly serve the cause of Italian unity. Needless to say, Mazzini's opposition to Piedmontese intervention made him *persona non grata* with the British government, which wanted Piedmont in the anti-Russian coalition. The conservative press targeted him as an undesirable alien, the Friends of Italy Society was forced to shut down, and Mazzini railed against the British ruling class that governed, he charged, without regard for the interests of the people.

Cavour played a minor role at the Paris Peace Congress that ended the Crimean conflict, but his stay in Paris was useful in other ways. Piedmont gained stature simply by being at the peace table and having the 'Italian Question' brought to the attention of governments. When not attending sessions of the congress, or indulging himself at the gambling tables, Cavour busied himself meeting personages who might be politically useful to him. The Venetian exile Daniele Manin was one. Manin had served as head of the Venetian republic in 1849, but his republicanism owed more to the historical legacy of Venice and the circumstances of 1849 than to strong republican convictions. He was a practical man with a visceral distrust for utopian conspirators like Mazzini. While Mazzini looked for national revolutions that would give power to the people, Manin looked for the least arduous way to achieve Italian independence. His chief collaborator was the Lombard nobleman Giorgio Pallavicino, whose dislike of Mazzini exceeded even Manin's. Cavour, Manin, and Pallavicino laid down the groundwork for political collaboration between republicans and monarchists. The programme of 'national unification' that they announced proved attractive to a broad spectrum of patriotic opinion. The term 'national unification' implied an open-ended process of unspecified duration, while Mazzini's demand for 'national unity' suggested a fixed goal. Unification implied moderation and patience, unity impatience and tempestuous action. Unification implied inclusion, unity exclusion. In Pallavicino's phrase, the politics of inclusion reassured the 'gentlemen of revolution' who wanted no more Mazzinian surprises.[29]

On 25 May 1856 *The Times* of London published Manin's letter condemning 'the doctrine of political assassination' and 'the theory

[29] See Baccio Emanuele Maineri (ed.), *Daniele Manin e Giorgio Pallavicino. Epistolario politico* (Milan, 1878), pp. 501–6, and Giorgio Pallavicino, *Memorie* (Turin, 1882–95), III, p. 250.

of the dagger'. Manin did not mention Mazzini's name, but every informed reader understood that he was attacking Mazzini and the Party of Action. Mazzini denied having a theory of violence, accused Manin of defaming the Italian people, and proposed that all patriots rally under a 'neutral banner'. That summer, moderates formed the Italian National Society. Announcing that it stood for 'Italy and Victor Emmanuel', the National Society accepted Piedmontese leadership, constitutional monarchy, and a piecemeal approach to unification. Garibaldi offered his services, his republican convictions notwithstanding, thus positioning himself to bridge the gap between republican and monarchist patriots that was his historical contribution to the politics of the *Risorgimento*.

Mazzini's response to these developments was to turn more decisively toward the popular constituency that he had previously sacrificed in pursuit of middle-class support. The Party of Action called on workers to play an active role in the politics of national unification, arguing that participation would earn them the right to be heard and govern after unification. Not all republicans agreed with that tactic, Mauro Macchi arguing, for instance, that political involvement was not in the interest of workers, and that workers should organize for economic improvements, not for political causes.[30] Mazzini found an ally in Carlo Pisacane, a Neapolitan officer whom he had met in 1848. In some ways they were an incongruous pair, because Pisacane was critical of Mazzini's spiritual bent and Mazzini rejected the materialist basis of Pisacane's ideas. But Mazzini admired Pisacane's courage, they agreed that doing was more important than theorizing, and that a courageous few could galvanize the masses. Pisacane was a socialist and perhaps even something of an economic determinist, but not so rigid a determinist as to rule out the role of human agency and individual initiative. On that basis, Mazzini and Pisacane were a match.

In December 1856 Pisacane proposed to Mazzini an armed expedition against the Bourbon regime in Naples. The idea was to land with a party of patriots, incite the peasantry to revolt, and topple the monarchy with the help of democrats in the cities. Mazzini actually hesitated, but promised to help when he saw that Pisacane was

---

[30] See Mauro Macchi, *La conciliazione dei partiti. Risposta a Giuseppe Mazzini* (Genoa, 1856).

determined to go ahead with or without him. When Garibaldi declined their invitation to lead the raid, Pisacane decided to do it himself. Mazzini seconded him with heart and soul, raising money, urging republicans to support the initiative, making plans for workers to attack military forts in Genoa to give Pisacane time to load men and supplies, and then paying a secret visit to the city to oversee the preparations. The attacks fizzled, but Pisacane managed anyway to sail away with a handful of men, only to be hunted down after making a landing near the town of Sapri in upper Calabria. Pursued by troops and peasants who mistook their would-be liberators for brigands, Pisacane killed himself, while his companions were killed or taken prisoner by their pursuers.

Defections, charges of recklessness, and a second sentence of death for Mazzini followed this clamorous incident. Mazzini agonized privately over the death of Pisacane, to whom he was sincerely attached, but not publicly: 'To me, to us, slanders and accusations make no difference. We recognize no judges except God, our conscience, and the Italy that will exist in the future.'[31] The 'initiative' was no longer his. In the months that followed he launched the periodical *Pensiero e Azione* to stimulate theoretical debate, worked on the publication of his writings, and generally kept a low profile. He had nothing to do with Felice Orsini's unsuccessful attempt of January 1858 on the life of Napoleon III. The beneficiary of Orsini's action was Cavour, who took advantage of the incident to work on the emperor's fear of republican agitation, thus opening the dialogue that led to the agreement of Plombières on 20 July 1858. Mazzini's first reaction to the prospect of a French–Piedmontese war against Austria was one of dismay. Another 'royal war' would end 'the heroic phase of the Italian *Risorgimento*' and surrender 'the nation to the discretion of the foreigner'.[32] Republicans were undecided whether to be partisan or patriotic, and Mazzini himself wavered as war approached. His fear that a 'Bonapartist–Italian war' would end all prospects for republican revolution was balanced by the anticipation that war would destabilize the political system. In that case, he could compensate for republican losses in the North by taking advantage of opportunities in the South. To take the pulse of the South he dispatched emissaries

[31] *EN*, LIX, p. 69.
[32] Mazzini, *Scritti editi ed inediti* (Milan, 1861–91), X, p. lvi.

to Sicily to direct toward the goal of national unity the insurrection
that his sources said was already underway.

Mazzini and the making of Italy

When war broke out in April 1859, Mazzini lingered in London; but
he rushed to the scene after learning that the French had unexpectedly signed an armistice with the Austrians at Villafranca on 11 July.
That was the break he was waiting for, because the armistice discredited Cavour's policy of cooperation with France, angered many
patriots, and justified republican claims that Italians must win
national unity by themselves. The notion that Italians could unify
without foreign help did not seem unrealistic at that moment. Uprisings unplanned by Cavour and unwanted by Napoleon had occurred
in central Italy; Garibaldi had at his disposal several thousand volunteers who had joined to fight Austria and presumably could be used
for republican operations elsewhere. The difficulty was that Garibaldi
was now a general in the Piedmontese army, and ostentatiously loyal
to King Victor Emmanuel. Still, Mazzini was convinced that if there
was a revolt in the South Garibaldi would support it with his volunteers. It was perhaps to soothe Garibaldi that he made the astonishing
offer of the presidency of the Italian republic to Victor Emanuel in
return for his collaboration with republicans. Mazzini's plan was to
gather volunteers in Tuscany, which was now in the iron grip of
Baron Bettino Ricasoli, known to favour unification. The watchword
was ready: *Al centro, al centro, mirando al sud!* (To the centre, to the
centre, on the way south!).[33]

The project envisaged a land operation led by Garibaldi which,
moving south from Tuscany, would link up with the Sicilian
insurgency, liberating Rome and Naples along the way. The project
foundered when Ricasoli ordered Mazzini out of Tuscany, Garibaldi
withdrew to Caprera, and Piedmont paused to digest the spoils of
victory after annexing Lombardy, the Central Duchies, and the
Romagna. Mazzini retreated to London to lick his wounds, while
Cavour's policy seemed vindicated, even if he had to sacrifice Nice

---

[33] *EN*, LXIV, pp. 57–66.

and Savoy to obtain French recognition for the new Kingdom of Italy. Mazzini protested the cession of Nice and Savoy, and chastised Cavour and the monarchy for failing to unify the peninsula. But he still hoped that republicans could regain the initiative with a 'splendid, daring deed' in the South.[34] He recognized that only Garibaldi could pull it off, for Garibaldi had by then a large enough following to act independently of the government, and Mazzini had developed an almost superstitious faith in Garibaldi's invincibility in the field. Garibaldi agreed to lead an expedition to Sicily in support of an uprising already said to be in progress on the island. Assured that an uprising was indeed underway by the Sicilian Mazzinian patriot Francesco Crispi (who may have fabricated the evidence), Garibaldi sailed for Sicily and into history with his volunteers. Mazzini's role in the launching of *I Mille* (The Thousand) was invisible at the time, but there is no denying that he did play a role. Garibaldi's plan differed from Mazzini's in sailing directly from Genoa to Sicily rather than waging a land campaign from the centre, but Mazzini's insistence that national unification be completed helped to keep the issue in the public eye. Mazzini championed Garibaldi's command of the expedition, sent emissaries to Sicily to stoke the insurrection that Garibaldi demanded, and used his contacts to prepare for Garibaldi's arrival. Garibaldi did carry out the venture under the banner of 'Italy and Victor Emmanuel' that was repugnant to Mazzini, but republicans were influential in Sicily and in the rest of the South during Garibaldi's dictatorship. Throughout this operation, Mazzini's best ally in Garibaldi's camp was Agostino Bertani, who did what he could to put a republican imprint on the liberation of the South.

Political expediency required that Mazzini keep a low profile while Garibaldi ruled the South in the name of Victor Emanuel. That was a role that Mazzini did not welcome. He joined Garibaldi in Naples, arriving unannounced and unheralded on 17 September 1860. First he had to look for his own hotel, then wait his turn to be received by Garibaldi. Moderate elements around Garibaldi urged him to leave the city voluntarily to avoid dissension. Mazzini refused, claiming that as a private citizen he had a right to be there and speak his mind. He did what he could to establish a republican presence in the city by founding a newspaper and organizing workers. He left the city after

---

[34] *EN*, LXV, pp. 44, 47.

Garibaldi departed and the Piedmontese took over. Before leaving Naples he and Garibaldi reached a fragile understanding to resume the campaign and complete the unification the following spring. Rome and Venice remained to be liberated, Rome from the pope and Venice from the Austrians. Mazzini promised to collect funds, mobilize public opinion, and refrain from raising the 'Institutional Question'. Garibaldi promised his services as long as he could work for unification in the king's name.

Not surprisingly, the cooperation agreed to in Naples never materialized. In fact, in the coming years Mazzini and Garibaldi would bicker, disagree, and fulminate against each other with regularity. The moving tributes that they exchanged during a London dinner in 1864 marked a rare moment of cordiality in their stormy relationship. Agreeing that Rome and Venice should be liberated, they disagreed on when and how to do it; agreeing that the pope was the enemy, they disagreed on the role of religion; Garibaldi's crude anticlericalism never sat well with Mazzini; Mazzini's spiritualism clashed with Garibaldi's earthy disposition; Garibaldi's respect for Victor Emanuel struck Mazzini as being little more than peasant deference toward authority; Garibaldi regarded Mazzini's strict adherence to republican principles as a hindrance to national unification. For Garibaldi, the acquisition of Rome and Venice meant completing national unification, while Mazzini agitated for Rome and Venice for the dual purpose of completing national unification and revitalizing republicanism. There was therefore more at stake in the fight for Mazzini than for Garibaldi. The ulterior motive behind his agitation and conspiracies in the 1860s was to embarrass the government and persuade the Italian people that republicans were inherently more patriotic than monarchists. When he insisted that there was no incompatibility between *patria* and *libertà* he meant that republicanism was the necessary humus for both: 'Prepare, preach, and work for both simultaneously; seize the one that comes first, in the knowledge that one will hasten the advent of the other.'[35]

---

[35] *EN*, LXXXIII, p. 222.

Against monarchy and socialism to the end

The decade of the 1860s saw Mazzini fighting a double battle against monarchy on one side and socialism on the other. In 1860 he published *Doveri dell'uomo* (Duties of Man), a collection of writings designed to show the organic unity of his social thought. By far the most popular of Mazzini's works (several editions and an estimated one million copies were produced in the century after its publication), the book addressed workers directly, urging them to be mindful both of their duties and their rights. But the title indicates that it was fulfilment of duties that Mazzini thought most important. He reminded workers that they were citizens first and workers second, and that as citizens they had obligations to their country which took precedence over their claims as workers, however legitimate their claims to economic justice might be. The stress on duties, the preachy tone and paternalistic language, the call for cooperation across class lines, easily disguise the radicalism of Mazzini's message, which was a call to political action. Italian governments in the 1860s feared that Mazzinianism was a danger to the state second only to clericalism. Anarchist and socialist agitation lagged far behind on the scale of government concerns during that difficult decade. Anarchism lacked organization and socialism directed the resentments of workers against their employers, while Mazzinian propaganda targeted government as the enemy and urged workers to agitate for political power. Mazzini's republicanism, his call for universal suffrage, and for accountability by elected officials, reflected his understanding that power is ultimately political, and that social problems require political solutions. Backing that message was a thick network of cooperatives and mutual aid societies that gave Mazzinianism a real social dimension.

While rejecting socialist materialism, Mazzini upheld the associational values that he saw as the essence of genuine socialism. In the name of association he called on workers to make common cause with other oppressed groups. Women, slaves (Mazzini wholeheartedly supported the abolitionist cause), serfs (serfdom was abolished in Russia in 1861), and members of oppressed nationalities were the natural allies of workers, but for their alliance to endure it must be based on questions of principle because the economic interests of oppressed groups did not necessarily coincide. He had seen how conflicts of interest disrupted the revolutionary movements of 1848, pitted men against women in the factories, and divided workers along national lines. The commitment to action that led Karl Marx to appeal to the economic interests and the international solidarity of workers prompted Mazzini to adopt an ideology of revolution based on patriotic ideals and principles of justice. Revolutions required coalitions, and successful coalitions required shared ideals. At the heart of his disputes with Bakunin and Marx in the 1860s and with the Paris Commune of 1870–71, which he condemned after concluding that it had been taken over and diverted from its legitimate goals by socialist agitators, lay Mazzini's conviction that ideals unite and material interests divide.[36]

On 20 September 1870 the Italian army took Rome from the pope. On the day that Mazzini should have celebrated as marking the crowning achievement of his life he was under arrest, confined to the fortress of Gaeta after a final, pathetic attempt at insurrection. When released, he refused to visit the city that he deemed defiled by the presence of royal troops. After a brief stay in London, he returned to Italy where he spent the last months of his life under an assumed name, perhaps out of conspiratorial habit, but more likely as a gesture of defiance against the state. He died on 10 March 1872, venerated by a few, but considered a relic of the past by a younger generation of radicals that would not forgive him his condemnation of the Paris Commune and his rejection of Bakunin and Marx. In his last years, some democrats valued him mostly as an impediment to the spread of socialism. The cause of Italian unity to which he had dedicated his life had won out, but the outcome was not to his liking. The ruling parliamentary monarchy offended his revolutionary conscience, the majority of his erstwhile followers disappointed him, and the appeal of socialism filled him with apprehension for the future. At the end of his labours, the man who would later be hailed as the soul of modern Italy preferred to think of himself as the monarchy's outlaw; *il proscritto della monarchia*.

---

[36] See *Doveri dell'uomo* in the 1860 Naples edition reproduced in *EN*, LXIX, pp. 29, 73, 97, 145.

Cavour and Piedmont

Anthony Cardoza

The extraordinary wave of revolution that had raised patriotic hopes on the Italian peninsula in 1848 concluded the following year in bitter disillusionment, defeat, and disarray for both moderate and democratic proponents of reform and national independence. The defeat of the Piedmontese army by Austrian forces at Custoza and the abandonment of the national war by the princes in the summer of 1848 drove moderate political forces everywhere into retreat. Those constitutional liberals who were not dismissed or overthrown faced mounting popular opposition and often wound up allying with their reactionary adversaries in defence of order and property. Democratic forces in the isolated republican bastions of Venice and Rome enjoyed a certain prestige and popularity for their determination to fight on, but ultimately they fared little better, succumbing in 1849 to the superior military might of Austria and the France of Louis Napoleon.

Not surprisingly, the failure of the revolutions was followed by a second restoration on the peninsula championed by Austria with the support of Pius IX and Tsar Nicholas I of Russia. As early as May 1848, frightened Neapolitan moderates supported a *coup d'état* by Ferdinand II that led to the suspension of parliament and a return to royal absolutism in the Kingdom of the Two Sicilies. Most other Italian princes followed suit, abrogating the constitutions they had reluctantly granted in 1848 and relying on Habsburg forces to reassert autocratic power in their respective states.

The one exception to the triumph of absolutism and reaction in Italy after 1848 was Piedmont under the House of Savoy. In the short run, three circumstances distinguished the Piedmontese situation from that of other states on the peninsula. First, the House of Savoy emerged from the revolutions as the only dynasty in Italy that was not dependent on Austrian influence and military might. Such independence was largely the result of geo-political concerns of the Great Powers who needed an autonomous Piedmont to continue serving as a buffer state between France and Austria. Secondly, Piedmont was the only post-1848 Italian state to retain a constitution, the *Statuto*, with an elected parliament sharing governmental responsibilities with the monarchy. The interests of both the Habsburg Empire and House of Savoy dictated this extraordinary circumstance. Austria agreed to the comparatively moderate *Statuto* and a lenient peace treaty with the Savoyard monarchy to avoid inflaming internal unrest in Piedmont and risking armed intervention by France. For his part, the autocratic new Savoyard ruler, Victor Emanuel II, accepted constitutional procedures in order to pre-empt the democratic opposition at home and to placate liberal moderates whose support was necessary for the monarchy's anti-Austrian policy. Despite its narrowness, the *Statuto* allowed political development in Piedmont to diverge in significant ways from the rest of the peninsula during the next decade. Lastly, with the entrance of Count Camillo Benso di Cavour into political life after the revolutions of 1848, Piedmont gained an exceptionally able leader who distinguished himself both as a dynamic reformer at home and as the outstanding statesman on the peninsula in the 1850s.

The distinctive features of the Piedmontese situation in 1849 rested, in turn, on a set of older institutional arrangements and structural developments that together laid the foundations for the small state's claims to national leadership in Italy. To begin with, in the nineteenth century the House of Savoy was the only indigenous monarchy on the peninsula, with a court and state system based in Turin, that had employed Italian as its administrative language from the sixteenth century onwards. As a result, it enjoyed unusual institutional stability as well as an independence that permitted the pursuit of an anti-Austrian foreign policy in the 1850s. Savoyard rulers could also count on the loyal support of Italy's only martial service nobility, the backbone of an army that gave them the most powerful regional military force after 1730.

The Piedmontese state also benefited from important economic changes in the century preceding unification. Agricultural advances, new manufacturing, and commercial investments in the late eighteenth century increased the circulation of non-agricultural goods, ensured that wealth was not as concentrated as in other regions, and strengthened the influence of the middle classes. Beginning in the 1830s, Piedmont participated in a general transformation of the European economy. The use of fertilizers and the expansion of irrigation and drainage projects brought further improvements to agriculture, while manufacturing profited from the mechanized spinning of cotton and wool and the rise of a metallurgical industry. Finally, recent scholarship suggests that the reign of Charles Albert (1831–48) witnessed a programme of bureaucratic modernization which transformed the monarchy from an arbitrary, despotic regime into a consultative and administrative system.[1] As a result, the Savoyard state was able to make social and economic improvements that gave it a breadth of public support without parallel on the Italian peninsula in the decade preceding 1848. This combination of structural factors and immediate political circumstances set the stage for Piedmont's emergence as the most liberal, progressive state on the peninsula and the unchallenged leader of the Italian national movement in the 1850s.

Historiographical context

Despite, or perhaps because of, the pivotal role of Cavour and the Piedmontese state in Italy becoming a modern, unified nation in 1861, most historical assessments of their achievements have been shaped and conditioned by the subsequent experiences of war and fascism as well as by the shifting interests of rival political camps and ideological agendas. The decades immediately after unification, and later the Fascist era, for instance, produced a celebratory literature that glorified Cavour and the monarchy in order to nourish patriotic sentiments, strengthen national identity, and legitimize the political status quo. From the end of the Second World War through the 1970s,

---

[1] See N. Nada and P. Notario, 'Il Piemonte sabaudo: Dal periodo napoleonico al Risorgimento'. In G. Galasso (ed.), *Storia d'Italia*, Vol. VIII (Turin, 1993), pp. 210–62.

virtually all treatments of Cavour and Piedmont subordinated them to ongoing ideological disputes between liberals and Marxists and to the preoccupations of historians with the unified Italy's troubled modernization, the failures of the liberal state, and the origins of Fascism.

In this context, the policies and decisions of the Piedmontese leadership in the *Risorgimento* became a means for explaining not so much Italy's relatively successful unification as the country's subsequent deviation from European 'norms' of modernization. Marxist and liberal intellectuals heatedly debated the relative responsibilities of Cavour and the moderates for the economic 'backwardness', 'distorted' social development, and endemic political corruption that weakened the new Italian nation and ultimately paved the way for Fascism. Marxists sought to link liberalism to Fascism by locating the roots of Mussolini's regime in the policies of the Piedmontese leadership during the *Risorgimento*. Above all, they stressed the part played by Cavour and the moderates in carrying out a 'passive revolution' that compromised with 'feudal' remnants in order to defeat the republican left. The resulting power bloc produced systems of political transformism and economic protectionism that corrupted parliamentary life and distorted industrial development. Predictably, liberals defended the achievements of Cavour and the monarchy in the face of enormous obstacles inherited from the past. The subsequent problems of the new state they ascribed either to external events such as the First World War or else to Italy's longstanding disunity, its deeply entrenched economic backwardness, and the tenacious resistance of reactionary elements.

During the past two decades, this historical paradigm has come under serious attack from a younger generation of 'revisionist' historians who have accused it of teleological assumptions, politically inspired interpretations, and unilinear models of modernization. Their work has largely abandoned political events, focusing instead on long-term structural changes in economy, society, and state formation. Ironically, the cumulative effect of these tendencies has not been to provoke any major reinterpretation of the *Risorgimento* so much as it has been to shift the research agenda on modern Italy away from the *Risorgimento* altogether and, more specifically, to diminish drastically scholarly interest in Piedmont and Cavour. As a result, there has been virtually no new research on the Piedmontese state and leader in the last twenty years. Even the latest and most thorough surveys of their role in the *Risorgimento* have had to depend almost exclusively on a body of work published before 1980.

As Lucy Riall has recently observed, however, the structural approach of the revisionists offers no real answer to the question of why Italian unification happened at all, let alone when and in the way that it did.[2] These questions are important, since the achievement of unity did mark a critical moment of rupture in the history of a country characterized by centuries of political fragmentation, with profound repercussions on Italian economic and social life. The initiatives taken by Cavour and the House of Savoy that culminated in national unification certainly did not constitute the inevitable or obvious solution to the crisis that overwhelmed Restoration Italy. On the contrary, the moderate forces were at best a largely unrepresentative minority without an especially coherent programme. Accordingly, to understand how they were able to play such a pivotal role in Italian unification requires a careful examination of two interrelated topics: first, the remarkable political and economic transformation of Piedmont in the decade after 1848 and, second, the responses of Cavour and the House of Savoy to the sudden opportunities and challenges that confronted them in the decisive years between 1859 and 1861.

Piedmont in the 1850s

The history of Piedmont in the decade after the revolutions of 1848 has an importance that extends well beyond the immediate borders of the small regional state nestled in the north-west corner of the Italian peninsula. To begin with, developments there anticipated in microcosm a host of subsequent national developments. The Savoyard state provided a setting in these years in which a number of larger administrative, juridical, political, and religious issues were confronted. Significantly, the methods and solutions developed by the Piedmontese in response to these issues served as models for the economic system, constitution, legal codes, and bureaucracy of the

---

[2] L. Riall, *The Italian Risorgimento: State, Society, and National Unification* (London, 1994), pp. 1–10, 65–6.

new unified nation-state after 1861. At the same time, the policies pursued by moderate governments after 1850 transformed Piedmont from one of the more autocratic and backward regimes into the most liberal, progressive state on the peninsula. Moreover, this transformation occurred without any abandoning of the strengths the state derived from the Savoyard monarchy and military nobility. It was this unique blend of reform and tradition, liberalism and military force, that permitted the Piedmontese government to develop an alternative to the Restoration and republican nationalism and to become the leading force in the campaign to unify Italy.

Despite the modernizing efforts during the reign of Charles Albert, Piedmont still offered only modest indications of economic vitality or political dynamism at the end of the 1840s. In fact, it was a small country struggling to recover from the defeats of 1848–49. Even the new constitution was a narrow document that gave the autocratic-minded Victor Emanuel II ample authority to nominate the members of the new upper chamber or senate, to impose ministers of war, and to engage in his own secret diplomacy. Likewise, men whose careers had been forged in an era of absolutism continued to occupy the highest positions in the judiciary, army, and diplomatic corps. Piedmont also lagged behind other states on the peninsula in curbing the authority of the Catholic Church. In contrast to the situation in Naples, Austrian Italy, and Tuscany, there were few limitations on clerical power in Piedmont where ecclesiastical courts still existed and the Jesuits exercised enormous influence.

Nonetheless, the survival of the *Statuto* meant that Piedmont entered the new decade with a constitutional framework which imposed legal limits on absolutism and linked the governability of the country to a system of parliamentary representation. Timely collaboration between Victor Emanuel II and his moderate prime minister, Massimo D'Azeglio, at the end of 1849, enabled Piedmontese leaders to rein in a bellicose democratic opposition and win a mild peace settlement, without recourse to an alliance with Austria or the abolition of the *Statuto*, a solution favoured by some reactionary elements. Instead, a new governing order took shape, capable of sustaining a strong executive while gradually eroding monarchical independence and assuring the political participation of those middle-class elements engaged in commerce, banking, public employment, and the professions.

The chief beneficiary of this new order was Count Camillo Benso di Cavour, the principal architect of Piedmontese modernization, secularization, and liberalization in the 1850s. Cavour had remained largely outside politics until his late thirties, when he was elected to parliament in 1848. Thereafter, he enjoyed a meteoric rise to public prominence that ended only with his premature death at the age of 50 in 1861. Entering his first cabinet in 1850 as minister of trade and agriculture, he quickly established himself as the dominant figure in a series of successive governments that kept him at the centre of power throughout the decade.

The second son of a prominent old-line aristocratic family, Cavour combined many of the stereotypical virtues of both the nobility and the bourgeoisie. Such a blend was already a characteristic of the family in his father's generation. The Benso di Cavour had lost much of their patrimony in the wake of the French occupation of the late 1790s. During the Napoleonic era and the Restoration they amassed a vast new landed fortune, much of which they owed to their ability to act as aggressive agricultural entrepreneurs. The Benso di Cavours' entrepreneurial talents did not prevent them from taking advantage of strategic marriage alliances, a standard means of enrichment favoured by the old nobility, to help achieve their rapid economic recovery in the early nineteenth century. Nor did Cavour's father hesitate to exploit his aristocratic connections and influence at court in order to advance his own career in state service.

Cavour was an even more iconoclastic nobleman who disdained court life and resisted family controls. After resigning his commission in the largely aristocratic officers corps, he became a successful commercial farmer on his family's estates, a respected expert in political economy, and an early advocate of railroads before embarking on a career in politics in 1847. At the same time, his cousin described Cavour as 'an aristocrat by birth, taste, and nature' who considered the old nobility to be 'by nature superior to the bourgeois classes.'[3] And despite his impatience with the more stifling aspects of titled society, he still paid implicit homage to his noble origins through his preference for dropping Benso and using only Cavour, the name of his family's former fief.

This blend of aristocratic and bourgeois attitudes and values

---

[3] Quoted in D. Mack Smith, *Cavour* (London, 1985), p. 102.

shaped Cavour's moderate political principles. By the 1830s he had begun to formulate his central notion of the *juste milieu* or middle path, in which government could avoid the extremes of absolutism and anarchy by following a programme of gradual, orderly progress. Reflecting his temperament and the social milieu in which he was born and raised, Cavour assigned a leading role in public life to the landed upper classes, whose principal tasks included the avoidance of revolutionary change and the preservation of established institutions like the monarchy. In line with these views, he was an outspoken foe of democratic and republican ideas and movements, which explains his hostility toward such political figures as Mazzini and Garibaldi. Especially in the 1840s, the Piedmontese left, for its part, distrusted and despised Cavour whom they viewed as an arrogant and abrasive aristocratic conservative.

Cavour, however, also fitted squarely into the traditions of nineteenth-century liberalism in his deep commitment to the values of free trade, secularism, and constitutional parliamentary government. As a product of the Enlightenment, he was a firm believer in the inevitable triumph of reason and progress over 'the exponents of obscurantism'.[4] He had little sympathy, then, for those conservative and aristocratic elements who sought to prevent all change, convinced that their reluctance to compromise only increased the likelihood of revolutionary upheavals. He was equally averse to the excessive influence of Catholic traditionalists in public life, which he considered a major obstacle both to innovation and to freedom of thought in general. His travels abroad, and especially his long stays in Great Britain, convinced him of the need for free trade and economic development, together with timely social reforms, to improve the conditions of the masses and give them a stake in the established order.

Cavour found ample opportunities to translate his political principles into practice from 1850 onwards when he embarked upon an ambitious programme of reforms to modernize the economy, political life, and church–state relations in Piedmont. Initially he had his greatest impact in the economic arena, first as minister of trade, agriculture, and navigation after October 1850 in the government headed by D'Azeglio, and then as minister of finance, an additional

---

[4] See R. Romeo, *Vita di Cavour* (Bari, 1984), p. 31.

portfolio he assumed the following year. In these capacities he set out to achieve three interrelated objectives: to improve state finances, to raise the standard of living of the population, and to increase private profits. As minister of trade, Cavour implemented a policy of free trade to facilitate Piedmont's entrance into European markets, stimulate export of her 'natural' products, and reduce the cost of imported machinery and manufactured goods. Accordingly, he arranged new commercial agreements with nearly a dozen countries in western and central Europe during his first two years in office. These agreements opened the way for Cavour to introduce a new general tariff schedule that lowered duties on a wide range of agricultural and manufactured products. Its ratification by a sizeable majority in parliament in the summer of 1851 effectively transformed Piedmont from protectionism to free trade. While customs revenues fell, they were more than offset by the growth in trade and a general improvement in the Piedmontese economy. A rise in international agricultural prices sparked farm exports, while the availability of imports favoured mechanization of the textile industry. Significantly, the apparent success of Cavour's policies in the 1850s established a precedent that was extended to the new Italian nation in 1861 where free trade doctrines would hold sway until the protectionist turn of 1887.

Upon taking charge of the ministry of finance, Cavour also turned his attention to the problem of the state's budgetary deficit, which had surpassed its revenues in 1850 due to wartime expenditures and reparations to Austria. Rejecting the English model of a progressive income tax as too risky for the small and fragile economy of Piedmont, the new finance minister instead adopted a series of fiscal measures aimed at previously exempted activities and privileged segments of the population. Direct taxes were introduced on a host of new items, while the remaining feudal privileges like *fidecommessi* and primogeniture were eliminated. In addition, he tightened up management of state monopolies and made the financial bureaucracy more efficient in order to increase state revenues. To meet the immediate financial needs of the treasury, he expanded the sale of state bonds and negotiated an international loan from foreign banks.

Cavour's policies extended well beyond the elimination of obstacles to trade and balancing budgets, however. He boldly involved the government in various infrastructural improvements to encourage and stimulate economic development and private initiative in

Piedmont. To reorganize the system of credit, he doubled the capital of the *Banca Nazionale* (formed in 1849 through a merger of the Banks of Genoa and Turin) in 1852 and the following year made it the central bank of the state. During the same period, he also promoted the establishment of additional private financial institutions and oversaw the expansion of the existing savings banks (*casse di risparmio*), both with an eye to increasing the availability of commercial credit in the country. The founding of stock exchanges in Turin and Genoa between 1850 and 1855 worked in a similar direction by encouraging the growth of new joint-stock companies and additional instruments of capital formation. Taken together, these measures paved the way for joint public–private collaboration in investments, often orchestrated directly by Cavour, to expand rail lines, modernize the port facilities of Genoa, develop irrigation projects, and build new roadways. Railroad construction and the expansion of transatlantic shipping, in particular, stimulated the development of a Piedmontese machine industry, heavily dependent from its inception on state subsidies and contracts.[5]

The pursuit of these many projects was not without risks. Cavour's reliance on foreign and domestic private loans to finance his initiatives, for instance, produced an alarming increase in the public debt, which climbed from less than L.120 million in 1847 to 725 million by 1859, when interest payments were absorbing more than a fifth of state revenues. Moreover, his preference for joint ventures to encourage the modernization of credit facilities and the development of new heavy industrial enterprises favoured the growth of a small, politically connected, economic oligarchy that dominated these sectors and blurred the distinction between private enterprise and public power. Still, the rewards of Cavour's financial and economic policies were undeniably impressive. The Savoyard kingdom's railroad system, which had been virtually non-existent in 1851, was larger than that of any other Italian state by 1861, covering 850 kilometres, 40% of the total for the entire peninsula. The same years saw the value of Piedmontese trade triple with the increased export of textiles, oils, wines, and rice, while local industries flourished. By the end of the decade, Piedmont had emerged as economically the most modern state on

---

[5] R. P. Coppini, 'Il Piemonte sabaudo e l'unificazione (1849–1861). In G. Sabbatucci and V. Vidotto (eds), *Storia d'Italia*. Vol. I, *Le premesse dell'Unità* (Bari, 1994), pp. 354–8, 362–3.

the peninsula, serving as the model that all other Italian states attempted to follow by lowering tariffs and pursuing foreign investment.[6]

Cavour encountered considerably fiercer opposition to his efforts to curb the privileged status and independent authority of the Catholic Church within the Savoyard kingdom. Relations between the papacy and the Piedmontese state had markedly deteriorated even before the aristocratic moderate entered the government in 1850. Tensions between the two grew steadily from 1848 onwards over issues of principle and policy. After the revolutions of that year, Pope Pius IX became an uncompromising anti-constitutionalist and defender of the Church's temporal power, precisely at a time when the House of Savoy was adopting a new constitutional system and displaying expansionist ambitions in northern Italy. The initial measures of the Piedmontese parliament in 1848 did little to allay papal fears and distrust. The easing of censorship in the Savoyard kingdom further aggravated the situation, since it opened the way for the publication of a host of articles in the local press highly critical of the Vatican and the Church. For their part, most Piedmontese moderates saw the special status of the Church in their country not only as a direct violation of the guarantees of civil equality in the *Statuto*, but also as a threat to the secular authority of the new constitutional regime.[7]

The moderate campaign to remedy this situation took the form of a series of reforms introduced into parliament between 1850 and 1855. The first and most important came in 1850 when the D'Azeglio government, with strong support from Cavour in the Chamber of Deputies, proposed the so-called Siccardi Laws to eliminate separate courts for clergy, abolish the right of criminals to sanctuary in churches, give the state the authority to veto gifts and donations of property to the Church bodies, and limit the number of religious holidays. Two years later, the government introduced another measure legalizing civil marriage. Finally, in 1854 Cavour pushed a law abolishing religious orders and monasteries that performed no charitable or educational functions, and selling off their properties to help cover state budgetary deficits.

---

[6] Coppini, 'Il Piemonte sabaudo', pp. 363–7; V. Zamagni, *The Economic History of Italy 1860–1990* (Oxford, 1993), p. 16; S. J. Woolf, *A History of Italy, 1700–1860: The Social Constraints of Political Change* (London, 1979), p. 441.

[7] E. E. Y. Hales, *Pio Nono* (New York, 1954), p. 179; Woolf, *A History of Italy*, p. 438.

In contrast to Cavour's economic reforms, the moderate campaign against the Church produced only mixed results. The Siccardi Laws marked a landmark in the secularization of Piedmont. The rather modest proposal for civil marriage, however, was not enacted into law due to strong opposition from clergy, conservatives, and the crown. Similarly, three years later, the government managed to win parliamentary approval for only a watered-down version of the measure abolishing religious orders.

In fact, the anti-ecclesiastical campaign was distinguished less by its legislative successes than by the bitter conflicts it unleashed. The paucity of moderate conquests in this arena was due in no small part to the uncompromising opposition of Church authorities, who mobilized their substantial influence in the countryside and at court against the government. Despite the fact that the Vatican had already accepted, in other Catholic countries, most of the changes in church–state relations proposed in the Savoyard kingdom, the Piedmontese Catholic hierarchy refused to concede anything that limited its prerogatives and instead attempted to sabotage the reforms at every turn.

The moderates did not hesitate to respond in kind against their clerical adversaries. Harsh measures were taken against the excesses of the Catholic press, while intransigent clergy met with arrest, imprisonment, and even expulsion. To neutralize the power of Catholic opposition in parliament, Cavour went so far as to manipulate electoral laws to exclude ecclesiastics voted into the Chamber of Deputies and to invalidate election results where parliament deemed that the clergy had used their spiritual authority to influence their parishioners. Although such measures enabled Cavour to outmanoeuvre the clerical right in the short run, their long-term effects were less salutary. First of all, the bitter struggles between Church and state in the Savoyard kingdom guaranteed the identification of Piedmontese liberalism with anticlericalism. The two adversaries became locked into intractable positions of principle that discouraged negotiations, precluded compromises, and justified extreme measures on both sides. Once Piedmont became the nucleus of the movement to unify Italy, bad relations worsened as the Savoyard state not only extended its secularist laws unilaterally to newly annexed provinces, but also became a mounting threat to the temporal power of the Church. As a result, after 1870 the antagonism between Piedmontese moderates and clerics became a national problem of enormous importance: the hostility of the Catholic Church and its faithful to the unified Italian state.

The efforts of Cavour and the moderates to secularize the Pied-montese state not only affected church–state relations; they also shaped in fundamental respects the structure of political alignments as well as the institutional division of powers between throne and parliament in the 1850s. First of all, they helped to overcome the rigid polarization of the left and right in the years 1848–49, paving the way for the *connubio* or marriage between the centre-left and centre-right that assured Cavour of the parliamentary majorities for reform at home and a national policy abroad. At the same time, religious con-troversies provided the setting in which the ambiguous relationship between the monarchy and parliament in the *Statuto* came to be defined in ways that curbed the independence of the king and ensured the primacy of the Chamber of Deputies. Much as in the case of economic and religious matters, these political arrangements in Piedmont in the 1850s were then extended to the rest of the country and became some of the defining features of the new Italian state after 1861.

The major realignment of political forces in Piedmont that found expression in the *connubio* of 1852 grew out of the diverging reactions of the parliamentary right and left to Cavour's reforms. An important group of constitutional conservatives headed by Cesare Balbo and Ottavio Thaon di Revel, who had previously supported the govern-ment, became apprehensive over the pace and direction of Cavour's free-trade policies. More ominously, they voted with the clerical right against the D'Azeglio government's secularist legislation in 1850 and began to pressure for laws to restrict the electorate and limit press freedoms. The same reform measures, and the government's reluctance to impose further limits on freedom of expression, met with an increasingly positive reception from centre-left elements of the parliamentary opposition, led by Urbano Ratazzi, who wished to escape the political isolation and impotence to which they had been condemned in 1849. The growing convergence of interests between Cavour and the centre-left encouraged the two to collaborate on a common programme of additional reforms. The resulting alliance of the centre-left and the moderate right in 1852 provided the parlia-mentary base for Cavour's governments during the rest of the decade.

Conflicts over the role of the Catholic Church in the Savoyard state also offered some of the principal occasions for Cavour to ensnare a reluctant monarch within a constitutional order dominated by parliament and parliamentary procedures. Victor Emanuel II had inherited the *Statuto*, which he considered a sign of monarchical weakness; he detested constitutional restraints on his royal prerogatives and engaged constantly in the first years of his reign in extraparliamentary machinations to reassert his own authority. To make matters worse, he displayed a personal animosity toward Cavour while maintaining close ties to Pius IX.

Victor Emanuel II's overriding preoccupation with the prestige of the dynasty and with his own popularity, however, gave Cavour and the moderates the means to contain his autocratic tendencies, undermine his relations with the clerical right, and gradually manoeuvre the sovereign into accepting parliamentary government. The monarch suffered his first setback during the crisis of the D'Azeglio ministry in the winter of 1851–52, brought on by clerical and royal opposition to civil marriage. Initially, the king attempted to resolve the crisis by pushing the idea of a conservative minority government. When that idea failed to win sufficient political support, he had little choice but to accept the *connubio* and invite Cavour to form a new ministry on terms largely negotiated by the aristocratic moderate.[8]

A far more pivotal constitutional conflict between the throne and the moderate government developed during the crisis of 1855 over legislation to close the religious orders. Once again, Victor Emanuel II attempted to circumvent parliamentary procedures, this time by means of a private understanding with Pius IX and the replacement of Cavour's ministry with a pro-clerical minority government. But in the absence of an acceptable alternative to Cavour, and confronted by clerical intransigence, warnings from a wide range of the moderates, and the disapproval of Napoleon III, the king had little choice but to back down and recall the old ministry. His defeat had fundamental consequences both for Church–state relations and for the role of the monarchy in the Italian political system. In the wake of the crisis, relations between Victor Emanuel II and the Church hierarchy deteriorated, while a permanent split developed on the far right between royalists and clerics. At the same time, the resolution of the crisis confirmed the political supremacy of the Chamber of Deputies

[8] Nada and Notario, *Il Piemonte sabaudo*, pp. 377–8.

over the autocratic aspirations of the throne and thus assured Cavour greater power and freedom of action in the ensuing years.[9]

The willingness of Victor Emanuel II to accept constitutional limitations on his personal power at home was inseparably linked to his expansionist ambitions on the Italian peninsula. The monarch came to recognize that his own popularity, as well as the prestige of his dynasty, depended ultimately upon a working relationship with Cavourian moderates who, unlike the clerical conservatives, shared his anti-Austrian orientation in foreign policy. The moderates alone enjoyed the base of support at home, elsewhere on the peninsula, and abroad that made credible Savoyard pretensions to national leadership. It was precisely this convergence of interests between monarchy and liberalism that permitted Piedmont to embark upon a new campaign of expansion and unification in the second half of the decade.

Cavour, Piedmont, and Italian unification

At first glance the unification of Italy between 1859 and 1861 seems to offer a striking example of how exceptional individuals can have a profound impact on the course of history. There is little question that the emergence of a new Italian nation-state in these years would have been inconceivable without the contributions of Cavour and the Piedmontese state. After the wars of 1848–49, the small border kingdom became irrevocably associated with the cause of Italian independence. In the 1850s, it was the only state in Italy which combined the free institutions, economic resources, military might, diplomatic expertise, and political will to unify the peninsula.

The centrality of the role played by the Piedmontese leadership in these years, however, does not mean that there was anything preordained or inevitable about what they accomplished. On the contrary, the campaign to unify Italy was an extremely contingent and unpredictable process that could have been easily derailed on a number of occasions. To make sense of that dynamic process, then, entails a shift of focus away from underlying structures and long-term

---

[9] See Mack Smith, *Cavour*, pp. 78–81; Woolf, *A History of Italy*, pp. 438–9; Coppini, 'Il Piemonte sabaudo', pp. 386–91; Romeo, *Vita di Cavour*, pp. 302–3.

developments and towards immediate events and their often unintended consequences. In this context, Cavour's real genius lies less in his long-range planning than in his talent for exploiting opportunities, and improvising in the face of unforeseen international and domestic challenges and constraints that confronted him in these years.

The idealized image of Cavour that emerged after 1861 as the architect and executor of a preconceived programme of unification bears little resemblance to the reality of his evolving thinking on the national question. While he agreed with most other moderates in the early 1850s that Italian independence from Austria was a desirable goal and that Piedmont needed allies among the Great Powers, he had little knowledge or experience in foreign affairs. During his first years in government, Cavour devoted most of his energies to his domestic reforms. He showed scant interest in foreign affairs, generally, before the Crimean War (1855) and seemed to have no strong feelings about either the rest of Italy or Italian unification. In 1852, for instance, he proposed a new commercial treaty with the Habsburg Empire, much to the annoyance of patriotic public opinion.

On the whole, Cavour was reluctant to confront Austria in the first half of the decade and did so only in response to pressure from influential emigres or to neutralize the initiatives of the Mazzinian democrats. Piedmontese hospitality drew thousands of political exiles to Turin after 1849, making the capital an increasingly 'Italian' city. Their importance emerged after the Austrian government seized the property of Lombard refugees residing in Turin in 1853; the prime minister immediately lodged an official protest at the Austrian action with the Great Powers and had parliament set aside a special fund to help compensate the victims. In this fashion, he used the incident to undermine Mazzini's influence, highlight endemic discontent on the peninsula with Austrian rule, and increase the prestige of Piedmont in Italy.

Traditionally, the Crimean War has been viewed as the major turning point in the development of Cavour's new national policy. According to this older view, the aristocratic prime minister enthusiastically committed Piedmont to the war in 1855 to win the support of France and England as the first stage in his grand scheme to liberate Italy.[10] More recent research suggests, however, that he was a late and

---

[10] W. R. Thayer, *The Life and Times of Cavour* (Boston, 1911). pp. 316–22.

reluctant convert to the idea of Piedmontese participation. In fact, he initially opposed involvement in the war against Russia, fearful that it would deprive his country of needed wheat imports and encourage Victor Emmanuel to reassert his independence from parliament. His views changed only in response to foreign constraints and domestic threats. Both France and England put intense pressures on Piedmont to enter the war largely to reassure Austria and gain her participation in the anti-Russian coalition. When Cavour's government decided to join the coalition, it did so not in pursuit of national objectives, but out of fear that a Franco-Austrian alliance would leave Piedmont encircled and in regional isolation. Closer to home, a bellicose king, who was intriguing to dismiss his ministry and replace it with a conservative pro-war government, pushed him to take pre-emptive action by committing Piedmont to war on terms largely dictated by France and England. Even after the war ended, in the winter of 1855–56, Cavour remained a reluctant nationalist. He did go to the peace conference in Paris, but with little enthusiasm and modest territorial demands that were in any case rejected by the Great Powers.

Although the war produced few immediate gains for the Piedmontese, their participation in the military operations and the Paris peace conference elevated the stature of the Savoyard state on the peninsula and encouraged fundamental changes in Cavour's thinking on the Italian question from the spring of 1856 onwards. Both international and domestic circumstances favoured the adoption of a more assertive foreign policy in this regard. To begin with, the war itself provided a more promising diplomatic setting. The hostilities left in shambles the conservative bloc of Austria, Russia, and Prussia that had guaranteed territorial arrangements on the Italian peninsula. The defeat of Russia, in particular, transformed one of the staunchest defenders of the old order into a revisionist power alongside the French emperor, Napoleon III, who aimed to exploit nationalist sentiment in Italy to redraw the map of Europe and enhance the influence of France. As a result, Austria emerged from the war isolated as the sole defender of the diplomatic status quo of 1815. By introducing a new fluidity into European relations, then, the breakdown of the Concert System created opportunities for Cavour to exploit differences among the Great Powers to advance his state's interests on the peninsula. At the same time, the war and its aftermath triggered a surge of pro-Piedmontese sentiment among both moderates and segments of the democratic left in other Italian states that found expression in the National Society, an organization launched in 1857 to promote Savoyard leadership of the independence movement. Together, these European and regional developments encouraged the prime minister to adopt a foreign policy designed initially to extend the boundaries of the Savoyard state and establish its predominance over the rest of Italy. This shift in the thinking of the Piedmontese leadership was a major change, for it marked the first time that a group actually in power had agreed to embrace the cause of Italian nationalism, a cause that now acquired a new respectability since it was no longer associated exclusively with the revolutionary left.[11]

In the years between 1856 and 1859, Cavour embarked upon a daring, but ambiguous and opportunistic foreign policy whose principal objective was not so much national unification as the dislodging of Austria from Italy. On the one hand, his government broke diplomatic relations with Austria (1857) and sought to increase instability on the peninsula by encouraging discontents, exploiting insurrectionary movements, and rallying patriotic support to Piedmont in the other regional states. On the other hand, Cavour fully recognized the limits of his government's freedom of action and its dependence on international diplomacy. Accordingly, he simultaneously attempted to convince the Great Powers that Piedmont was the securest bulwark against revolution and the most reliable guarantor of European diplomatic interests on the peninsula, in order to cultivate closer ties with Napoleon III, while maintaining good relations with Russia and Prussia as a counterweight to the English Tory government's support of Austria. Such policies did not reflect as yet a clear vision of the Italian question; rather they were designed to disrupt the status quo on the peninsula and position Piedmont to take advantage of any new opportunities that might arise.[12]

The radical left unwittingly provided Cavour with his first great opportunity in the early months of 1858, when a dissident Mazzinian, Felice Orsini, attempted to assassinate Napoleon III. Even before the incident, the emperor had spoken informally with associates of Cavour about an eventual alliance with Piedmont against Austria. As the story goes, however, the assassination attempt and Orsini's

---

[11] Riall, *The Italian Risorgimento*, p. 69.
[12] Woolf, *A History of Italy*, pp. 446; Coppini, 'Il Piemonte sabaudo', pp. 389–412.

pre-execution appeal converted Napoleon III to the Italian cause. What had been vague talk turned into secret contacts between the two governments in the spring of 1858 that culminated in a direct understanding in July of that year based largely on discussions shaped by the Piedmontese prime minister. During meetings with Cavour at the French spa of Plombieres, the emperor guaranteed French military cooperation with Piedmont if the latter found a diplomatic pretext for a war with Austria. In the event of victory, the two agreed to the division of the peninsula into four states. The House of Savoy's domains would be expanded into a kingdom of upper Italy with the annexation of Lombardy, Venetia, the former duchies of Parma and Modena, and perhaps the Papal Legations in Romagna. This enlarged Savoyard state would become part of an Italian confederation that also included a central kingdom, the Papal States, and a Kingdom of Naples in the South. In compensation, Napoleon III expected to receive the regions of Nice and Savoy from Piedmont and to dominate the new confederation. To seal the agreement, a marriage alliance was arranged between the two dynasties. These terms were confirmed in a formal, but secret 'offensive and defensive' treaty signed in January 1859, whose purposes were 'to liberate Italy from Austrian occupation' and to create 'a Kingdom of Upper Italy with 11 million inhabitants.'[13]

Even with this formal agreement, the international situation remained fluid and uncertain in the spring of 1859 as Cavour began to prepare the Piedmontese military for war. Indeed, his carefully laid plans threatened to unravel completely in April when Napoleon III capitulated to pressure from England and Russia, and called upon Piedmont to demobilize its army. Only a last minute ultimatum from Austria sabotaged the peace initiative and guaranteed the outbreak of hostilities.

Initially, the war produced results that seemed to exceed Cavour's expectations. The defeat of the Austrian forces at the battles of Magenta and Solferino ensured Franco-Piedmontese occupation of Lombardy, albeit at a terrible cost in lives. The withdrawal of Austrian troops, in the meantime, created a power vacuum in central Italy where the flight of the old rulers from Tuscany, Parma, Modena, and the Papal Legations converted frightened local elites to the idea of

---

[13] See sources cited in Coppini, 'Il Piemonte sabaudo', p. 411.

union with Piedmont as the only alternative to democratic revolution.

Cavour's plans, however, suffered a major setback after his French allies abandoned Piedmont in early July 1859 when Napoleon III unilaterally proposed a truce, which the Austrians accepted a few days later. A variety of circumstances moved the emperor to go back on his agreement: the enormous carnage of the war and the prospect of even more casualties, distrust of Piedmontese machinations in central Italy, and most importantly, fear of Prussian armed intervention. To make matters worse, the terms of the resulting armistice of Villafranca were drawn up by the two emperors without any consultation from the Piedmontese. The House of Savoy still received Lombardy, but Venetia remained in Austrian hands while the duchies of Tuscany and Modena as well as the Papal Legations were supposed to be restored to their old rulers.

The Treaty of Villafranca marked a critical turning point in Cavour's thinking on the Italian question. The prime minister, who had initially embarked on his anti-Austrian campaign as part of a policy of Savoyard expansionism within a federal Italy, appears to have embraced the idea of national unification by early July. Accordingly, when Victor Emanuel II initially voiced satisfaction with the terms of Villafranca, a furious Cavour broke with his king, denouncing the treaty as a complete betrayal by the French and immediately tendering his resignation in mid-July.[14]

In the wake of Cavour's resignation and his replacement by a timid new cabinet, Piedmont ceased temporarily to play a leading role in the national movement on the peninsula. For the remainder of 1859, the real diplomatic and political initiative shifted to the British abroad and to the elites in central Italy led by Bettino Ricasoli and Luigi Carlo Farini. The insistence by a new and more sympathetic Whig government in England that the Great Powers not intervene on the peninsula precluded any quick restoration. Meanwhile, in Tuscany and the duchies it was Ricasoli and Farini, rather than the Piedmontese government, who sabotaged the Villafranca settlement and kept the unification cause alive.

Cavour's absence from the political and diplomatic scene proved to be short-lived. Indeed, favourable international circumstances not

---

[14] Mack Smith, *Cavour*, pp. 175–6; Romeo, *Vita di Cavour*, pp. 431–2.

only paved the way for his return to the prime minister's office early the next year, but also enabled him to carry to apparent conclusion his programme of territorial expansion. Anglo-French pressures were in fact critical to overcoming internal opposition, both from Victor Emanuel and from Cavour's political enemies, to his reappointment in January. Exploiting the temporary accord between England and France, he moved to support plebiscites based on universal manhood suffrage in Tuscany and Emilia that took place in mid-March and legitimized the annexation of central Italy, which immediately became part of the Kingdom of Piedmont. Of course these gains came at no small cost. In order to secure the backing of Napoleon III, the Piedmontese leader arranged a secret treaty ceding the historic territories of Savoy and Nice to France, a move that alarmed the British and antagonized important segments of Piedmontese public opinion.

Even with this sacrifice, Cavour could be rightly proud of what he had achieved by the end of March 1860. In a period of less than two years, he had overseen the creation of a greatly enlarged state that now included Lombardy, Emilia, and Tuscany, the most modern and prosperous regions on the Italian peninsula. Moreover, all this had been accomplished by a military–political campaign, largely orchestrated by him, that exploited the energy and enthusiasm of the democratic and revolutionary forces while keeping them in a subordinate role.[15]

The Piedmontese prime minister had little time to rest on his laurels, however, as unexpected events in southern Italy quickly confronted him with new problems and challenges. The danger that revolutionary forces might escape his control and seize the initiative appeared to become a reality after revolts erupted in Sicily in April 1860. In order to support the uprisings and liberate the island, Garibaldi organized and led an expeditionary force, the famous one thousand 'Red Shirts', which arrived in Sicily the next month and proceeded to win a series of remarkable military victories. Buoyed by these successes in Sicily, the Red Shirts launched an invasion of the mainland in August with British support.

Cavour, who had never shown any real interest in the South up to this time, was understandably alarmed by developments over which

---

[15] Romeo, *Vita di Cavour*, pp. 456–7.

he exercised little control. Garibaldi's expedition and his more grandiose vision of an Italian nation represented, in fact, potential threats
to the moderate leadership on a number of fronts in the summer of
1860. Not only did they introduce the possibility of constituent
assemblies and a democratic republican regime in the South, and
revolutionary agitation elsewhere, but they also raised the prospect of
eventual attacks on Rome and Venice that risked provoking war with
both France and Austria. Still, Cavour could not openly oppose the
expedition which enjoyed the backing of the king and the public. As a
result, he decided to give Garibaldi enough support to justify intervening in the movement in order to keep it within internationally
acceptable limits. But even this strategy met with scant success. The
envoy Cavour sent to negotiate with Garibaldi in Sicily antagonized
the military hero and wound up being expelled from the island, while
attempts to organize a pro-Piedmontese uprising in Naples prior to
Garibaldi's arrival failed miserably.

Developments in the South made it imperative that Cavour
appropriate the Mazzinian ideal of a unified Italian nation, but he did
so in the name of monarchy. In anticipation of Garibaldi's defeat of
the Bourbon army and his occupation of Naples in early September,
Cavour prepared a bold, but risky plan to recapture the initiative
from the left and forestall any hostile foreign intervention. Days after
Garibaldi entered the southern capital, he launched an unprovoked
invasion of the Papal States by the Piedmontese army that led to the
occupation of two-thirds of the pope's territories by the end of
September. Cavour justified such a revolutionary challenge to the
diplomatic status quo as the only means of forestalling revolution
and blocking any Garibaldian advance on Rome. At the same time, he
arranged for Victor Emanuel to head the invading army to exploit
the king's influence over Garibaldi.

Cavour's daring gamble paid off on both the domestic and diplomatic fronts. His decision to have the king lead the army proved
especially astute, since a devoted Garibaldi handed over all the territories he had conquered to Victor Emanuel in late October, thereby
precluding any armed confrontation between the two military forces.
Cavour moved swiftly to consolidate these gains and avoid any constituent assemblies by holding plebiscites that approved Piedmontese
annexation of all the new territories by early November. The process
of political unification culminated in the first months of 1861 with the

election of the first parliament and its recognition of Victor Emanuel as King of Italy. Significantly, these events did not provoke any hostile foreign intervention. Although Russia broke diplomatic relations and Austria strengthened her military presence in Venetia, the British remained openly sympathetic to Italian unification while Napoleon III privately approved of the Piedmontese initiatives if only to avoid any embarrassing conflicts over the Roman question.

Although the history of Piedmont officially ends with the creation of the Kingdom of Italy in 1861, the influence of its institutions and leaders did not, since Turin and Cavour remained at the centre of power, especially in the pivotal first six months after unification. During this period, the leaders of the new nation had to construct an administrative apparatus, army, legal code, system of political representation, and network of communications. The solution they chose reflected the manner in which the peninsula had been unified, namely as the territorial extension of the Savoyard state: Cavour and the moderates simply imposed on Italy a centralized political structure from above, extending in a uniform manner the Piedmontese constitution, legal system, and bureaucracy to the rest of the country.

It has long been fashionable for historians to blame this rapid 'Piedmontization' of the Italian state for aggravating many of the problems that beset the country in the decades following unification. In particular, the enormous gulf between the new state and Italian society after 1861 has been attributed, in no small part, to Cavour's rejection of all regional claims and differences and to the extremely restricted suffrage of the Piedmontese electoral system. In the last months of his life, the prime minister not only dismissed all proposals for regional autonomy, but also refused to honour promises of administrative decentralization within a political order that denied real participation to 98% of the population. Rooted in the ignorance, and arrogance of the Piedmontese elite, such policies purportedly accentuated the already narrow political base of the new state at the same time that they wound up inflaming rather than dampening regional rivalries and conflicts. As a result, they bred popular resentment, apathy, and resistance that found its most tragic expression in the brutal civil war which engulfed the South in the first half of the 1860s.

A newer body of scholarship has revised somewhat this highly critical interpretation of Piedmontese state-building by shifting the focus from long-term consequences to the immediate pressures and constraints in 1860–61 that shaped and limited Cavour's choices. The Piedmontese moderate's personal preference was, in theory, for a decentralized state as the most liberal, efficient, and cheapest alternative. The extraordinary and unexpected political and military events of the years 1859–60, however, confronted Cavour's government with the task of devising a new system of administration for the entire country as rapidly as possible without the luxury of long preparation and careful deliberation. In this context, 'Piedmontization' represented a quick solution that permitted Italy to present a unified front to the Great Powers at the same time that it assured a uniform system of basic civil and political freedoms to the rest of the peninsula. Cavour's reluctance to accept a federal solution also rested on a legitimate concern that in the Italian setting decentralization would only perpetuate municipal rivalries and jealousies as well as enhance the influence of the Mafia and the most retrograde local elites.

Even with all its shortcomings and long-term liabilities, the unification of Italy remains a remarkable and improbable achievement in a territory with a millennial history of political fragmentation. There is little question that the new nation which emerged in 1861 was a largely unplanned product of war, diplomacy, and popular revolution carried out against all odds by a large cast of often mutually hostile forces that ranged from Bonapartists to Mazzinian democrats. Still, whatever coordination and coherence this chaotic and uncertain process enjoyed, it derived principally from the leadership of Cavour and the Piedmontese state. In the final analysis, they alone combined the military might, diplomatic expertise, institutions, and political flexibility to exploit the opportunities created by the collapse of the Concert System, the crisis of the Restoration regimes, and the growing popularity of cultural nationalism on the Italian peninsula.

Garibaldi and the South

Lucy Riall

Introduction

The South played a vital role in the unification of Italy. Indeed, without the administrative collapse of the Bourbon Kingdom of the Two Sicilies, without the peasant revolt in Sicily in the spring of 1860, and without Giuseppe Garibaldi's successful invasion in support of the revolution, Italian unification would not have happened. Yet ironically, in the years after unification, the South came to be seen as an obstacle to Italian unity. Administrative normality proved difficult to reconstruct, the population unwelcoming and the economy curiously resistant to the benefits of liberal government and free trade. Law and order were only re-established using (a great deal of) military force. After 1860, what came to be seen as the 'barbarous' conditions prevailing in the South were increasingly juxtaposed to the values and interests underpinning Italian national identity. And the pervasive sense of a 'North–South divide', of a 'Southern Question', defined as a problem of economic, political, and cultural 'backwardness' relative to the more developed North, developed in Italy during the decades following national unification.

How did the South, the fulcrum of national unity in 1860, become the apparent antithesis of everything the Italian nation sought to be thereafter? The sources of this paradox are to be found partly in the origins and circumstances of unification itself. For southern Italy, as we shall see, the events of 1860 marked merely the culmination of a protracted crisis. This was a crisis with its origins in a process of economic and political modernization and which, beginning in the late eighteenth century and during the French and Napoleonic periods (1798–1815), profoundly destabilized the Kingdom of the Two Sicilies. Neither the Bourbon government nor, as the revolutions of 1848–49 showed only too clearly, the political opposition were able to resolve this crisis or direct it to their own advantage. Arguably, the most fundamental political problem with the South, after unification as before, was that it was difficult to control uniformly and effectively. In this chapter, we will try to explain why.

1848 and beyond

On 12 January 1848, a revolt broke out in the streets of Palermo. Starting in Palermo's Piazza della Fieravecchia, the popular uprising was led by Giuseppe La Masa and spread rapidly into the surrounding streets. Over the next few days, and reinforced by armed gangs (*squadre*) from the surrounding countryside, La Masa managed to gain control of key strategic points in the city. A week after the revolt in Palermo, revolt also broke out in the countryside of the Cilento region near Salerno, on the southern mainland. Towards the end of January, there were even public demonstrations in the capital, Naples, calling for a constitution, a parliament, and press freedoms. Under pressure at home and from abroad, the Bourbon king, Ferdinand II, reluctantly agreed to grant a liberal constitution on 29 January.

As was the case elsewhere in Italy, the events of 1848–49 mark a turning point in the history of the Kingdom of the Two Sicilies. The initial success of the revolution showed clearly the weaknesses of the Bourbon kingdom. Ranged against the monarchy was both a body of liberal public opinion and a growing revolutionary movement. The declining legitimacy of Ferdinand's government was perhaps best symbolized by the welcome given in 1847 to Luigi Settembrini's contemptuous pamphlet, 'A protest by the people of the Two Sicilies' (*Protesta del popolo delle Due Sicilie*), which accused the monarch of corruption, 'superstition', and 'ineptitude'.[1] Other leading Neapolitan

---

[1] A. Scirocco, 'Dalla seconda restaurazione alla fine del Regno'. *Storia del Mezzogiorno*, iv (1986), p. 715.

intellectuals also openly criticized Bourbon policy. Opposition to Ferdinand manifested itself in a different form through the proliferation of political conspiracies. These were responsible for revolts in Messina and Reggio Calabria in September 1847 and for the more successful January revolt in Palermo, which was organized (and even announced) in advance by democratic committees in Rome, Naples, and Palermo.

Revolution in 1848 also came at a time of intensifying social unrest. Disturbances in Palermo and Naples were connected to rising unemployment; they were fuelled by the deteriorating economic situation common to much of Europe in the mid-1840s and produced a temporary alliance between the urban poor, artisans, intellectuals, and political activists. In rural areas, an entirely distinct situation prevailed, but it was arguably more serious still. Despite the use of police and military campaigns, the government proved largely unable to control the activity of bandits and armed gangs in the countryside, especially in Calabria, Basilicata, and western Sicily. Moreover, attempts at reform during the previous decades had provoked a series of social and political tensions within rural communities. Administrative centralization, introduced at the beginning of the nineteenth century (and somewhat later in Sicily) to bolster central government's hold over peripheral areas, was resented by traditional power-holders and, simultaneously, used by some as a tool for individual aggrandizement. Hence, the administrative responsibilities of local government did little to enhance the power of central government; in the provinces themselves, they led often to a struggle for power between members of the local elite. This situation profoundly destabilized rural communities. Within these same communities, peasant agitation over the expropriation of land created even greater tension. Especially in the grain-producing areas (*latifundi*), peasants were angered by the government's failure to protect them from the consequences of agrarian reform. In particular, the failure to compensate the peasantry for the abolition of customary rights (such as grazing or wood-gathering) and the enclosure of common land caused terrible hardship; bad harvests, exploitative landlords, and an inequitable tax system further intensified popular resentment. Violent 'civil war' in parts of the rural South—factional conflict, the collapse of local government, land occupations, crop destruction, and the burning of land and tax registers—were the consequence of all these problems during the spring and summer of 1848.

The Bourbon government itself, finally, was temporarily wrong-footed by the broader Italian and European situation. The election of an apparently liberal pope, Pius IX, in 1846 altered the atmosphere in favour of reform throughout Italy. During the crisis of January 1848, Ferdinand came under great pressure from the British government (with substantial economic interests in the area) to cede to Sicilian demands for a separate constitution. Especially after the European-wide revolutions of February and March, when the monarchy in France was overthrown, the Austrian regime in northern Italy suffered setback after setback, and administrations in the German states, Austria, Piedmont, and central Italy were forced to reform themselves, King Ferdinand in Naples seemed swept along by the general 'patriotic consensus', pulled away from the political structures of absolutist monarchy and towards constitutional government.

Ferdinand's concession of a constitution at the end of January thus provoked a temporary mood of enthusiasm and popular unity. In this respect, the first months of 1848 represent the highpoint of liberal optimism in southern Italy, and the climax of its political *Risorgimento* ('resurgence'). One revolutionary, Giuseppe Sodano, expressed the sentiments of many when he remembered that 'not to have witnessed those days meant never to have witnessed anything of real importance and grandeur'.[2] Liberal and democratic periodicals flourished both in the capital and the provinces. In Naples, plans for a national guard to replace the Bourbon *gendarmerie*, and for an expeditionary force to fight the Austrians in northern Italy, were drawn up. Elections for the new parliament were also organized and in Sicily, evacuated by the Bourbon army (apart from the Messina citadel) since the beginning of February, a new provisional government was established in the capital, Palermo. Under the veteran autonomist, Ruggiero Settimo, the government set out its demands, which were the restitution of Sicily's 1812 constitution and total separation from Naples.

Yet the 1848–49 revolutions in both Sicily and the southern

---

[2] M. Petrusewicz, *Come il meridione divenne una questione. Rappresentazioni del Sud prima e dopo il Quarantotto* (Catanzaro, 1998), p. 105.

mainland also revealed the constraints on effective change. For the revolutionaries, the experience was what one historian has called a period 'of dramatic and unexpected ascendancy followed by traumatic defeat'.[3] Not all the demands made in January and February were equally welcome. The Sicilian desire for separation from Naples was viewed with suspicion not just by the Bourbon monarchy, but also by the liberals in Naples as well. As time went on, Sicilian separatists, too, found it increasingly difficult to agree amongst themselves on the form of their independent government. And although dislike of Sicilian 'municipalism' led many Neapolitan liberals to look to a greater 'Italian' solution as an alternative to territorial disintegration, reliance on Italy exposed them to the whims of Italy's monarchs: to the pope and Piedmont's Charles Albert who, like King Ferdinand himself, were to prove fickle friends of liberalism. At least in Naples, moreover, Ferdinand still maintained a firm grip on the reins of power. As his coup of 15 May showed, when the army prevailed over the revolutionaries on the Naples barricades, liberals had been unable either to capitalize on their initial gains or to present themselves as a working alternative to absolutist government.

What weakened the revolution most of all, however, were internal divisions within the liberal movement. Moderates in Naples, led by La Troya and Pignatelli, were largely content with January's compromise between monarch and parliament, and looked for a rapid return to stability based on very limited popular participation in politics. But if, according to one democrat, moderates 'feared the masses above everything else',[4] democrats—men like Ricciardi, Musolino, and Petruccelli on the mainland, or Friscia, Calvi, and Pilo in Sicily— sought a direct link with the masses through universal manhood suffrage. They also favoured a republican form of government and supported (to a greater or lesser extent) a programme of social reform. This disagreement within the opposition became clear, and caused the most damage, after the king's victory over them on 15 May in Naples. Democrats abandoned the capital and transferred their energies to the provinces, where leaders such as Costabile Carducci mobilized guerrilla action against the Bourbons. Encouraged by democrats, peasant revolt and agitation over the land question spread

---

[3] C. Lovett, *The Democratic Movement in Italy* (Cambridge, MA., 1982), p. 117.
[4] Ibid., p. 153.

throughout Calabria and into the Cilento, parts of Basilicata, and Puglia. But unfortunately for them, these attempts to establish links with the rural poor simply fragmented and weakened the political opposition. Democratic revolt in the countryside cemented the division with the moderates who had stayed in Naples. It also intensified the fears of the property-owning classes and thereby strengthened Ferdinand's hand at the centre of power in Naples.

The reconquest of Sicily, which began in the autumn of 1848, was a further indication both of the strength of monarchical reaction and of the failure to coordinate political opposition. At the same time, a counter-revolutionary 'terror' against the democrats in Calabria and elsewhere destroyed the radical network in the Two Sicilies, as its leaders were executed or forced underground and into exile. The king's decision to dissolve the Naples parliament in March 1849, and the organization of a conservative government in the summer, merely confirmed an existing *fait accompli.*

Nevertheless, and notwithstanding the apparent triumph of reaction in 1849, nothing was ever the same again afterwards. The king never recovered his popularity; perhaps especially in Sicily, political stability was never fully re-established. The economic malaise and social discontent which lay behind mass participation in the 1848 revolution did not diminish; the problem of Sicilian separatism meant that there was a constant threat of territorial disintegration. However, fragmented and disillusioned by their failure, political opposition to the Bourbon monarchy hardened after 1849. Both at home and abroad, public opinion turned decisively against the whole regime. For all these reasons, the roots of revolution in 1860 can be found in the defeats of 1848–49.

Decline and dissent, 1849–59

What is known in nationalist circles as the 'decade of preparation' (*il decennio di preparazione*) before the unification of Italy in 1860, was a decade of decline for the Bourbon monarchy. However, this decline was far from being a straightforward process. Instead, a particular kind of crisis prevailed where an ineffectual and despotic form of government met with an uncompromising, but equally weak, opposition. Thus, the decade after 1849 was characterized, above all, by a power vacuum.

The immediate effect of 1848–49 on the Bourbon monarchy was to accentuate its repressive aspects. Although Ferdinand II had always resisted liberal calls for a constitution during the 1830s and 1840s, he had still attempted to satisfy the demand for economic and social reform and had even made some limited political concessions. All this changed after 1849. Transformed into a 'police state', the monarchy purged the bureaucracy and state personnel of all intellectuals, reintroduced censorship and Church control of education and, through the Ministry of Police, organized a complex system of surveillance to spy on the population. Political suspects were placed on a special list; political arrests and trials also continued throughout the decade. Both on the mainland and in Sicily (where the infamous Salvatore Maniscalco was chief of police), the police recruited 'professional' criminals (bandits and others) to inform on the behaviour and whereabouts of political activists.

However, the impact of all this repression was largely counter-productive. It led liberals throughout Europe publicly to denounce Bourbon reaction: William Gladstone famously condemned the regime as 'the negation of God erected into a system of government' after visiting Neapolitan liberals in prison in 1851.[5] Internally, if less perceptibly, repression also fed a sense of growing disillusionment with the regime. It seemed as if the citizens of the Kingdom of the Two Sicilies languished in their own internal exile, enclosed or 'segregated from the rest of the world by a Great Wall of China or, more accurately, a Great Wall of Naples', with all their prominent intellectuals (Settembrini, Spaventa, De Sanctis, Poerio, Michele Amari) in prison or abroad.[6] In this context, the police, and the whole apparatus of repression, became a visible symbol of Bourbon misgovernment, a tangible reminder of the monarchy's problems which served actually to focus public attention on its weaknesses.

Even among the middle, property-owning classes who should have been the regime's keenest supporters, the closed world of post-'49 Naples could be compared unfavourably with the process of peaceful reform introduced in liberal Piedmont (where so many Neapolitan

---

[5] D. Beales, *England and Italy, 1859–1860* (Edinburgh, 1961) p. 27.
[6] Petrusewicz, *Come il meridione divenne una questione*, pp. 113–16.

and Sicilian exiles went to live after 1849). Middle-class discontent with the Bourbon monarchy was also sharpened by growing evidence of the kingdom's economic problems. Ferdinand II continued to invest extravagantly in his army and navy; by the mid-1850s, close to half of total government expenditure went on the armed forces and a further fifth serviced the growing public deficit. This left very little money available for public works, education, and welfare. In Sicily, where initially Lieutenant (*luogotenente*) Prince Carlo Filangieri made some concessions to demands for autonomy, support for the Bourbons was undermined by a disastrous famine in 1853–54 and by the cholera outbreak of 1855. A growing perception of economic 'backwardness' relative to northern Europe and, by the 1850s, the liberal Kingdom of Piedmont, came to be blamed on government policy. The failure to invest in railway-building, and the broader inability to develop a coherent strategy for economic development and public welfare, seemed more than ever—and to more people than ever—a damning indictment of post-'49 government in Naples.

Hence, the longer-term effect of the 1848–49 revolution in the Two Sicilies was to destroy the bases of consent hitherto enjoyed by the Bourbon monarchy. Moreover, in the other crucial area of government policy—international diplomacy—Ferdinand II met with a series of setbacks as well. Here, too, he found himself consistently outflanked by Piedmont: in this, as in other ways, the Bourbon government was to prove no match for the Piedmontese prime minister, Camillo Benso di Cavour. The turning point came with the Crimean War, when the Naples government favoured its traditional links with Russia, and refused to cooperate with the Anglo-French alliance. The subsequent breakdown of the conservative alliance of Austria and Russia and the growing diplomatic isolation of Austria, the closest ally of the Two Sicilies, led Ferdinand into serious difficulties. He severed diplomatic relations with France and Britain when, at the Congress of Paris in 1856, both the French foreign minister, Count Walewski, and the British foreign secretary, Lord Clarendon, denounced the repression and 'despotism' of the Naples administration. The declining international standing of the Two Sicilies was mirrored in the growing reputation of Piedmont. In 1859, in what was to be almost his last act as monarch before his death, Ferdinand refused to enter into an alliance with France and Piedmont in the forthcoming conflict with Austria. With this otherwise admirable act of loyalty to his Austrian ally, Ferdinand sealed the diplomatic fate of his kingdom.

However, in many respects the decade after 1849 was to prove equally disruptive for the political opposition. Especially on the left, the defeat in 1849 provoked a period of reassessment which, together with the hardship and loneliness of political exile, led to some substantial political realignments. It is possible to discern at least four currents among the Neapolitan and Sicilian exiles. During the early 1850s, a group of exiles began to support what was called *murattismo* ('Muratism'); that is, the idea of attracting French support by making Luciano Murat (the son of Joachim Murat, who had ruled Naples in the Napoleonic period) king of Naples to replace Ferdinand. By the mid-1850s, when Napoleon III's reluctance to endorse such a policy had become clear, Muratism ran out of steam. A second group, made up largely, but not exclusively, of moderates, met with greater success. Often living as exiles in Piedmont, they looked to its moderate liberal government, to the king, Victor Emmanuel II, and to the prime minister, Cavour, for assistance in the struggle against Bourbon reaction. They also looked to Piedmont for an 'Italian' leadership as a way of overcoming their own internal divisions. Among them was Giuseppe Massari, who was elected as a deputy in the Piedmontese parliament and became the friend and biographer of Cavour. During the 1850s, the Sicilian democrats Giuseppe La Farina and Filippo Cordova abandoned their radical convictions to become enthusiastic supporters of the moderate Piedmontese 'solution'. In 1858, La Farina became the leader of the Italian National Society, an organization dedicated to popularizing and disseminating the ideal of Italian unification, and transformed it largely into a propaganda vehicle for Piedmontese domination. Even Sicilian autonomists living in Piedmont—the Marchese di Torrearsa, Michele Amari—came more or less reluctantly to endorse the possibility of Sicilian autonomy within a united Italy dominated by Piedmont.

A third, loosely allied group of democratic exiles remained loyal to some, but not all of the ideals of 1848. These democrats increasingly emphasized national unity and became ever more committed to the ideal of a united Italy. They were represented perhaps most effectively by the brilliant Sicilian lawyer (and future Italian prime minister),

Francesco Crispi, who claimed to 'love Italy above all else'.[7] Expressing the disillusionment felt by many about the possibility of democratic revolution following the defeats of 1849, these southern democrats followed the Mazzinian policy of a 'neutral flag', that is, broad support for any organization, as long as national unification was the declared objective. In practice, this position led them also to accept Piedmontese leadership, although not always happily, and a more moderate policy.

A minority of southern democrats, however, refused to accept any kind of compromise with a monarchical state. Indeed, the most radical among them, Carlo Pisacane, wrote in 1857 that 'the constitutional regime in Piedmont is more damaging to Italy than the government of Francis II' because, while equally repressive, it possessed far greater stability.[8] So, 'far from advancing the *Risorgimento* in Italy', the Piedmontese solution 'actually' retarded its progress.[9] For exiles like Pisacane and the Sicilians Rosolino Pilo and Pasquale Calvi, the events of 1848–49 confirmed the need for a revolutionary alternative to monarchical Piedmont, and the need to establish and mobilize greater grass-root support amongst the rural poor. Social revolution was to them a higher priority than national unity. This group, dispersed in Malta, Genoa, and Marseilles, was responsible for a great deal of conspiratorial activity during the 1850s, notably in Sicily and Calabria. Pisacane, in particular, proposed the idea of an expeditionary force which would lead a huge peasant revolt, and bring about the downfall of the Bourbons in Naples. However, in 1857 his plans met with disaster at Sapri. He and his followers failed entirely to provoke revolt and met their deaths in the face of peasant indifference and fear. These events led to great disillusionment and a shift by more democrats towards a tacit alliance with Piedmont.

After 1849, the southern Italian opposition may have agreed on the need to get rid of the Bourbon monarchy. But that was all they agreed upon. The divisions within the opposition movement continued to undermine their political effectiveness, especially when, as sometimes

[7] L. Riall, *Sicily and the Unification of Italy: Liberal Policy and Local Power 1859–1866* (Oxford, 1998), p. 79.

[8] E. di Ciommo, *La nazione possibile. Mezzogiorno e questione nazionale nel 1848* (Milan, 1993), p. 299.

[9] Riall, *Sicily and the Unification of Italy: Liberal Policy and Local Power*, p. 78.

happened, political disagreements were backed up by personal enmity. Increasingly, they looked outside the kingdom for practical help and political inspiration. Perhaps for all of them, the experience of exile led to a sense of alienation from their homeland, and to a growing feeling of pessimism about the prospects for change there.[10] There was, as a result, next to no agreement about what to do when the Bourbons were gone.

Garibaldi and the South

Ferdinand II's death in May 1859, shortly after the outbreak of the Franco-Piedmontese war with Austria, precipitated a new crisis of Bourbon government. Much of the residual legitimacy felt towards the throne by the southern Italian elites died with him. Moreover, his young and inexperienced son, Frances II, made a series of crucial mistakes which subsequently narrowed the options open to his government. At a time when liberalism seemed triumphant throughout much of northern and central Italy, Francis chose to emphasize tradition and the continuity between his regime and that of his father by appointing the 75-year-old Prince Carlo Filangieri as prime minister. He reaffirmed his father's policy of neutrality in the conflict with Austria, and used troops to quell popular demonstrations in Naples celebrating the Franco-Piedmontese victory at Magenta. Francis also ordered the disbanding of the Swiss regiments, the best soldiers in the Bourbon army (who had played a crucial role in the coup of 1848), after an attempted mutiny over pay. Finally, in the spring of 1860 he sent the bulk of his army north to protect the frontier with the Papal States. All of this left the monarchy dangerously bereft of military force in the event of armed conflict, and isolated internally and externally. And, as a deeply religious and retiring man, Francis spent more and more time at prayer as the crisis confronting his kingdom worsened.

In April 1860, an insurrection by Mazzinian conspirators in Palermo was easily uncovered by the Bourbon police, and its principal leaders were quickly arrested. Yet, this failed insurrection had fatal consequences for the Bourbon monarchy. On the one hand, the

---

[10] Petrusewicz, *Come il meridione divenne una questione*, pp. 135–58.

execution of the conspirators and the general behaviour of Bourbon soldiers who 'rampaged' (according to the British vice-consul)[11] through the streets of Palermo provoked another round of international condemnation. On the other, repression proved ineffective as popular disturbances spread in waves throughout the surrounding countryside. Excited crowds hoisted the tricolour flag in neighbouring towns, and angry peasants attacked government offices and local officials, refusing to pay taxes and rents. There was an immediate increase in the number of armed gangs and 'lawless people' (*i facinorosi*), who disrupted mail and telegraph communications between Palermo and the provinces and often 'liberated' local prisons in order to swell their numbers. Under the strain, local government ceased to function. Hence, the effect of the April revolt was effectively to destroy any semblance of normal government in Sicily.

Theda Skocpol's explanation of social revolution as a structural crisis of the state is in many respects true of the 1860 revolution in southern Italy. In 1860, the Bourbon state came under increasing international pressure with the defeat of Austria in 1859 and the subsequent revolutions in central Italy. Internally, it was destabilized by the serious, and deteriorating, financial situation and could no longer rely on the support of southern ruling elites. As a result, the Bourbon administration was unable to control or withstand the revolution in the Sicilian countryside. In one crucial sense, however, the events of 1860 reveal the limitations of Skocpol's assertion that revolutions are not 'made' or caused by people, that they simply 'happen' as the result of greater structural forces.[12] For it is only by reference to the ideas, and the actions, of its principal protagonists that the complex, and largely unanticipated outcome of the political crisis in 1860 can be explained.

By the end of April, there was some evidence of a return to order in Sicily. But while shops in Palermo re-opened for business, and daily life appeared to resume, the government was less successful in extinguishing the revolutionary forces. Conspiracies continued unabated. Political exiles—notably Rosolino Pilo and Francesco Crispi—returned to Sicily with arms and money to prepare for a new revolt. While Pilo concentrated on mobilizing the countryside, Crispi began

---

[11] Riall, *Sicily and the Unification of Italy*, p. 67.
[12] T. Skocpol, *States and Social Revolutions: A Comparative Analysis of France, Russia and China* (Cambridge, 1979), esp. pp. 14–32.

to organize an expedition of northern Italian volunteers to come in aid of their Sicilian colleagues. It was this expedition of a 'Thousand' men (*I Mille*) which he persuaded Giuseppe Garibaldi, the heroic defender of the Roman republic in 1849, to lead. Garibaldi set sail from Genova in April, by his own account convinced that any expedition of this kind had 'little chance of success'.[13] Yet, a reluctant Garibaldi succeeded where Pisacane had failed. Shortly after landing in Marsala, on Sicily's west coast, Garibaldi's force prevailed over Bourbon troops in a crucial, but otherwise minor skirmish near the town of Calatafimi. The Bourbon commander withdrew his men to protect his lines of retreat and a victorious Garibaldi declared himself the 'Dictator' of Sicily. Offering land to every peasant who came to fight for him, he subsequently mobilized the countryside against Bourbon power. Only a few weeks later, in a surprise midnight manoeuvre, he managed to take control of Palermo; the Bourbon army prepared once again to evacuate the island. Garibaldi's new government, set up under the guidance of Crispi, began to organize a new administration and to introduce a programme of economic and social reform.

Garibaldi's sucess in Sicily completely transformed the political situation throughout Italy. Not only did he save the dying revolution in Sicily itself but, at the head of a large and growing volunteer army, he shook and, ultimately, destroyed the Bourbon kingdom on the mainland as well. Although the events in Sicily initially had little impact on Naples, by the summer of 1860 all this was to change. For in August, Garibaldi crossed the straits of Messina and landed in Calabria. Making rapid progress up the peninsula, by September 1860 he had entered Naples unopposed and in triumph; from there, he began to plan a new expedition to take Rome from the Pope, and make it the capital of united Italy. The Bourbons retreated, meeting defeat at the decisive battle of Volturno and arriving, subsequently, at the temporary safety of Gaeta where Francis and what remained of his army hoped in vain to prepare the reconquest of their lost kingdom.

Garibaldi's success over the Bourbon army also shook the confidence and control of Cavour, forcing a rapid rethink in Piedmontese policy towards the southern half of the Italian peninsula. Garibaldi and Crispi, as moderate democrats, had claimed the South in the

[13] Riall, *Sicily and the Unification of Italy*, p. 79.

name of 'Italy and Vittorio Emanuele'; and their expedition was partly assisted by the pro-Piedmontese National Society. Nevertheless, Cavour continued to suspect them, and others in the new Palermo administration, of being republicans and followers of Mazzini. He was not slow to see that he had largely lost the initiative both to the South and to the democratic movement. Hitherto uninterested in the South, or in Italian unification per se, he now saw that the only way to restore moderate and Piedmontese control was through the unconditional annexation of the ex-Kingdom of the Two Sicilies. Throughout the summer, Cavour schemed tirelessly to achieve this end. He used his influence in Palermo both to promote the interests of Piedmont and to persuade the administration that rapid annexation—not a negotiated union—was the only possible political future for the island. In Naples, too, he attempted (unsuccessfully) to engineer a moderate seizure of power before Garibaldi arrived.

By September, the tide had turned once again decisively in Cavour's favour. He sent Piedmontese troops south through the Papal States, so as to stop Garibaldi from marching on Rome. In October a popular vote (or plebiscite) was held throughout the South on the question of annexation: this resulted in an overwhelming vote in favour of union with Italy under Piedmont. It is in this respect that the unification of Italy in 1860 must be seen as a strategy to restore Piedmontese domination of the peninsula, and as a defeat for Italian democrats. 'Few people', Mack Smith remarks, were as surprised by Italian unification as Cavour and 'few more disappointed than Mazzini and Garibaldi, the two men who had looked forward to this moment more keenly.'[14] As a result, the unification of Italy actually accentuated the internal conflict between moderates and democrats.

One reason why Cavour was able to outmanoeuvre Garibaldi and the *garibaldini*, and impose his own politics on Italian unity, was because of pre-existing divisions within southern politics. As we have seen, differences between moderates and liberals, and the divergence between Palermo and Naples, meant that the opposition had never spoken against the Bourbons with a single voice. In 1860, the opposition was equally unable to offer an alternative to leadership by Piedmont. A moderate line ultimately prevailed with regard to the

[14] D. Mack Smith, *Cavour and Garibaldi: A Study in Political Conflict* (Cambridge, 1954; 2nd edn, 1985), p. 1.

land question and social reform, and despite the efforts of Garibaldi's pro-dictator (deputy) in Sicily, Antonio Mordini, the government tended increasingly to marginalize peasant demands and repress any sign of popular disturbance. Over the crucial question of the region's political future and its relationship to the rest of Italy, those in and around Garibaldi's government—pro-Piedmontese annexationists, Sicilian autonomists, Mazzinian nationalists, and socialist democrats—all disagreed with each other. 'During the revolution of 1860', the leading autonomist, Torrearsa, later remarked, 'we talked of unification and annexation, but we never had a clear notion of what it entailed'.[15] This lack of consensus allowed Cavour to step in and direct the issue to his own advantage.

In Sicily, Cavour was also able to profit from the prevailing financial, administrative, and social chaos, which largely discredited Garibaldi's government. In many districts, those who had held power under the Bourbons simply switched sides at the appropriate moment in order to stay in government. Not surprisingly, throughout the summer of 1860 the representatives of local and provincial government often refused to obey the new directives on taxes, conscription, and land reform; they thought of themselves, in the words of one official, 'as independent and entirely in control . . . [and] in the name of liberty committed acts of the most total anarchy and the most unbridled licence.'[16] Many local administrators in the Sicilian countryside continued to manipulate official powers to their own private advantage. Particularly damaging to Garibaldi were the problems in organizing new police forces, so that peasant unrest over the land question—which grew worse and more violent as peasant hopes of effective land reform were increasingly disappointed—and over conscription was impossible to control. At the same time, attempts to repress crime and social unrest using military force (most infamously in General Bixio's repression of the revolt at Bronte) undermined the popular appeal of Garibaldi's army, and blurred the ideological and political differences between the *garibaldini* and Cavour's moderates.

On the southern mainland, king Francis's decision to grant a constitution in June 1860 (before the arrival of Garibaldi) threw the

---

[15] In S. Carbone and R. Grispi, *L'inchiesta sulle condizione sociali ed economiche della Sicilia (1875–76)* (Rome, 1968), p. 528.

[16] Riall, *Sicily and the Unification of Italy*, p. 98.

administration and policing system into chaos, leading to the mass exodus of officials and officers. On the one hand, this allowed the rapid transfer of power at a local level from the Bourbons to the liberals, a process forced through by the formation of liberal national guards. Yet, on the other hand, those who came to power were not prepared necessarily to follow the new government's directives. In many provinces, local government was controlled by the moderates who favoured the interests of property owners over the peasants. Even those provincial governors who supported Garibaldi found themselves frustrated by practical problems, such as the absence of administrative personnel, security forces, or adequate resources.

All of these difficulties limited the effectiveness of Garibaldi's government, and strengthened the position of Cavour and Piedmont. Many of them were also unavoidable. They were caused by the same problems which had undermined Bourbon government—the demand for local (or regional) autonomy, lack of money, and social conflict in the countryside. They were also considerably worsened by the chaotic aftermath of revolution and by political differences within the new government. In 1860, conditions in the South worked in favour of Cavour, whose government appeared to possess efficiency, wealth, and power in great abundance, and who offered considerable autonomy for Sicily and law and order for everybody. This, for southern property owners, was the great appeal of the Piedmontese 'solution'. As early as the following year, however, Cavour's successors were forced to confront the limitations of all he had already promised.

The birth of liberal Italy

The so-called 'brigands' war' in the mainland South during the early 1860s, and the widespread crime and unrest prevailing in rural Sicily for much of the same period, were in many ways entirely predictable. Peasant land-hunger did not diminish with national unification, and unification itself brought a series of new economic and fiscal hardships. The government's decision in 1861 to disband Garibaldi's volunteer army caused enormous upheaval and resentment, while the introduction of military conscription was widely resisted. Together with the release of prisoners on a wide scale during 1860, these factors created a vast pool of displaced poor and escaped convicts which the new administration had little hope of controlling. They also offered an opportunity to the Bourbons (and, indirectly, the Vatican) to mobilize popular opposition to the Italian government through a kind of 'guerrilla' war.

Even as Garibaldi entered Naples, a pro-Bourbon reaction began in Calabria, Basilicata, and Puglia. During the summer of 1861, peasant disturbances in many of the mainland provinces were the harbinger of more organized resistance to the new Italian government. In Basilicata, the main centre of disturbances, around 39 armed bands were identified and the most famous of these, led by Carmine Donatelli ('Crocco'), seized and occupied the towns of Venosa and Melfi during April. Crocco's band also joined briefly with soldiers led by the pro-Bourbon Spanish mercenary, Borjes, and other bands were active in Abruzzo and Salerno.[17] The whole situation was not brought under control until 1865. In Sicily, where support for the Bourbons was weak and there was less brigandage than on the mainland, republicans took advantage of the breakdown in law and order to organize a series of disturbances throughout the 1860s. The most notable was a huge anti-government revolt in Palermo during September 1866, in many ways a repeat of the events of January 1848 and April–May 1860. Bandits seized the city, forcing government representatives (including the prefect and mayor) into hiding for a week, in fear for their lives. Military reinforcements had to engage in bloody street fighting in order to restore government authority.

Thus, the crisis in southern society and in government authority, which had brought about the collapse of the Bourbon kingdom, continued long after the Bourbons had gone. In many ways, moreover, this crisis was prolonged by the unification of Italy. Cavour's victory over Garibaldi in 1860 was based on a cynical, short-term strategy. He and his successors knew next to nothing about the South, and they lacked any kind of policy for dealing with the crisis that confronted them. Confident that the policies of liberal government and free trade which had brought success to Piedmont could work equally well in southern Italy, and too far removed in Turin to appreciate the scale of

[17] J. A. Davis, *Conflict and Control: Law and Order in Nineteenth-century Italy* (London, 1988), pp. 172–5.

the crisis in the South, Cavour planned simply 'to impose unity' on what he called 'the most corrupt and weakest part of Italy' with 'moral force and, if this is not enough, with physical force'.[18] The plan, according to the Lieutenant General (*luogotenente generale*) in Naples, was to 'establish monarchic authority, morality, and good sense in Naples and Sicily'.[19] In practice, government attention was fixed firmly elsewhere in northern Italy, on the question of Rome and on its mounting financial problems. The situation in the South was generally neglected.

Ironically, it was the government's overwhelming commitment to law and order, and to administrative and economic uniformity which undermined its ability to achieve these same aims. Initially at least, Garibaldi was considered more of a security threat than Francis II, so Cavour's new government 'purged' more *garibaldini* than Bourbons from administrative, military, and judicial positions. This purge caused further upheaval and instability, and often left those most hostile to the government in control. To build an efficient administration in Sicily, Cavour went back on his promise of autonomy and, in a policy reinforced by his successors, simply imposed Piedmont's centralized system on the island. In so doing, he alienated the autonomists—the most powerful political group in Sicily. More generally, central government made little effort to appeal to the southern landowning elites, who had first abandoned the Bourbons and then later forsaken Garibaldi. It was especially dismissive of the men Cavour called 'little village doctors'—the local power holders in the countryside—whose support was vital to the maintenance of government authority.[20] New economic policies, notably the introduction of free trade that damaged many southern industries and southern grain agriculture (but not the more lucrative market-gardening areas) also proved deeply unpopular. The overall effect was to weaken the central administration by putting it on a collision course with both urban and rural elites; and lack of support severely hampered government's ability to uphold and control law and order, as both the brigands' war and the revolt in Palermo showed only too clearly.

On his deathbed in 1861, Cavour instructed his successors to rule

[18] Riall, *Sicily and the Unification of Italy*, pp. 123–4.
[19] Ibid., p. 124.
[20] Ibid., p. 125.

the South 'with liberty', not repression.[21] Yet they were neither willing nor able to follow his advice. More and more troops were needed to contain the disorder; indeed, it is estimated that close to two-thirds of the Italian army was used in the brigands' war during the 1860s. In 1862, following Garibaldi's attempt to march on Rome, the government declared 'a state of siege' (martial law) in southern Italy and Sicily. The freedom of the press and of association was suspended and vigorous efforts were made to discover and arrest 'disorderly gatherings' and armed bands. During the following year, the government brought in the Pica Law, which gave the civilian authorities extensive military powers of arrest and detention to deal with provinces declared 'in a state of brigandage'. These powers were used widely, and were widely abused. Summary executions were commonplace; villages were besieged, and whole families held hostage in the search for one fugitive. Assorted 'vagrants' and 'criminal types', as well as bandits, were targeted by the military. In Sicily, the powers of the Pica Law were even used to enforce the conscription laws through a series of military operations, and in 1865 they helped the authorities in a campaign against a perceived threat from organized criminals known as the 'Mafia'. Following the Palermo revolt in 1866, another state of siege was declared. Under the command of General Cadorna, a veteran from the brigands' war, the military took control of civilian government, set up military courts to try civilians, and sent troops into the countryside to round up wanted men.

It is hard to overestimate the costs of the war which was fought in the South immediately after the unification of Italy. The war was hugely expensive in terms of men and money, and it produced a mood of public disillusionment with the new Italy that proved hard to erase. It also helped to create a distorted, but remarkably enduring, image of southern Italy as backward and crime-ridden, impervious to real change, and a source of political subversion. Thus, the war contributed to perceptions of a 'Southern Question', to a sense of southern 'difference' which came to dominate historical and contemporary understandings of the South. At the same time, the war tarnished the moderate liberal image at home and abroad. Together with administrative centralization and the disregard of parliamentary procedures, both characteristic features of government in these years, it harmed

---

[21] Riall, *Sicily and the Unification of Italy*, p. 3.

the internal unity of the governing party, or 'Historic Right' as it came to be called, and made its leaders seem dictatorial and repressive, uncaring about the constitutional guarantees they had sworn to uphold.

In reality, it was only the weakness of government opponents that prevented a more serious political crisis. Despite its capacity to disrupt and undermine government authority, Bourbon reaction never quite justified all the alarm it caused. After the mid-1860s, the Catholic Church withdrew ostentatiously from political life. Republicans, and other extra-parliamentary revolutionaries, did little more than (greatly) embarrass the government, and even the parliamentary left was, in the words of Clara Lovett, 'lamentably ineffective' during the 1860s.[22] Internal divisions and differences between the parliamentary and revolutionary left also undermined their activities.

Perhaps the most damaging aspect of government action in the South was that it, too, was ineffective. As we have seen, administrative 'normalization' was not re-established and law and order was a persistent problem. Moreover, military action caused new problems: disruption which undermined economic activity, a terrible cholera epidemic introduced by troops to Sicily in 1865–66, and mass arrests which turned overcrowded prisons into an added security risk. Many who escaped arrest became fugitives and joined armed bands. In general, repression created resistance which necessitated further repression, which seemed, in turn, to encourage anti-government feeling. Above all, the use of the military, however vigorous and decisive, could never entirely hide the reasons for their presence: the collapse of political authority, the unwillingness of local authorities to cooperate with the government, and the broad extent of elite disaffection and popular hardship. Hence, the use of emergency legislation and military force served merely to emphasize the weakness of the new government and the betrayal of Cavour's promises of law and order, 'self-government' and political autonomy.

---

[22] Lovett, *The Democratic Movement*, p. 197.

From *Risorgimento* to 'Southern Question'

In the years after Italian unification, and especially in the decades towards the end of the century, the events of the *Risorgimento* and the protagonists of 1860 were celebrated in monuments, public spaces, and other elaborate rituals. Statues were raised to Garibaldi; squares and streets were renamed after him. His exploits and the story of 'the Thousand' became part of a broader mythology of the *Risorgimento*, which emphasized both the selfless motives of its participants and the unity produced by the nationalist struggle. But, for the South at least, this heroic narrative was at best a piece of wishful thinking. At worst, it masked a harsher, more uncomfortable reality.

The causes of the revolution in the Kingdom of the Two Sicilies can be clearly attributed to social unrest and to the 'disintegration'[23] of the Bourbon monarchy. The outcome is more difficult to explain. Why were neither the democrats nor the moderate liberals able to re-establish political authority and restore order after the Bourbons had gone? One reason was that the crisis itself had deep roots, involving a painful and divisive process of political and social change, which affected the peripheral areas of the countryside just as much as the centres of power in Naples and Palermo. It was also characterized by conflict on different levels: between rival factions within local communities, between local elites and the central power, between social classes, and between competing political visions and ideologies. Equally striking was the absence of a unified political leadership to deal with these problems. However genuinely committed to political change, liberals in southern Italy remained unable to achieve it; in 1848 and thereafter, they never agreed to come together as an effective alternative to Bourbon 'misgovernment'. The success of Garibaldi's expedition to Sicily surprised everyone, and was far more the result of government weakness than of opposition strength. Union with Piedmont was also conceived and imposed on southern Italy largely by outsiders (Crispi was an exception) with an agenda of their own; this was a solution pursued by southern moderates and southern

---

[23] The term favoured by A. Spagnoletti in *Storia del Regno delle Due Sicilie* (Bari/Rome, 1997).

democrats only in the absence of any alternative, and partly as a means of defeating each other. Not surprisingly, therefore, national unification became a reflection and an expression of the issues which divided southern Italians.

The so-called 'parliamentary revolution' of 1876, when the Historic Right was defeated with the help of southern deputies and the parliamentary left came to power, brought the period of political turmoil in the South, initiated by the 1848 revolutions, to a close. On one level at least the new prime minister, Agostino Depretis (Garibaldi's pro-dictator in Sicily in 1860), proved more sensitive to the economic and political demands of southern elites than his political predecessors. In a policy imitated by almost all his successors, Depretis traded control at a local level in the South in return for political support at the national level and in parliament. Later, in 1887, tariff protection for southern grain agriculture was also introduced. Depretis made a compromise/alliance with southern elites the cornerstone of his hold on power: this 'historic bloc' was to be, henceforth, a fundamental basis for political life and government administration in liberal Italy.

The compromise of 1876 also represents an important turning point in the modern history of southern Italy. However limited in its scope and divisive in its impact, the prolonged crisis which preceded 1876 had been the product of political innovation and social mobility. The deal struck by Depretis was very different. It was an endorsement of the (often weak and corrupt) status quo, and a confirmation of the existing, unequal distribution of power and wealth. Depretis' solution to the apparently chronic instability of the South was thus in many respects a conservative one. He integrated specific (largely landowning) sections of the southern elites into the system by exploiting their need for economic and political protection; but this deal was not based on any fundamental agreement about the south's political and economic future, nor did it represent a resolution of the conflicts which divided the South. Instead, the existing divisions within southern society were preserved and guaranteed, by a political process which effectively stalled any possibility of internal renewal or reform. It was in this way that the aspirations for a southern *Risorgimento*, expressed so eloquently if chaotically in the early months of 1848, ended in the monotonous, apparently immutable realities of Italy's 'Southern Question'.

6

Politics in the era of Depretis and Crispi, 1870–96

Christopher Duggan

Italy in the 1870s

On 20 September 1870 Italian troops breached the walls of Rome and entered the Eternal City. It was hardly a very glorious affair. There was some fighting; and there were casualties; but it was not the heroic inauguration of the Third Rome—the Rome of 'the people' and of the 'national principle'—that Mazzini and his followers had dreamed of. There was no popular rising in the city; and no great feat of arms on the battlefield. Indeed it was only because the French emperor, Napoleon III, had had to withdraw his garrison of troops from the city earlier in the summer with the outbreak of the Franco-Prussian war, and then been roundly defeated and forced to abdicate after Sedan, that the Italian government had felt able to risk taking Rome at all. And even then there was some trepidation and not a little guilt: it was later claimed (maliciously and probably unfairly) that the prime minister, Giovanni Lanza, had wept tears of contrition before the French ambassador when telling him of his government's intentions.[1]

It was all rather galling. Publicists tried to put a brave face on it:

---

[1] E. Tavallini, *La vita e i tempi di Giovanni Lanza. Memorie ricavate da suoi scritti*, 2 vols (Turin/Naples, 1887), Vol. 1, pp. 179–80.

when King Victor Emanuel visited the city at the end of the year he was reported to have declared: 'We have finally arrived!' In fact the train had been late; it was raining; and the drive to the Quirinal Palace had been tedious; the remark was made in petulance (and in Piedmontese dialect) and not in triumph, as the writer Alfredo Oriani, one of many on the left who were to feel bitterly disappointed at the lack of idealism and 'poetry' in the new Italy, later recalled. Furthermore, the completion of Italian unity occurred against the backdrop of the dramatic unification of Germany: why could Italy not have affirmed itself in such emphatic style? The Prussian monarchy had seemed single-minded in its commitment to the national principle and had scored a series of brilliant victories in 1864, 1866, and 1870. The Piedmontese monarchy, by contrast, had relied largely on French and Prussian successes—in 1859, 1866, and 1870. And in 1866 it had been humiliated by Austria at the battles of Custoza and Lissa.

The manner in which the new capital of Italy was acquired may have been disappointing; and it left the Garibaldian goal of a revolutionary 'march on Rome' tantalizingly unrealized. But at least territorial unity was broadly complete. There were still the so-called 'unredeemed' lands (*terre irredente*) of the south Tyrol and Trieste; and there was talk in some quarters from time to time of Italy's claims to Corsica and Nice; but 1870 effectively marked the end of the *Risorgimento*. Relations with Austria were periodically to be soured by 'irredentism', as the movement to acquire the south Tyrol and Trieste was known; but compared to the 1860s, when the issues of Venice and Rome had overshadowed the entire political agenda, the decades after 1870 were to be largely free of the politics of national unification. Attention now turned to other questions.

The first problem was the pope. Pius IX had already refused to recognize the legitimacy of the Kingdom of Italy; and Catholics had been formally enjoined to abstain from voting in national elections. The loss of the city of Rome hardened him in his hostility. He remained inside the Vatican, a self-proclaimed 'prisoner'. The destruction of the temporal power fatally compromised the Church's spiritual mission, he declared: how could the successor of St Peter possibly hope to maintain his independence and authority surrounded by liberals and Freemasons? For the next thirty years relations between Italy and the Vatican were fraught. Every now and then there was talk of 'conciliation': Pius's successor, Leo XIII, certainly tried hard on occasions to reach a settlement, most notably in 1887. But passions were still running high. Inside the curia were many so-called 'intransigents', while in the government were politicians who had been schooled in the *Risorgimento* and who saw in Roman Catholicism an incorrigible enemy of freedom and the national principle. Only around the turn of the century, with both sides facing a common enemy in socialism, did relations begin to improve markedly.

The government sought to mollify the papacy (and international opinion) by passing a law in 1871 regulating the position of the pope. The Law of Guarantees, as it was known, accorded the pope the status and honours of a sovereign. His person was declared inviolable; he was allowed his own diplomatic representation in the Vatican; he was granted freedom of communication with Catholics throughout the world; and he was assigned an annual income of 3 million lire in perpetuity. The state also renounced many of the controls that it had formerly exercised over the clergy in Italy. The aim was, as far as possible, to uncouple Church and state, and hopefully—at least in the long run—to convince the pope that without the encumbrance of the temporal power (had not the corruption and obscurantism of the Papal States become a source of growing embarrassment to him in an age of democracy?) his spiritual mission would be enhanced. (Cf. pp. 189–94 below.

This was quite logical; and the Vatican soon came to accept that in many ways it was much better off than before (though it would not admit it: it repudiated the new law). Indeed, as many of those on the left who had opposed the Law of Guarantees pointed out, the Church was now in a dangerously strong position. The Italian state had effectively disarmed itself in the face of its most powerful enemy: the pope, the clergy, and the Catholic press were free to denounce the Kingdom of Italy, and all that it stood for, with near impunity. And the Vatican was not slow to take advantage of this, setting up the *Opera dei Congressi* in 1874 to foster and coordinate initiatives and to mobilize Catholics at the local level. The ban on Catholic participation in national politics remained in being; but Catholics were encouraged to take part in municipal politics.

The challenge from the Church was a source of great anxiety to Italy's rulers. During the 1860s there had certainly been a feeling that the new kingdom was living on a near knife-edge: republicans and reactionaries within, France and Austria without, had all posed a threat (if at times rather exaggerated so as to justify the hasty imposition of Piedmontese rule). But this feeling had been offset by a consolatory belief that many of the new kingdom's problems might be transient: centuries of despotic government had left many Italians (certainly southern Italians, it was felt) corrupt and impoverished; but the moral and material benefits of liberalism would soon become apparent and bind the masses to the new order. Such confidence, however, evaporated after 1870 as the sheer scale of the country's social problems emerged and as the economy headed into recession. The danger from internal enemies such as the Church seemed greater than ever: they had deepening reservoirs of discontent on which to draw.

Socialism was not yet a problem; and it was frequently argued that it would not become one since Italy was overwhelmingly a rural society and had little industry. But there were growing concerns about the activities of the anarchists, or 'internationalists' as they were usually known, especially in southern Italy where the famous Russian revolutionary, Michael Bakunin, had succeeded in attracting a number of able followers to his cause in the later 1860s. The Romagna, too, was disquieting. It had been the scene of violent tax riots early in 1869, which had left several hundred people dead and thousands in prison. In the 1870s it was to develop into a major centre of left-wing militancy. Prefects spoke in their reports to Rome in sometimes near apocalyptic terms about the dangers posed by internationalism in their provinces (and there were a couple of attempted risings, of a rather farcical character, in the Romagna and the Beneventano). The dangers were less than supposed; but the fears were real.

Fears were heightened by ignorance: the cultural and economic gap separating Italy's small and largely urban ruling class from the mass of impoverished and illiterate peasants was enormous. In 1873 one of the leaders of the left, the future prime minister, Francesco Crispi, visited his remote rural constituency of Tricarico in the region of Basilicata. It was an arduous undertaking. It lay over steep and often ill-made roads, two days' carriage journey from the nearest railway station, Eboli. He was appalled by what he found. The landowners were unable to market their produce because of the ruinous transport costs and their crops were being left to rot; the clergy were almost the only educated people; and the peasantry were close to starvation. They were weighed down by taxes, and were angry at the government. They presented a frightening spectacle when they turned out in the piazza to protest. As Crispi told a friend:

I will not describe to you the shouting, the swearing and the tears. All I will say is that the Italian government is cursed and hated. And if brigandage were to break out again, could we hold it against them? And if they overturn [Italy's] unity, would we dare to punish them? It is enough to make you despair . . . What has the government done to bring civilization here and win the friendship of the population? Nothing.[2]

The 'social question' and the 'Southern Question'

The existence of a 'social question' came to be recognized increasingly in the mid-1870s. The problem was felt to be particularly acute in the South. This was not simply because the South had exceptional levels of poverty—which it did—but also because it had deep-seated patterns of violence that could pose a threat to the state. The horrors of brigandage had already been seen on the southern mainland in the 1860s; and in Sicily a major insurrection had broken out in September 1866, with Palermo in the hands of some 40,000 insurgents for a week. Sicily, indeed, was felt to be a particular problem. It had an alarming track record of revolts: 1820, 1837, 1848, 1860; it had been in near constant unrest since 1860; it had a fierce tradition of insular patriotism that could easily transmute itself into a desire for political separation from the mainland; and, it was now discovered (the first writings on the subject date from these years), it had its own peculiar form of vicious criminal organization, the Mafia.

The particular problems of the South—the 'Southern Question' as it came to be known—were analysed by a number of highly intelligent and influential observers from the mid-1870s. They included Pasquale Villari, Giustino Fortunato, Pasquale Turiello, Leopoldo Franchetti, and Sidney Sonnino. The latter (his mother was British)

---

[2] Archivio centrale dello stato, Carte Crispi, Ex-Archivio di stato di Palermo, fasc. 114, Crispi to Bertani, 14 October 1873.

had been in Paris at the time of the commune in 1871 and was convinced that a similar disaster lay in store for Italy if something drastic were not done to help the poor. He was dismayed by a government enquiry into the condition of Sicily in 1875—which had effectively denied the existence of a social question—and the following year he and a fellow Tuscan, Leopoldo Franchetti, travelled to the island to conduct their own survey. Their brilliant investigation exposed the scale and complexity of the island's plight: the corruption of local government, the prevalence of private violence, the ineffectiveness of the police, the excessive taxation of the poor, the shortage of smallholders and the concentration of property in the hands of great landowners, many of them absentee, the inequities of agricultural contracts, the primitive nature of farming methods, the absence of roads, the chronic indebtedness of the peasantry, and the shortage of credit facilities.

Many of these problems were common to all of southern Italy—indeed to much of Italy as a whole. What was the government's response to them? The Right, which had been in power since 1860, was well aware of the situation. Its exponents—typically northern landowners with a strong sense of the state and a commitment to sound administration and public finances—saw their main task after 1870, however, as being to grapple with the country's debts (which had partly been inherited from the pre-1860 states). A balanced budget was after all one of the shibboleths of nineteenth-century liberalism. In pursuit of this goal they adopted a policy of fiscal prudence and sought a low profile in foreign affairs (so as to avoid incurring heavy military expenditure). They remained wedded to free trade—though were quite ready to accept a measure of state intervention in the economy if they felt it justified: it was a proposal to nationalize the railways that triggered the downfall of the Right and the advent to power of the Left in 1876.

The high priority given by the Right to sorting out the budget deficit in the early 1870s (Quintino Sella, Italy's north-European educated finance minister, called it 'a matter of "to be or not to be"') gave rise to growing discontent. During the 1860s the widely accepted need to complete and cement national unity had to a degree masked opposition to fiscal rigour. Now it took centre stage. The South was particularly aggrieved. Its parlous economic situation was clear. Yet the much-hated grist tax hit the grain-growing South disproportionately hard; and taxes on urban houses affected southern peasants more than their northern counterparts, as the former tended to live largely in towns; and the fact that taxes were being funnelled increasingly towards the centre, and burdens were being placed more and more on local government, caused many of the South's under-resourced administrations to go bankrupt. In 1874 the government tried to address the problem of the distribution of land taxes. This was the last straw for many southern landowners, who admittedly often paid less than they should have done—because their assessments were based on old and faulty registers—but who could legitimately claim that they ought to pay less given their restricted profit margins.[3]

Growing opposition to the government (in the elections of 1874 its majority fell to around 40: two-thirds of opposition deputies now came from the South) may have been triggered largely by economic discontent; but there was a more general feeling of dissatisfaction with the Right: with the narrow franchise on which its power rested, its perceived authoritarianism, its centralizing tendencies, and its northern bias. The men of the Right, it is true, often seemed more committed to the letter of liberalism than to its spirit: Piedmont, from which many of their leaders continued to come, had strong autocratic and military traditions that informed the rather heavy-handed response of governments to problems, especially in the South. But in fairness to them, Cavour's successors had faced a monumental task after 1860: how to introduce the practices of freedom to 22 million people, the vast majority of whom had had no experience of liberalism and most of whom were more likely to be deferential to a local priest, a tyrannical landlord, or even some local bandit, than to a high-minded exponent of constitutionalism. In such circumstances, could decentralization and a broader suffrage be justified? Would this not be simply playing into the hands of the enemies of the state?

---

[3] On the issue of tax distribution, see R. Romanelli, *L'Italia liberale (1861–1900)* (Bologna, 1979), pp. 187–8. For the growth of southern opposition in these years, see G. Procacci, *Le elezioni del 1874 e l'opposizione meridionale* (Milan, 1956).

The parliamentary 'revolution' of 1876 and the Left

In March 1876 the Right was defeated in parliament and forced to resign. The new prime minister was Agostino Depretis, a cautious, grey-bearded former Mazzinian of progressive principles but conservative instincts. He was Piedmontese—which endeared him to the king—and like the great majority of his party he was deeply loyal to the monarchy: the republicans had by now been reduced to a rump. The accession of the Left caused much excitement; but in reality there was to be no dramatic rupture with the past. 'Left' and 'Right' were not so much disciplined and tight-knit parties with clear programmes, as coalitions of interests, held together by the bargaining power of ministers; and individuals and groups were for ever cutting loose and forming fresh alliances. In the 1860s sections of the Left had peeled away to support the Right—and entered government; and in 1876 it was the defection of a largely Tuscan group of deputies, worried about the nationalization of the railways, that brought down the Right.[4]

This said, the Left did share a general commitment to greater democracy. They favoured decentralization and a widening of the franchise. And they tended to advocate (though with varying degrees of enthusiasm) such policies as stipends for deputies, progressive taxation, lay education, a slimmed down central bureaucracy, an elected senate, and an end to the interference of the executive in the administration. Their democratic principles—certainly those of the leadership: men like Depretis, Crispi, Cairoli, and Nicotera—were grounded in an essentially romantic view of 'the people'. 'The people', they believed, were intrinsically virtuous. They may have been somewhat vitiated by centuries of tyranny and Catholicism (the Left was more robustly anti-clerical than the Right), but if trusted and treated with kindness they would gravitate spontaneously to the institutions and turn their backs on priests and subversives. Any

---

[4] For the advent of the Left to power (and the subsequent evolution of party politics), see G. Carocci, *Agostino Depretis e la politica interna italiana dal 1876 al 1887* (Turin, 1956).

rough edges could soon be smoothed off. It was largely a matter of time—and of those in power setting a good example and educating Italians to liberalism and to virtuous citizenship.

This romantic optimism began to wane in the 1870s. The often insensitive and repressive conduct of the Right, especially in the South, scandals, and humiliations in foreign policy, had done nothing to win public confidence. And now time seemed to be running out: the economic situation was worsening and extremists were gaining in influence and support. The attempt in November 1878 on the king's life by an anarchist cook (the assassin's knife was parried, ironically, by the ex-republican prime minister, Benedetto Cairoli) was particularly traumatic. In the wake of this episode, and of a series of terrorist bomb attacks that followed, Crispi announced that he was no longer in favour of administrative decentralization: until such time as Italians had become 'politically educated' (i.e. loyal to the institutions), the state, he said, needed centrally appointed prefects and sub-prefects to monitor and control what was going on locally.[5] 'The people', in other words, were not yet ready for unfettered liberty and democracy.

However, pressure from public opinion to broaden the suffrage was becoming too great to be resisted in the late 1870s. And most on the Left continued to believe the institutions would be strengthened by drawing new social groups into the state. The Right (with some notable exceptions) was uncertain of this: it tended to harbour much less generous feelings towards 'the people' (it is no coincidence that Joseph-Marie de Maistre came from Piedmont). But even the most progressive on the Left were prey to dark forebodings, and few of them advocated unqualified universal suffrage: most wanted voters to be able to read and write, which meant excluding a significant percentage of the adult population, especially in the South. They argued that if a man could not fill in the ballot paper in person (there was almost no discussion of women being given the vote at this time) the way would be open to fraud. Their real concern, though, was with vulnerable peasants being manipulated by reactionary landowners or priests.

A new electoral law was passed in 1881. It was the highpoint of a rather meagre first few years in power for the Left. The only other

---

[5] Atti parlamentari, Camera dei Deputati, Discussioni, 15 February 1879.

reforms of note to have reached the statute book since 1876 were the Coppino Law, making primary education free, compulsory, and lay (up to the age of nine), and a law abolishing the reviled grist tax. The new electoral law increased the number of voters from 620,000 to over 2 million. Literacy replaced wealth as the main criterion. A tax threshold (19.80 lire) was retained: but only about a third of the electorate now qualified on the basis of wealth. Previously the figure had been around 80%. The debates in parliament revealed just how frightened many deputies were about the new law. They were particularly worried about the petty bourgeoisie and artisans of the cities, who were the main beneficiaries of the reform: might they not vote for radical, even socialist, deputies? It was partly to minimize this risk that a new system of larger electoral colleges and voting by *scrutin de liste* was introduced: the aim was to dilute urban votes with safe conservative rural ones.[6]

The elections of 1882—the first under the new suffrage—proved to be less of a 'leap in the dark' than feared. The far Left, or *estrema*, of radicals, republicans, and (for the first time) one socialist, doubled their number of seats: but they still had only about 40. Many voters had no doubt themselves been anxious about the future composition of the chamber and had erred on the side of caution. Despite this relatively reassuring outcome, Depretis (who was to be prime minister uninterruptedly from 1881 to 1887) now decided to draw in his horns and move to the Right. For some time he had been flirting with the conservatives under Marco Minghetti: in the spring of 1883 he reshuffled his government and brought them into his majority. This was the official beginning of '*trasformismo*'—the 'transformation' of the Left and Right into a single constitutional bloc which Minghetti, Depretis, and others had for several years been arguing was logical, given the lack of substantive differences dividing the old parties.

The rationale of *trasformismo* was to engineer a flexible centrist coalition that would leave the extremes isolated. Its aim was to ensure stable government and avoid weakening the institutions by overly brusque lurches to Left or Right. It was not a new approach: Cavour had attempted something similar in Piedmont during the 1850s. But

---

[6] For the 1881 reform, and electoral issues generally in this period, see P. L. Ballini, *Le elezioni nella storia d'Italia dall'Unità al fascismo. Profilo storico-statistico* (Bologna, 1988). For Italy in the broader European context, see P. Pombeni (ed.), *La trasformazione politica nell'Europa liberale* (Bologna, 1986).

whereas Cavour had occupied the centre ground largely so as to be able to push through a radical agenda, Depretis was doing so mainly in order to avoid radical changes: calm in the country, he felt, would be best ensured by calm at the top. *Trasformismo* was not necessarily deleterious, but unfortunately it fed into the increasingly heated debates that were taking place in the 1880s about the supposed malfunctioning of the Italian parliamentary system. It became a term of abuse, a synonym for opportunism and corruption.

The idea that Italian parliamentary politics were corrupt had already taken root by the end of the 1860s. This was partly because the old Mazzinian left contained a strong vein of austere anti-materialism: the charge of corruption was levelled readily (sometimes too readily) at opponents. But it was also the case that the boundaries between private and public interests were not always well respected by deputies. The episode of the tobacco monopoly scandal in 1868–69—when a number of politicians (and probably the king, too) had stood to make huge personal gains from a rather dubious financial deal contracted with the state—had raised a storm of protest from the left and denunciations of the moral 'quagmire' and 'mud' (terms that were to recur frequently in the anti-parliamentary diatribes of the next fifty years) into which Italy had sunk.

Criticisms of Italy's parliamentary government intensified in the 1870s as the anti-materialism of the old Left elided with a growing sense of disillusionment at the unfulfilled dreams of the *Risorgimento*. Where was the 'Third Rome' that Mazzini had prophesied? Fashionable Social Darwinist ideas also fed into the equation and helped underpin a belief that Italy was a 'decadent' nation, inclined through history, climate, and perhaps even race, to cowardice and passivity. The best known poet of the age, the former Mazzinian, Giosuè Carducci, railed against what he saw as the country's prosaic and timid leadership: Italy had wanted Rome—virile and glorious—he wrote famously; instead it had been given Byzantium, weak and corrupt. Many wondered how a country that had made such a miserable spectacle of itself in the war of 1866 and limped apologetically into the capital in 1870 could hope to compete against the likes of Germany, France, or Britain. Perhaps Italians needed strong and assertive leadership to correct their vices rather than representative government that would simply mirror them. (This was one of the arguments advanced by the former follower of Garibaldi, Pasquale Turiello, in his celebrated book, *Governo e governati in Italia*, of 1882: its premise was that Italians were congenitally prone to indiscipline (*scioltezza*).)[7]

Many commentators felt that the advent to power of the Left in 1876 lowered the moral tone of parliament. This was, to a degree, sour grapes on the part of the Right; and also snobbery: northern deputies were often scornful of their less cultivated southern counterparts. But there was also some substance to the charge. The surge of support for the left in the South had been grounded in economic hardship. What southern electors wanted was a government more sympathetic to their plight: that took the fiscal pressure off them, propped up wheat prices (tariffs on wheat were first introduced in 1878), and provided public works. Deputies from the South were expected to cater to the material needs of their constituents—or rather their voters, who even after the 1881 reform were still only a fairly thin slice of the population. If they failed to do so, they risked losing their seats. As a result parliament came, in the 1880s, more and more to resemble a cattle market, as deputies haggled with ministers over the price of their support, especially on key votes. One politician described the scene in 1886:

You should see the pandemonium in Montecitorio [the seat of the Chamber of Deputies] when the moment approaches for a solemn vote. The government's agents run through the rooms and corridors trying to win support. Subsidies, decorations, canals, bridges, roads—everything is promised; and sometimes an act of justice, long denied, is the price of the parliamentary vote.[8]

Trasformismo seemed a further nail in the coffin of parliament's credibility: principles and programmes sacrificed on the altar of expediency. And the fact that after the passing of electoral reform in 1881 the government appeared unable or unwilling to press ahead with radical measures to help tackle the country's mounting social and economic problems added to the feeling that Italy's parliamentary system was deeply flawed. Politicians, political scientists, and sociologists picked over the shortcomings of what was rather disparagingly referred to as 'parliamentarism': Pasquale Turiello (*Governo e governati in Italia*, 1882), Gaetano Mosca (*Teorica dei*

---

[7] In the introduction to the revised edition of 1889, Turiello talked explicitly of the need for war to cure Italians of their indiscipline. See P. Turiello, *Governo e governati in Italia*, Vol. I, *Fatti* (new edn, Bologna, 1889).

[8] F. Crispi, *Discorsi elettorali 1865–1886* (Rome, 1887), p. 230.

governi e governo parlamentare, 1884), Vittorio Emanuele Orlando (*La decadenza del sistema parlamentare*, 1884), Ruggero Bonghi (*La decadenza del regime parlamentare*, 1884), to name but a few. Among the country's elite it became almost commonplace to scorn parliament and to wonder whether the country might not be better off without it. The diary of the well-connected politician of the Right, Alessandro Guiccioli, is full, from the late 1870s, of such remarks as: 'When I look at our Chamber, I understand more and more Cromwell and Napoleon's way of dealing with Parliaments' (5 July 1878).[9]

The absence of clear-cut parties, party programmes, and a two-party system; the venality of deputies (and electors); the instability of governments; the clogging-up of parliament with petty local business; the meddling of the executive in the workings of the administration (the judiciary was not formally independent, and prefects were continually intruding into local government, using the police in a partisan manner, backing government candidates at election time, etc.)—these were just some of the issues highlighted by critics. Of course, as was sometimes pointed out, it was perhaps unfair to expect Italian parliamentary government to mirror its British counterpart— as if that were the ideal type to which all parliamentary regimes should conform. If Italy did not have two well-defined parties, one conservative, the other progressive, might that not be because it did not need them? And was it not the case that France and even Britain in the 1880s were experiencing problems of their own, with ill-disciplined chambers, volatile governments, scandals, and parties that split and 'transformed' themselves?[10]

What was the Italian nation?

The comparison with other countries, however, fed into another debate of the period, one which raised further doubts about Italy's political system. If countries, like species, were the product of slow evolution (and the Darwinian model of development was now

[9] A. Guiccioli, 'Diario 1878', in *Nuova Antologia*, 16 August 1935, p. 590. See also, for example, the entries for 20 April 1880, 20 January 1890, 16 September 1892.
[10] These arguments were quite common at the time. They were reiterated famously by Benedetto Croce in his *Storia d'Italia dal 1871 al 1925* (Bari, 1928).

becoming widely accepted), why should they adopt regimes that might in the abstract seem rational but which in practice could be utterly ill-suited to the character of a people? In France this thesis was being explored by the historian and philosopher Hippolyte Taine in his monumental work, *Les origines de la France contemporaine* (1875–94)—a work that proved immensely influential in Italy in the 1880s. Taine's central argument was that the French Revolution had imposed 'doctrinaire liberalism' onto a nation whose historical development had not predisposed it to such a system, and thereby established a dangerous disjuncture between the 'nation' and its political institutions.[11]

What, though, was the Italian 'nation'? Without a unified history before 1860 there was no set of traditions (at least not acceptable ones) on which to fall back. Accordingly, attempts from the 1880s to overcome the cleavage between what were called 'legal' and 'real' Italy had had to have an essentially forward-looking trajectory: the Italian character had yet to be fashioned. This idea helped to underpin a growing conviction among politicians and commentators of both Left and Right after the 1870s that the state needed to adopt a strongly educative role. It needed to identify and inculcate national symbols and values and thereby 'make' Italians. This, indeed, might be a possible solution to the country's political problems: if Italians could be taught to think in patriotic terms and to subordinate private to public interests, evils such as corruption, clientelism, and the excessive focus on local and regional issues, might be resolved.

In the 1880s and 1890s the state did a great deal to promote patriotism. The *Risorgimento* was made into Italy's founding myth, its narrative carefully doctored to hide the bitter rifts that had in reality separated the moderates and the democrats. In school textbooks and in speeches, in 'official' histories and biographies, Left and Right were presented as two sides of the same coin, forces that had worked in an almost miraculously complementary way for the common goal of a united Italy. A huge cult was created around the figures of Victor Emanuel and Garibaldi (who died in 1878 and 1882, respectively)— statues, commemorative plaques, paintings, hagiographies, newspaper articles, and for Victor Emanuel a national 'pilgrimage' to his

[11] On the influence of Taine in Italy in this period, and also the cultural climate in general, see L. Mangoni, *Una crisi fine secolo. La cultura italiana e la Francia fra Otto e Novecento* (Turin, 1985).

tomb in the Pantheon in 1884. Their selfless devotion to the cause of unity (genuine in the case of Garibaldi, highly doubtful in that of Victor Emanuel) was glorified and their close partnership taken as symbolic of the alliance of people and monarchy on which Italy rested.[12]

These efforts to engender patriotism were of course part of a general European trend: nationalism was in the air. But in Italy the indifference or hostility of the great mass of the population towards the institutions made 'political education' seem particularly urgent. The credibility of parliament was low—and falling. And the monarchy's grip on the public imagination was uncertain (the most popular member of the royal family in the 1880s and 1890s was the fair-haired and intelligent Queen Margherita, around whom a huge publicity industry developed: the king, Umberto, was irremediably colourless). Social unrest was spreading fast. Violent strikes became common in the Po Valley from 1882 as the agricultural crisis deepened. Disenchanted peasants were beginning to emigrate in droves from the South. In the Romagna the socialist leader Andrea Costa set up a *Partito socialista rivoluzionario* in 1881; and in 1885 another revolutionary party, the *Partito operaio italiano*, was founded in Lombardy.

Francesco Crispi

The strongest advocate of 'political education'—of the need to 'nationalize' the masses and bind them to the state—was the man who was to dominate Italian politics from 1887 until 1896—Francesco Crispi. Crispi was a Sicilian by birth. During the 1850s he had been in exile in France and Britain and had become acutely aware of the extent to which the greatness of these two countries depended on a deep and pervasive sense of patriotism. He had been one of the main architects of Italy's material unity: in the revolution of 1860 he had been Garibaldi's secretary of state. But after 1860, as one of the leaders of the Left in parliament, his main concern was to bring about what he and others often referred to as Italy's 'moral unity'. He wanted a state

[12] The elaboration of the 'cult' of the *Risorgimento* is well explored in U. Levra, *Fare gli italiani. Memoria e celebrazione del Risorgimento* (Torino, 1992).

that invited the respect of Italians, built on justice and the rule of law, a parliamentary regime that operated effectively, with clear-cut parties and party programmes, and a government that could provide strong and principled leadership in both foreign and domestic policy.

Crispi was a committed supporter of the monarchy: given the conservative instincts of much of the population he knew there was little mileage in a republic. In 1864 he declared famously: 'The monarchy unites us, a republic would divide us.' He was aware of the enormous symbolic potential of the crown, and was among the chief exponents of the cult of Victor Emanuel and of the 'nationalization' of the House of Savoy. It was he who, as minister of the interior in 1878, insisted on Victor Emanuel being buried in the Pantheon in Rome, rather than in Turin; and it was he who ensured the new king was styled Umberto I and not Umberto IV: the identification of the monarchy with the old Piedmontese state needed to be broken. He was conscious of the power of the crown to excite the popular imagination and opposed attempts by some of his colleagues to reduce the civil list: the monarchy was nothing if it was not splendid.

Crispi was also an advocate of a strong foreign policy. There were several reasons for this. In the first place, he ascribed to the Mazzinian concept of 'mission', according to which nations had a duty to spread sacred ideals; and just as France had imparted the gospel of liberty, equality, and fraternity to the world, so it was now Italy's turn to disseminate the 'principle of nationality'. Hence Italy should actively seek the dismemberment of old empires, such as the Ottoman Empire, and the formation of free and independent nation-states (e.g. in the Balkans). Secondly, Crispi saw the conduct of foreign policy—and of war in particular—as closely linked to the standing of the monarchy. This was the case in most European countries, but it was underscored in Italy by the pronounced military traditions of the House of Savoy and by the fact that under the constitution (the 1848 Piedmontese *Statuto*) foreign policy was technically a royal preserve—something that Victor Emanuel tried (with embarrassing consequences) to take advantage of in the 1860s. If the monarchy was to be strong in Italy it needed, in Crispi's view, to be identified with a successful foreign policy.

But foreign policy was also a means of generating patriotism. Like many of the old left Crispi was fascinated by the links between war and nationhood, military service and citizenship. Revolutionary

France provided an almost mesmerizing example of national self affirmation through war, of 'the people' mobilized for a sacred mission. The idea of 'the nation in arms' was a cardinal tenet of the democrats during the *Risorgimento*: Garibaldi had believed in it passionately. And training young men to defend their country was seen as self-evidently desirable: after the 1870s there were many local and some national initiatives to create sports, gymnastics, and rifle-shooting associations; and there were calls from some, Crispi included, for military training to be made a compulsory part of the school curriculum. The good soldier was the good citizen, selfless and obedient; and a willingness to fight and die on behalf of the nation was one of the best indicators of patriotism—and one of the best ways of engendering it.

Italy's failures in foreign policy after 1860 were as dispiriting for the Left as for the Right. In the war of 1866 Crispi had called in parliament, to rapturous applause, for the nation's 'baptism of blood': the subsequent defeats of Custoza and Lissa were traumatic. For several years after 1870 there had been general support for a low-key foreign policy: Italy needed to address its domestic problems, it was felt. The Congress of Berlin in 1878 inaugurated a new phase, one in which there was growing concern about the country's security in the Mediterranean. At the congress, the Italian government under Cairoli had refused to press any territorial claims and had come away with what was high-mindedly referred to as 'clean hands'. Meanwhile, Austria had picked up Bosnia-Herzegovina, and Britain, Cyprus; and France had been given a free hand in North Africa. Italy, it seemed to many, had been treated as a nullity: Austria now dominated the Adriatic; and in 1881 France occupied Tunisia, thereby installing itself just 100 miles to the south-west of Sicily. Italy was being encircled—or so it felt.

The French occupation of Tunisia led to the downfall of Cairoli's government. A foreign policy of detachment and isolation no longer seemed viable in an age of realpolitik. In 1882 Italy entered the Triple Alliance with Austria and Germany. This was intended to provide the country with some guarantee against future aggression by France—though it was much more likely that France would attack Germany, and Italy thus be drawn into a war on behalf of its ally. It was also hoped that with the central European powers behind her, Italy would be able to cut more ice on the international stage—and particularly in Africa, where the scramble for colonies was just beginning. There was a domestic consideration, too: the fears caused by the enlargement of the suffrage in 1881 made the friendship of two safe conservative powers seem prudent: a declared aim of the treaty was to uphold the existing social order and the institution of monarchy. The alliance naturally had its price. First, Italy was obliged to renounce its irredentist claims against Austria. Second, it was driven into higher defence spending. And third, and perhaps most important, it lost the freedom to manoeuvre between rival European powers that had traditionally been seen as so advantageous—indeed almost essential—given the country's economic and military weakness and its geographical vulnerability.

During the 1860s the Right had tended to be sympathetic to France—Napoleon III had after all been Victor Emanuel's ally in the war of 1859—the Left to Prussia. It was generally acknowledged by the Left that Bismarck's Prussia was a little short on liberalism, but as the standard bearer of German unity it could be easily seen as an exponent of the 'national principle'. Napoleon III was universally abhorred on the Left: he was seen as a despot whose only wish in 1859–60 had been to replace Austrian with French influence in the peninsula. The situation became more complicated after the fall of Napoleon in 1870 and the establishment of the Third Republic. The Right now began to gravitate towards Germany, while the Left divided between those (and they were mainly on the party's republican wing) who looked to France and those who supported Germany.

Crispi was one of the strongest advocates of the alliance with Germany. He believed history had made the French nation almost incorrigibly imperialist: it wanted to dominate Continental Europe— hence its secular struggle with Germany—and it wanted to control the Mediterranean, hence (or so he maintained) its deep-seated aversion to united Italy (though there was also the question of the pope to keep French Catholic opinion inflamed). After the occupation of Tunisia Crispi's strident attacks on France, and more generally his calls for greater military spending to make Italy strong, touched a chord with growing sections of public opinion. Even Depretis found himself nudged into a more assertive foreign policy. In 1885 a detachment of troops was sent to the small port of Massawa on the Red Sea. Here, according to the foreign minister, lay 'the keys to the Mediterranean'. But many observers felt that Italy was getting itself involved needlessly in a region that offered no obvious strategic advantages, that could prove difficult to hold militarily, and whose occupation might well set Italy on a collision course with Britain, which regarded the Upper Nile valley as its sphere of interest.

There was some talk that Italy required colonies for economic reasons: in particular that its surplus population in the South should have somewhere to emigrate to rather than North America. But in reality prestige was the most important factor. Italy's self-esteem was low, its ambitions to greatness considerable; its institutions—the monarchy, the army, parliament—needed bolstering, and the masses diverting from their economic problems and the inflammatory rhetoric of the far Left. And had not all the other major European powers, including Belgium, begun to stake out territory for themselves in Africa? Unfortunately Italy was ill-prepared for its colonial venture. It knew little about Ethiopia and its military power, and it greatly underestimated the determination of the emperor and the local warlords to maintain their independence. Early in 1887 a detachment of 500 Italian troops from the under-equipped garrison at Massawa was intercepted and massacred by an Ethiopian force at a place called Dogali. Much was made of the fact that the soldiers had died heroically, in a disciplined line facing the enemy; but it was hard to disguise the fact that this was yet another national humiliation.

Crispi was turned to as the man of the hour. He alone, it was widely felt, had the energy, the determination, and the authority to salvage Italy's pride and restore the prestige of the beleaguered institutions. In the previous few years he had been a leader of an opposition group known as the *Pentarchia*; but in reality he had ploughed his own rather solitary furrow, setting himself up as a Cato-like figure in parliament, lambasting Depretis and his 'transformist' followers for their decadence, corruption, and inertia, and calling for Italy to assert itself in the world and fulfil the noble mission entrusted to it by the *Risorgimento*. In the spring of 1887 he agreed to enter Depretis's last administration as minister of the interior. Depretis was a sick man, and from the start Crispi was recognized as the de facto head of the government. When in July Depretis died, Crispi slipped into his shoes unopposed. Never before had an Italian prime minister enjoyed such widespread support in both parliament and the country as a whole.

Crispi's popularity had to a degree been carefully orchestrated. He had long hoped that parliament could provide the country with 'political education'. Events from the late 1870s persuaded him otherwise. He looked instead (and with quite clear self-referential intent) to a 'man of genius'. The idea of the great man who could alter the course of world events had its roots deep in the romantic culture of the democratic Left. Cromwell, Napoleon, Mazzini, Garibaldi—all could be construed as figures chosen by providence for the progress of mankind. For Crispi and his circle—among whom were a number of talented young writers and intellectuals eager, like Carducci, to assert the primacy of the 'aesthetic' and the 'ideal' over the material in politics—the messianic leader was particularly well suited to Italy, given the cultural predisposition of the Catholic masses to the veneration of saints. This was part of the reason why Crispi set out quite deliberately in the 1880s to build up his image as a great man, denouncing the government and the chamber constantly for its cowardice and its pettiness (or 'micromania' as he called it), reminding the public repeatedly of his key role in the *Risorgimento* and his friendship with such giants as Garibaldi and Mazzini, and delivering well choreographed set-piece speeches to ecstatic audiences of 10,000 or more.

The 'cult' (the term was dear to the old Left) of the great leader was part of a more general conception of politics as secular religion which again had its roots deep in democratic culture. The French Revolution was the obvious historical model: it had shown the value of festivals, ceremonies, symbols, and anniversaries for mobilizing the masses. In the 1870s, and even more in the 1880s and 1890s, the need to sacralize politics and squeeze out the rival religions of Catholicism and socialism was keenly felt by many within Italy's ruling elite. The fact that the Roman Catholic Church had been so conspicuously successful over the centuries in appealing to the imaginations of ordinary people through great buildings, statues, processions, vestments, holidays, rituals, shrines, pilgrimages, and saints, made the task appear particularly important (and difficult).

The religion of *la patria* was encouraged in a variety of ways. Victor Emanuel and Garibaldi were the most conspicuous 'saints' (when Garibaldi died, great pressure was placed on the family to have the hero interred in the Pantheon and to stop his body being cremated: the masses, it was argued, needed something tangible to venerate). But many other paragons of liberal virtue from the

Risorgimento (and earlier) were honoured with statues, street names, and hagiographic lives (in primary and secondary schools particular emphasis was placed on the use of biographies for teaching). Anniversaries were commemorated with sometimes lavish celebrations (for example, those marking the twenty-fifth anniversary of the expedition of the *Mille*, in 1885, or the sixth anniversary of Victor Emanuel's death, in 1884, when a national 'pilgrimage'—this was how it was officially described—was organized for tens of thousands of people from all over Italy). In 1895, 20 September, the date on which Rome had been captured, was made into a public holiday; and that year the anniversary was marked with huge festivities at Porta Pia (where the city walls had been breached in 1870) and on the Janiculum hill, where the great equestrian statue of Garibaldi, gazing out in brooding serenity over the Vatican below, was inaugurated amidst huge publicity.[13]

Crispi's first term as prime minister, from 1887 to 1891, was one of remarkable energy. This was partly because Crispi felt it important to rectify the years of inertia under Depretis, and to deal with some of the pressing social and economic issues that had been left unaddressed. Hence an extraordinary package of domestic legislation. A new and more liberal penal code was introduced: among other things this gave greater protection to labour against capital. A special tribunal was set up to provide citizens with redress against abuses by the administration. A prison reform law and a law to regulate emigration were passed. There was a major overhaul of the public health service, badly needed after recent cholera epidemics in the South. And the problem of welfare—crucial given the levels of unemployment and poverty in Italy—was tackled in a radical way. In the past assistance for the poor had been left largely to charitable bodies known as *opere pie*, controlled for the most part by local notables and clergy. In the late 1880s some 6 million Italians were estimated to be dependent on these bodies. A law of 1890 brought the *opere pie* under public control—to the indignation, naturally, of the Church—and made the welfare of the poor the responsibility of the state.

The energy of Crispi's administration—and it was very much Crispi's: he was simultaneously prime minister, minister of the

---

[13] Some aspects of the development of 'patriotic education' in the 1880s and 1890s are examined in B. Tobia, *Una patria per gli Italiani* (Bari, 1991). A fuller study is needed.

interior, and foreign minister—had another purpose as well: to generate 'enthusiasm', something that Crispi and his circle believed would help bridge the gap between 'real' and 'legal' Italy. The need to bind the masses emotionally to the institutions was particularly important given Crispi's long-held determination to extend democracy in local government, a much greater 'leap in the dark' than the 1881 electoral law, as the clergy (and increasingly the socialists, too) were highly active at the municipal level. The local government law of 1889 roughly doubled the number of those eligible to vote in administrative elections, to around 4 million (more than could vote in national elections) and for the first time made the office of mayor elective in larger communities: in smaller centres the mayor remained a state appointee. This was a brave reform, but one fraught with dangers, as the proliferation of what were felt to be 'subversive' local administrations in the 1890s showed.

Crispi knew that he was taking a risk, and he looked to mitigate the dangers of increased democracy by strengthening the powers of central government in several key areas. This was somewhat paradoxical, but it reflected a growing conviction that he and many others had held for a decade or more that the state needed to exercise a strong tutelary role until such time as the country's 'political education' was complete. Prefects thus retained their essential function as agents of the executive in the provinces and were given new powers of intervention at a local level: a 'socialist' or 'clerical' town council could thus be almost summarily dissolved. The executive's leverage over the administration (and parliament) was augmented with the introduction of a new tier of government, that of under-secretaries of state, who were answerable to ministers, and by such measures as one allowing for deputies to be appointed as prefects. Crispi felt this was necessary, given the tendency for civil servants, including prefects, to disregard the spirit if not the letter of a minister's instructions out of concern for their future careers: officials were often afraid to act in a way that might make them unpopular with opponents of the current administration and lead to their transfer or dismissal after the next (all too frequent) government crisis.

Crispi was trying to ensure more effective and stable government, and counter the lack of consonance that had become a major feature of the Italian political system. The state was almost a patchwork of rival power centres. The king and the court pulled strings; ministers conspired behind the back of the prime minister (not least with the court); deputies plotted over how and when to bring down a government; the army had its own agenda (to a degree); and so, too, did the navy. There was little sense of an independent civil service, and new ministers felt obliged to import friends and relatives into key posts so as to have people around them that they could trust. The Foreign Ministry was a particularly well defined enclave of power. It was strongly aristocratic, Piedmontese, and Francophile in character.[14] Crispi did not trust it, and in pursuing his own vigorous foreign policy he resorted to secret channels of diplomacy that allowed him to bypass certain ambassadors—and also the king and the court—when it suited him to.

The attempt to concentrate power in the hands of the executive, and of Crispi in particular, led to accusations of 'despotism' and 'Caesarism'.[15] But in general Crispi commanded widespread support among the country's political elite and probably among the population as a whole—though the introduction of higher taxes to pay for increased expenditure on the army and navy did cause growing disquiet in 1889 and 1890. Crispi's position depended partly on the fact that there was nobody else of sufficient authority to hold the different factions in parliament together, and partly on a shared recognition by Right and Left that the prestige of the institutions needed reinforcing. But an enormous amount rested also on Crispi's high profile in foreign affairs.

A vigorous foreign policy was at the heart of Crispi's political agenda. He saw it as a way of reinforcing his own standing, of fulfilling some of the frustrated dreams of national greatness that had been generated by the *Risorgimento*, and of creating a sense of patriotism in the country and cementing the masses to parliament and the monarchy. If a vigorous foreign policy led to war, so much the better—provided, of course, Italy was on the winning side: a glorious war would be the affirmation of Italy's nationhood. And it would be a way of overcoming those defects in the national character—indiscipline, unassertiveness, and lack of aggression—that commen-

---

[14] On the role of the Piedmontese aristocracy in foreign affairs, see A. L. Cardoza, *Aristocrats in Bourgeois Italy: The Piedmontese Nobility, 1861–1930* (Cambridge, 1997), pp. 20–5, 71–6.

[15] The issue of 'Caesarism' was intensely discussed in Italy in the 1890s. See Mangoni, *Una crisi fine secolo*, pp. 171–2, 180–2.

tators such as Pasquale Turiello had identified as being at the root of Italy's slide towards decadence.

Crispi looked to turn the Triple Alliance to Italy's advantage. He paid a visit to Bismarck shortly after becoming prime minister, which caused immense consternation in France. Quite rightly so, for it was followed by a secret military convention between Italy and Germany setting out detailed arrangements for a joint war against France. Crispi then embarked on a huge programme of rearmament. Relations between France and Italy deteriorated rapidly, and Crispi deliberately cranked up the tension by every means he could: he launched a ruinous trade war between the two countries, and then picked a succession of quarrels over often very minor issues, accusing France—which naturally retaliated with some aggressive posturing of its own—of wanting to attack Italy. Public opinion in both countries was brought to almost fever pitch in the course of 1888 and 1889—in part through quite skilful manipulation of the Italian press by Crispi.

Crispi was quite prepared to trigger a war: in July 1889 he actually started mobilizing the army after claiming the French were about to attack Italy. But he was in a weak position. He could do nothing without the support of Bismarck: Italy was not strong enough to fight France on its own; and Bismarck was not prepared to be jostled into a war—though many around him, including the young kaiser and a number of senior generals would quite happily have fought France and Russia at this time—as Crispi was well aware. Crispi tried again a year later to spark off a war, claiming that France had signed a secret treaty that would allow it to annex Tunisia permanently and that this would upset the balance of power in the Mediterranean. Again Germany would not play ball. Crispi tried for compensation in Africa and begged the British to allow Italy to take Tripoli. But Lord Salisbury mistrusted Crispi deeply and would not consent.

By the second half of 1890 Crispi realized he had been led down a cul de sac by Bismarck. Bismarck genuinely liked and admired Crispi, and saw in him a kindred spirit. But Germany had no need to upset the European order—not yet, at least. It suited Bismarck to drive a wedge between Italy and France; he had no desire to accede to Crispi's dream of a Europe in which Italy controlled the Mediterranean, Germany the Continent. Crispi saw too late in the day that he had been manipulated. He tried to insinuate that he might leave the Triple Alliance if Italy did not get something. But it was no use. Three years of high taxes and massive military spending had resulted in no tangible gains. Crispi had nothing to show for three years of enormous expenditure on the army and navy. A largely court-orchestrated plot led to his fall from power early in 1891.

The crisis of the 1890s

Three years later, at the age of 75, Crispi returned as prime minister. Italy seemed to be on the verge of collapse. The economy was in deep recession, and state bankruptcy was a real possibility. Socialism had begun to assume frightening dimensions: the first national workers' party had been founded in 1892, and socialist organizations were burgeoning across northern Italy. In Sicily a socialist-led movement known as the *Fasci siciliani* was mobilizing rural workers and organizing strikes: by the end of 1893 violence had erupted across much of the western half of the island. Worse still, parliament was in the grip of a devastating banking scandal that threatened to discredit the entire political class. Groups on the far Left, led by the radicals, were in full cry, demanding thorough investigation of the scandal and exposure of all the guilty men. It was against this backdrop that Crispi was called upon to try and salvage the situation.

Crispi proclaimed martial law in Sicily and crushed the *Fasci* by force. But he also put in train measures to tackle the chronic shortage of smallholdings in the island by dividing up some of the large estates. This angered the major Sicilian landowners greatly. Stringent new police measures were introduced to deal with the civil unrest in the country. And the unrest was severe: terrorist bombs had become commonplace, certainly in Rome, and deputies were often forced to go around armed. Socialism (or 'anarchism' as it was frequently called, to make it sound more lawless) was declared illegal, and numerous working-class associations were shut down. Voting lists were also radically revised to exclude thousands of poorer people who, it was claimed (with some truth), had been illegally registered. None of these measures attracted much opposition, certainly from the middle classes; nor indeed in parliament. There was a widespread feeling that some sacrifice of liberty was inevitable given the state of the country.

The main battleground in parliament was over what was called the 'moral question'. The banking scandal had compromised dozens of leading politicians. During the 1880s a number of banks had speculated in the property market and been left holding worthless bits of paper. To avoid bankruptcy, some had resorted to printing money illegally. They had also given large loans on very favourable terms to deputies and other prominent people. When the scandal broke the suspicion was that these deputies had effectively been paid to keep silent about the banks' activities. It was not as simple as that. Politics had become an increasingly expensive business in the 1880s: political newspapers were making huge losses, and elections were becoming immensely costly, given that many voters expected as a matter of course to be bribed; and the electorate was now bigger than ever. Politicians desperate for money had thus found themselves face to face with unscrupulous banks desperate to lend. Most deputies were not corrupt in any strict sense; but they were hard put to prove they were entirely innocent.

Some of the intensity of the scandal probably derived from the fact that the king himself was suspected of being implicated.[16] This emboldened the republican elements of the *estrema* who were in the vanguard of those demanding political blood. Parliament became increasingly unruly, and at the end of 1894 Crispi prorogued it after one of his great rivals, Giovanni Giolitti—who had been caught up in the scandal—produced a sheaf of documents claiming to show that Crispi was also implicated. Crispi had certainly borrowed massively from the banks in the past to keep his newspaper afloat, but there was little to indicate that he had behaved unethically. For most of 1895 the country was ruled by decree. Crispi was among many who were now inclined to believe that Italy was unsuited to parliamentary government and that some more authoritarian system, perhaps along German lines, might be more appropriate and effective.

In a final effort to save the situation, Crispi turned to war, this time in Africa. Since the late 1880s Italy had been trying to extend its holdings in east Africa, but lack of resources and deep divisions among politicians and generals about what was feasible in Ethiopia had hampered progress. Crispi was desperate for military success.

[16] The unpublished letters of *The Times*' Rome correspondent, W. J. Stillman, in the News International Archives, London, show how widespread this suspicion was in political circles and how much it coloured Italian politics of the mid-1890s.

Apart from anything else this would help to shore-up the position of the monarchy, whose standing had fallen alarmingly in recent years. But Crispi pressed too hard. The commander in Ethiopia was a former member of the *Mille* called Oreste Baratieri. He was not a very competent general at the best of times. Crispi goaded him insistently, and on 1 March 1896 Baratieri, who was by now on the edge of a nervous breakdown, launched a reckless march on the town of Adua. More than 5000 Italian troops were massacred by Ethiopian forces— the worst disaster ever inflicted on a colonial power in Africa.

The defeat at Adua brought an end to Crispi's career and marked a watershed in Italian politics. It is true that the country remained racked for several more years by economic crisis (though Crispi and his finance minister, Sidney Sonnino, had done a great deal to sort out Italy's public finances); and socialism continued to grow in strength and be dealt with by severe repressive measures: the years 1898–1900 were particularly troubled. But the politics of prestige, the attempt to heal the fracture between people and institutions through a vigorous foreign policy, was for the time being discredited. A new approach was needed. The dramatic upturn in the economy at the beginning of the century offered a way forward. If Italians could not be made loyal to the national institutions through ideals, enthusiasm, and education, perhaps improved standards of living might do the trick instead. This is what Giovanni Giolitti attempted for a number of years; and in the long run it was to be a winning formula—but not until the 1950s. In the meantime, the politics of idealism, whose roots went deep into the democratic culture of the *Risorgimento*, had a protracted and painful history before them.

7

Religion and society, 1789–1892

David I. Kertzer

The Church and the emergence of modern Italy

Whether looked at from the viewpoint of culture or politics, the Roman Catholic Church looms large in the history of Italy in the nineteenth century. Not only was Italy an overwhelmingly Catholic land, but, as the home of the Holy See—with the pope and his curia—it lay at the centre of Roman Catholicism worldwide. Developments affecting the Church thus had implications far beyond Italy's borders, implications that in turn affected life in Italy in major ways. Moreover, in a large swath cutting across the centre of the Italian peninsula, that of the Papal States, the pope was not only a religious leader but the political leader as well, head of the government.

The nineteenth century saw the emergence of Italy as a unified state and as a modern political system, moving from the *ancien régime* of monarchs and feudal aristocracies to an elected parliament and civil rights. The Church served as a bulwark of the old order, closely linked to the aristocratic elites, committed to a Catholic state in which the Church had the responsibility of regulating what people believed, read, and said. The Church also embraced the view that the pope could only be free to perform his spiritual duties if he were also a temporal ruler, a 'pope-king' who presided over the Papal States. Since most efforts to create a unified Italian state—the dream of the

Risorgimento—meant some curtailment, if not elimination, of this temporal power, the Church stood as one of the most powerful obstacles to Italian unification.

But to understand the role of religion in Italy in this period it is not enough to look at the political role of the Church, important as it was. For the mass of Italians the Church and Catholicism were a central part of everyday life. More important than the activities of the pope and cardinals in Rome for them was the local parish church, the local patron saint, the rites that marked the agricultural cycle and the life cycle, and the beliefs that imparted a supernatural dimension to their otherwise humdrum existence. In this chapter we shall examine both the battle between the Church and the state that was central to nineteenth century Italian history, and also the ways in which religion was experienced at the local level. In doing so, we pay particular attention to the considerable regional differences in the organization of the Church in Italy. Of course, not everyone in Italy was Catholic: there were small Jewish and Protestant communities, which we will briefly consider. More importantly numerically, there was a growing tide of anticlericalism which we will also examine.

Catholic Italy

At the dawn of the nineteenth century, the clergy formed a significant portion of the entire population, especially in the South: the Kingdom of Naples, with about 4 million inhabitants, had 90,000 priests. By contrast, the nineteenth century saw a sharp reduction in the number of clergy. By the time of unification, in a population which in today's borders of Italy was about 25 million, there were some 100,000 Catholic clergy, or one per 250 people, compared to one to every 50 or 60 in the previous century.

The great majority of the clergy lived in rural communities, where the bulk of the population then lived. Many aristocratic families continued the tradition of sending one of their sons into the Church, where they often entered the Vatican diplomatic service or took high positions in the ecclesiastical hierarchy. Yet this practice declined as the century progressed. These well-educated priests had little in common with the bulk of the rural clergy, who came from the peasantry, with often only rudimentary education, and lived in primitive conditions. Priests in the rural areas almost always lived near where they had grown up, and moved very little. A study of 1500 rural priests in Veneto, in north-eastern Italy, at mid-century, revealed that most priests came from the locality where they were beneficed, and that following initial placement as an assistant parish priest for 8–13 years, they then typically remained in the same parish for the rest of their lives, typically more than 30 years.[1] The cities, though, did exert some attraction, at least for the more literate clergy, as priests sought positions connected to the chapels of noble families, often in exchange for providing Latin lessons to the family's children. Indeed, the formal education of young children was practically a monopoly of the Catholic clergy in most areas. Clergy were also evident at the end of life as well: funerals in urban centres often saw long lines of priests in their processions, the number of priests being regarded as a sign of the wealth and prestige of the family of the deceased.

In the rural areas, priests ministered to a largely illiterate population and, among them, were viewed with some deference for their literacy, their links to local elites, and their contacts with the wider world. It was through the local priest that most rural people experienced the Church through the taking of the sacraments, attendance at mass, participation in patron saint day, and other processions. It was the local priest, too, who came around each year during Lent to bless each home, invoked the protection of saints, and even performed exorcisms on sick livestock.

Local clergy also aided their parishioners by serving as power brokers with the larger world. Whether dealing with government offices or with private—often Church-run—charitable agencies, people turned to their parish priest not only for advice, but also support, without which aid could be difficult or impossible to obtain. For many benefits, as in the case of a family seeking a dowry for their daughter, or a woman seeking work as a wet nurse for a foundling home, people had to obtain a certificate of good moral conduct from their parish priest. And the Church itself was responsible for the bulk of the charitable institutions in society: from hospitals to homes for

---

[1] Angelo Gambasin, 'Il clero diocesano in Italia durante il pontificato di Pio IX (1846–1878)'. In *Chiesa e religiosità in Italia dopo l'Unità (1861–1878)*, Vol. 1 (Milan, 1973), p. 179.

deaf mutes, from schools for children and (in the evenings) for adults to the offering of food to the needy. Moreover, the parish priest served as the only link most people had to the Church hierarchy, a power that became especially important in the not uncommon case when a marriage was planned with a relative within the wide net of kin relations prohibited by the Church, and for which Church dispensation was required.

The Church, however, was not a seamless web of authority, nor did it take the same forms throughout Italy. Not only were there regional differences linked to the different secular authorities found in different parts of the peninsula and their relations with the Church; there were also tensions generated between different institutional segments of the Church in the same areas. There was a division between the parish and diocesan clergy on the one hand and the friars, monks, and nuns in various orders on the other; there were rivalries among the religious orders; and there were many ordained priests who had no parish and worked outside the Church.

A good example of such endemic tension was found in the South, with its peculiar system of *ricettizie* churches. These were churches which were separate from the diocesan structure—that is, they did not depend directly on the bishop of the diocese in which they were found. They were based on a common patrimony—generally of landholdings—and composed of a number of priests who were admitted to membership and who then jointly administered the church's property. Typically the regulations governing these churches allowed membership only to those who came from the locality in which the church was found; having a son become a member of such a corporation was seen as a major conquest for peasant families throughout the South. The history of the Church in the South in the eighteenth and nineteenth centuries was in good part the history of attempts of the Church hierarchy to exert greater control over these churches, and the tenacious efforts of the local priests to hold on to their independence. Three-quarters of all churches in the South were of this type in the eighteenth century, but over the course of the following century they declined under the combined weight of efforts by the new states to take over their property—a phenomenon found in different forms elsewhere in Italy—and the ever-increasing attempts of the Church hierarchy to rein them in. Yet even by mid-century, in the deep south regions of Puglia and Basilicata, 74% and

94%, respectively, of all parish churches were of the 'ricettizie' type.[2]

The Church in the South was also marked by the hyper-development of dioceses and the poor development of local parishes. At the beginning of the 1800s, southern Italy had 131 dioceses, each ruled by its own bishop. All of Catholic Spain then had only 54. Even in the last decades of the nineteenth century, southern dioceses had only on average 32 parishes each, compared to 150 parishes per diocese in the North.[3]

The impact of the French occupation

The years of French occupation of the Italian peninsula—from 1796 to 1814—were a time of turmoil for the Church in Italy. Although Napoleon himself initially sought to come to terms with Pope Pius VI, he ultimately took harsh measures against the Church and in 1798 forced the pope to leave Italy.

Revolts against the French occupation spread through the peninsula in 1799, and defence of the Church and the Catholic religion provided one of its major battle cries. When the revolts were put down by the French, a new period of negotiations began. The Holy See signed a concordat with France's satellite Italian republic of northern Italy in 1803, which confirmed the jurisdictions and economic resources of the bishops and proclaimed Catholicism the religion of state. However, the annexation of the Papal States in 1809 led to the banishment of the pope from Italy and a period of sharp conflict between Church and state ensued. Many Church properties were seized and auctioned off, religious orders were suppressed, and a variety of other restrictions on the activities of the hierarchy and the clergy introduced.

The conflict between the Church and the new French rulers in Italy reflected a much longer-term development. The view that the state should reign supreme, and the role of the Church be limited to the

---

[2] Vincenzo De Vitiis, 'Chiese ricettizie e organizzazione ecclesiastica nel Regno delle Due Sicilie dal Concordato del 1818 all'Unità'. In Giuseppe Galasso and Carla Russo (eds), *Per la storia sociale e religiosa del mezzogiorno d'Italia*, Vol. 2 (Naples, 1982), p. 413.

[3] Gabriele De Rosa, *Chiesa e religione popolare nel mezzogiorno* (Bari, 1978), p. 73.

spiritual realm, was one that an increasing number of European rulers had embraced in the eighteenth century. Insofar as the Church involved itself in what the rulers regarded as their proper sphere, attempts were made to reduce its influence. Most notable, perhaps, had been the reforms introduced in the 1780s by the Austrian ruler, Joseph II, which affected not only Lombardy, but also, through Joseph's brother, Grand Duke Peter Leopold, Tuscany as well. The office of the Inquisition was ended, properties of religious orders which were deemed to be not meeting public needs were seized and the orders disbanded, and other actions taken to assert the primacy of the state against the Church in Tuscany.

Following the defeat of Napoleon in 1814, Pope Pius VII made his triumphal return to Rome. The defeat of the French meant the restoration of the old regimes in Italy, including the Papal States. The legacy of the French occupation would live on, however; French revolutionary ideas about freedom of religion and freedom from religion were not forgotten.

The Restoration

The Vatican quickly moved to restore its old position. In doing so, it attempted to convince the rulers outside the Papal States that their interests lay in forming a solid alliance with the Church to protect the old order against the threat of renewed uprisings. Indeed, the Church blamed the secular rulers for the revolutionary upheavals, arguing that they were the consequence of Enlightenment ideas regarding separation of Church and state which many European rulers had embraced. The lingering tensions regarding the prerogatives of the Church and the attempts of the secular rulers to limit them led to continuing conflict between Church and state, especially in those territories under Austrian control.

Various lines of division within the Catholic world emerged in the first few years of the Restoration. The modest reform efforts of the secretary of state, Cardinal Consalvi, were repudiated by the most conservative elements of the Church hierarchy, who denounced them as evidence of contamination by liberalism and even branded them 'Jacobin'. Functionaries of ecclesiastical government from the pre-French era returned to office throughout the Papal States. Described as 'curialists' because they saw themselves as advocates of the power of the central Church hierarchy of the Vatican, they sought to defend their former privileges and fiercely opposed any attempts to enlist more laymen into the government bureaucracy. By contrast, the more liberal cardinals and lay Catholics saw the reform efforts as mere window dressing, and were especially distressed that all high government positions remained in clerical hands.

In the decades to come before Italian unification and the demise of the Papal States, there would be continuous unrest and uprisings. Major revolts in 1831 briefly challenged the position of the Church as the bulwark of the old autocratic order throughout the peninsula. Gregory XVI, who was elected pope amidst the disorders early in 1831 after almost 100 inconclusive ballots, called on Austrian troops to put down the revolts in the Papal States, and with his secretary of state, Cardinal Lambruschini, did everything possible to stamp out the liberal heresy.

Despite the massive loss of property as a result of the sale of Church holdings early in the century, by the mid-nineteenth century the Church still owned a sixth of all productive lands in Italy. Another consistent source of displeasure was the great opulence on display in Rome, where cardinals—themselves often from the nobility— travelled in lavish carriages surrounded by liveried attendants, making frequent social visits to noble families.[4]

The impact of the French reforms continued to be felt. Throughout the peninsula religious orders re-established themselves only with great difficulty. The diocesan structure was affected as well, particularly in the South where the abolition of feudalism in 1806 considerably reduced the bishops' incomes as well as the incomes of many parishes.

In general, the rulers who were restored to power following the French occupation felt the precariousness of their positions and saw in closer relations with the Church a means of shoring up their authority. In the case of the Bourbon court in Naples, for example, a new concordat in 1818 cemented these links, with Church and court collaborating closely to prevent popular uprisings. But tensions in lines of authority within the Church continued, with high clergy

---

[4] Giacomo Martina, 'Il clero italiano e la sua azione pastorale verso la metà dell'Ottocento'. Appendix 1 to Roger Aubert, *Il Pontificato di Pio IX (1846–1878)*, Storia della Chiesa XXI/2 (Milan, 1990), pp. 771–2.

tending to be closely identified with the local aristocracy and civil rulers, and trying to carve out some autonomy for themselves with respect to the curia in Rome.

Pius IX: from the revolution of 1848 to unification

When Pius IX was elected pope in 1846, a brief period of hope and excitement began. In contrast to the reactionary Gregory XVI (and the equally reactionary Cardinal Lambruschini, whom Pius IX narrowly defeated in the balloting) the new pope was viewed as a more open person, able to deal with modern times, and sympathetic—or so it was presumed—to the need to expel foreign troops and make Italian rulers more independent. The new pope's decision to introduce gas lighting and railways to the Papal States, measures that had previously been rejected as promoting public indecency, were seen as omens of a new openness to change.

The election of Pius IX had, in particular, been welcomed by those liberal Catholics who sought to reconcile a commitment to Italian independence with loyalty to the Church. Just three years earlier, in 1843, a Piedmontese priest, Vincenzo Gioberti, who had been exiled as a follower of Mazzini, caused a sensation with a two-volume work that called for Italy to achieve independence through a confederation of existing rulers under the guidance of the pope.

The hopes of liberal Catholics that Pius IX would reconcile the Church with Italian independence and modernity were soon dashed with the outbreak of the revolutions of 1848. A new period of revolutionary upheaval swept the Italian peninsula and took aim at the power of the Church. Pius IX himself fled Rome in November of that year for exile in the fortress of Gaeta, nearby in the Kingdom of Naples. In 1849, the new Roman government proclaimed the end of the old papal regime and the establishment of a republic. The constitution guaranteed the pope the freedom to exercise his spiritual office, but deprived his position of all its political powers and proclaimed the equality of all citizens regardless of their religion.

The pope did not have to wait long before the uprisings were put down, in the case of Rome by the arrival of French and Neapolitan troops later in 1849. The presence of French military forces around Rome as well as Austrian battalions elsewhere in the Papal States meant that the movement for Italian independence and against papal temporal rule would be as much an international struggle involving foreign powers as an internal battle.

By the time Pius IX returned to Rome, in 1850, whatever sympathies he had once had for liberal reforms (in truth, not many) were now long gone. The forces of liberalism and national independence were the enemy of the Church, and the Vatican relied on the continued military support of the French and the Austrians to keep these enemies at bay. Relations with the restored rulers were not always smooth, however. In the Grand Duchy of Tuscany, for example, although Grand Duke Ferdinand signed a new concordat with the Vatican in 1851, the pope continually rebuked him for the new freedoms being accorded the population, especially criticizing the lenient treatment of Jews and Protestants. The relations between the two in the 1850s have been described as a 'dialogue of the deaf ... with Florence continuing to reason from the perspective of the eighteenth century and Rome from that of medieval Christianity.'[5]

Relations between the Kingdom of Sardinia and the Church also began to deteriorate at mid-century, as the Savoyard state, as part of its modernizing policies, increasingly sought to limit the sphere of Church influence. In 1850, passage of the Siccardi Laws led to the suppression of the separate system of Church courts and to the legal immunity enjoyed by the clergy, and it extended state control over certain ecclesiastical property. Five years later a new series of laws led to the suppression of all those religious orders not directly involved in providing public education or charitable assistance. The bitter struggle between the Church hierarchy and the government in Turin in these years is examined in detail in the preceding chapter.

[5] Roger Aubert, 'L'Église en Italie avant et après Vatican I.' In *Chiesa e religiosità*, Vol. 1, p. 5.

The fall of the Papal States and the rejection of modernity

Deterioration of relations between Rome and Turin in the 1850s encouraged the papacy to adopt an increasingly intransigent approach to all forms of political change in Italy, and hence to make itself an enemy of the national movements which were growing throughout the peninsula. When the Piedmontese forces occupied northern portions of the Papal States in 1859, cardinal legates were driven off, papal flags lowered, and the tricoloured national flag hoisted in their place. The elites in the Papal States, seeing in the Savoyard kingdom the face of modernity and opportunities for new wealth, began to abandon Church rule and played a key role in hastening the annexation of the papal lands to what would become the Kingdom of Italy. The defeat of Austrian forces in 1859 in Lombardy, as well as in the Papal States, left the Vatican feeling increasingly beleaguered. The pope mobilized every resource he could to halt the dismemberment of his state and issued orders of excommunication against all those involved.

Yet, initially, not all those loyal to the Church opposed unification. For example, Garibaldi and his men enlisted the support of many local priests as they made their way through Sicily in 1860. And even in the North, where allegiance to the Vatican was stronger, many priests called for an end to the temporal power of the papacy, although these demands were quickly denounced by the Church hierarchy.

With the proclamation of the unified Kingdom of Italy in 1861, all that was left of the Papal States was the region immediately surrounding Rome. There followed nine more years of tension, since the nationalists considered unification to be incomplete without Rome. These were years marked not only by frenetic political activity, but also by important religious initiatives as well.

In 1864 the Vatican issued one of the most famous encyclicals of modern times, *Quanta cura*, with its accompanying Syllabus of Errors, a document that listed the principal errors of the day. Sent to bishops throughout the world, the syllabus warned loyal Catholics everywhere of the pernicious doctrines which the pope had identified and anathematized. Among these were the beliefs: that people should be free to profess whatever religion they thought best; that even non-Catholics might go to heaven; that it was permitted to disagree with the demand that the pope should enjoy temporal power over his own state; that there should be separation of Church and state; and that 'the pope should reconcile himself to and agree with progress, liberalism, and modern civilization.'[6]

The pope's apparent condemnation of progress and modern civilization shocked many Catholics—although it was loudly applauded by the conservatives in the Church. However, it proved a windfall for the Church's enemies in Italy and elsewhere, who cited it as evidence of the incompatibility between the Church and modernity.

Pius IX also launched another initiative aimed at restoring his authority, the convening of a Vatican council. Held in Rome in 1870 and attended by 774 bishops from throughout the world, the council opened with solemn ceremonies attended by many of the recently deposed secular rulers, including the Tuscan grand-duke and the former king of Naples, Francis II. In July 1870, the delegates voted to endorse the doctrine of papal infallibility. This meant that when the pope spoke on doctrinal matters he spoke with divine authority and could not be challenged. Two months later, troops of the new Italian state entered Rome and ended what remained of the pope's temporal domain.

The new Italian state and the Church

The leaders of the new Italian government, including the king, Victor Emanuel II, found themselves in a difficult position. The creation of the new state had been made possible by the defeat of the Church, but the continuing hostility of the pope made consolidation of their rule more difficult, for it was an impediment both to gaining the allegiance of their own population, and winning recognition from foreign governments. The members of the new Italian ruling class were themselves conservatives from privileged backgrounds, people who were far from social radicals and who were accustomed to having

---

[6] From the Italian text in Eucardio Momigliano and Gabrile M. Casolari (eds), *Tutte le encicliche dei Sommi Pontefici*, Vol. 1 (6th edn, Milan, 1959), pp. 262–80.

close ties to the Church. Moreover, they realized the magnitude of the task they faced in winning the allegiance of the mass of the population. The people were still overwhelmingly rural and illiterate, and were intricately connected to the Church through the capillary web of parish organization. But opposition to the government was not a stance that was very comfortable for the Church, either. The Church hierarchy had for centuries flourished by maintaining close, mutually beneficial relations with the civil authorities, and its own *modus vivendi* presupposed such ties.

In short, although there were forces operating on both sides that favoured a rapprochement, for a variety of reasons the hostilities increased rather than abated, with each side blaming the other for the breakdown. To understand the Church leaders' refusal to recognize the legitimacy of the 'usurper' state, as they called it, we need to avoid looking back with the privilege of hindsight. While today it is clear that the Church had lost its hold over the Papal States for good, this was not obvious at the time. Indeed, in the decades before unification, popes had lost their temporal power and gone into exile a number of times, from the Napoleonic years at the turn of the century to 1848, yet in each case, after a shorter or longer interlude, the pope had made his triumphal return. Why should 1859–61 be any different? There seemed no reason that the successful methods of the past should not be tried again: hence the refusal to recognize the legitimacy of the new state, the instructions to good Catholics in Italy to refuse to give it their allegiance, and the appeal to the Catholic powers in Europe to assist the Church militarily and diplomatically in restoring its lost temporal power.

The banner under which the new government policy took shape was 'a free Church in a free State', a phrase used by Cavour in his parliamentary addresses of 1861. However, from the very beginning it was clear that the new rulers wanted and expected to receive Church blessing for the new government. It had long been considered natural for rulers to be blessed by the Church, and for these rites to be major occasions through which the general population came to recognize the legitimacy of the government and its leaders. To the rulers of the newly emerging Italian state it was inconceivable that the transition to the new regime from the old would take place without proper ritual markings, and these rituals could only be provided by the Church. There thus began one of the more peculiar features of Italian unification, the battle between state and Church over Church participation in the rituals associated with state power.

Each transition point of the newly emerging Italian state in 1860–61 was to be marked by a series of solemn rites involving popular participation. The new government made it clear that these rites should involve ceremonies held in the churches throughout the country— from cathedrals to parish churches—and involve clergy from archbishops to parish priests. Connected with such events as the successful referenda for annexation to the Savoyard kingdom, and the marking of the anniversary of the new constitution, the celebrations were to be consecrated by the holding of Te Deum rites and by the ringing of church bells throughout the country.

For the Vatican, such participation of the clergy in the rites celebrating the new state was an outrage, and bishops were soon issuing orders to their parish priests to refuse any such collaboration with the new government. As increasing numbers of Catholic clergy refused to allow their churches to be used for the patriotic celebrations, tension increased; bishops and priests were arrested, anti-clerical sentiment was enraged, and loyal Church followers were scandalized by the new government's actions.

Despite these tensions, the new rulers were eager to reach some accommodation with the Church; but although negotiations with Vatican representatives were begun, they soon broke down. In the first years of the new state, the details of the Church strategy were not yet firmly in place. In 1861, the editor of one of the major Church daily newspapers launched the motto later embraced by the whole Church: 'Neither elected nor electors'; that is, loyal Catholics could neither stand for election nor vote. However, this policy—referred to by the Latin phrase *non expedit*—was not fully put into effect until 1868, and even thereafter the Vatican had occasional second thoughts about it. The policy, however, remained in effect throughout the rest of the century and into the next, and was a constant reminder of the continued refusal of the Church to recognize the legitimacy of the Italian government or the Italian state.

The ambiguous position of the new state regarding the place of the Church was evident in the constitution on which the new government was based. The first article proclaimed that 'The Roman Catholic religion is the only religion of the state. The other cults that now exist are tolerated insofar as they conform with the law.' Yet article 24 of the same statutes proclaimed the equality of all citizens before the law.[7] Then, in 1867, the government, in the belief that an accord with the Vatican was not possible, and seeing in the Church the principal obstacle to the consolidation of the new state, pressed ahead with a series of measures aimed at reducing Church power. Church property, with the exception of that belonging to parishes, and certain other buildings, was confiscated; monasteries and convents were closed or forced to operate under burdensome restrictions. Civil marriage was introduced, and marriages performed by priests were no longer recognized as valid by the state, producing in the short run a sharp rise in rates of 'illegitimacy' in Italy, for a wedding in church continued to be viewed by most people as a 'real' wedding, with the registration of the wedding in the town hall as an empty formality, often postponed. Non-Catholics were to be admitted to the military academies and given free access to all the other positions in society. The exemption of Catholic seminarians and clergy from military conscription was revoked.

The Church reacted with particular energy to the new efforts being made to reduce its influence over the socialization of youth. Each community was to have its own public elementary school, with the teachers hired by civil authorities. The traditional monopoly of the clergy over education was to come to an end, just as the proportion of the population attending schools would increase dramatically. The original law (the *legge Casati*, which went into effect in Piedmont and Lombardy in 1859 and then was extended to the rest of the Kingdom of Italy in 1861) guiding these schools, however, did provide for the teaching of religion. Yet when a new law in 1877 (the *legge Coppino*) supplemented the earlier one, and listed all required materials to be taught in the schools, no mention was made of religion. Rather, students were to be taught the 'first ideas of the duties of man and of the citizen', language reflecting that of the French Revolution. This led to renewed polemics, although in practice the great majority of students continued to be taught the Catholic religion in the schools.[8]

The battles over the schools extended all the way up to the universities. In 1865, at the University of Bologna, which under the Papal States had been under Church authority, 35 professors were fired

---

[7] Francesco Margiotta Broglio, 'Legislazione italiana e vita della Chiesa (1861–1878)'. In *Chiesa e religiosità*, Vol. 1, pp. 111–12.

[8] Ibid.

when they refused to take the required oath to the new government. In 1873, a new law abolished all faculties of theology in the country.

The tense relations between the Church and the new state were nowhere more evident than in the battle over approval of the appointment of bishops to preside over dioceses. The right claimed by the government to approve the Vatican's appointment of new bishops before they could take their positions was one that had long been associated with relations between Church and state. The new government, in short, claimed no more in this regard than the governments that preceded it. However, the Vatican was loathe to request such permission of a government it viewed as illegitimate, fearing that to do so would constitute an act of recognition of the government's authority.

The government, meanwhile, did not make it easy for the Church, and took its power of reviewing these appointments very seriously, feeling free to disapprove of any bishops who were thought to be anti-government. That this stance ill accorded with the stated policy of a 'free Church in a free State' caused the rulers little concern. The result was that by 1864, of the 225 dioceses in Italy, 108 had no bishop to lead them. The following year, as a result of the battle with the state, 10 bishops were undergoing trials or had already been found guilty—typically of resisting the orders of state authorities to authorize their parish priests to take part in state ceremonies, or of sending out pastoral letters deemed to be inciting resistance to the state—43 bishops were in exile, and 16 bishops had been named but had been prevented from taking up their posts. A decade later, in 1875, while 94 newly assigned bishops had either directly or indirectly requested the government's permission to take up their post, only 28 had received it. Another 41 had not requested permission and so also lacked authorization to take up their positions.[9] Finally, after over a decade and a half of skirmishing, some accommodation was reached in 1876, with the Vatican agreeing to request permission of the government for its bishops, and the government placing fewer obstacles to approval of the Church's appointments.

These battles with the Church had done little to burnish the international image of the new Italian state, which was being undermined

[9] Gregorio Penco, *Storia della Chiesa in Italia, vol. II: Dal Concilio di Trento ai nostri giorni* (Milan, 1978), pp. 337–8; and Mario Belardinelli, 'L' 'exequatur' ai vescovi italiani dalla legge delle Guarentigie al 1878'. In *Chiesa e religiosità*, Vol. 1, pp. 30–1.

by the pope's determination to portray himself as a prisoner. This image received new impetus in September 1870, when Italian troops broke through the city wall at Porta Pia and, following a modest battle in which a number of papal troops were killed, took over Rome, which was soon to be pronounced the capital of the Italian state. The pope sent a letter to papal nuncios throughout Europe asking whether they thought he should remain in Rome at all: there was ample precedent for the pope to flee Rome under such circumstances and set up the Holy See elsewhere. However, after some hesitation—Belgium in particular had some attraction as an alternative site—Pius IX decided to remain where he was and fight to recapture his temporal kingdom from his base in the Holy City. To reinforce the public image of the pope held hostage, Pius IX never again left Vatican City, that small patch of land including St Peter's which was surrounded by the city of Rome.

In part to address the concerns being raised internationally about the new state and its treatment of the pope, the parliament in 1871 passed the Law of Guarantees, which gave the pope (practically if not explicitly) the status of an independent sovereign power, guaranteed his freedom of communication with Catholics throughout the world, the freedom to conduct diplomatic relations with other countries, and assigned a large annual endowment (over 3 million lire) to cover the expenses of the Vatican. The law also abolished the requirement that the bishops swear allegiance to the king. Although the Vatican heaped scorn on the new law, in fact it did help to improve relations between Church and state.

The rise of the Catholic movement

The embattled political position of the Church had a major impact on the relationship between the clergy and the Catholic laity in Italy. When the Church had been in a position of political power—whether directly, as in the Papal States, or indirectly, through its close links to the rulers in most of the rest of the peninsula and islands—the relationship between clergy and the mass of the laity was clear: in matters regarding the Church and the faith, it was up to the clergy to command and for the laity to obey. While there were many Church organizations involving the laity—most notably the thousands of local confraternities throughout Italy—these were clearly intended as expressions of popular piety under strict hierarchical control and not intended to involve lay members of the Church in negotiating relations between the Church and the larger society.

All this was to change in the nineteenth century, as a result not only of the loss of the Church's political power, but also due to the advent of a mass press and, eventually, increasing literacy. Indeed, the mid-nineteenth century was a fertile period for the birth of the Catholic press in Italy, with the Church pioneering the publication of newspapers having a national audience. In 1848, in Turin, the newspaper *L'Armonia della Religione con la Civiltà* was founded by a priest, and began a 15-year battle (until its demise in 1863) against all forms of liberalism. Two years later, in 1850, after special dispensation, the Jesuits authorized the publication of the journal *Civiltà Cattolica*, published in Rome, which quickly established itself as the unofficial mouthpiece of the pope. It soon became the premier journal of Church opinion, dedicated in its first decades to the battle against liberalism, written in highly polemical style, and quoted at length by the Catholic press throughout Europe. In 1861, the quasi-official newspaper of the Vatican, *l'Osservatore Romano*, began to publish. By 1872, the burgeoning Catholic press, preoccupied with the battle against liberalism and the new state, included 17 daily newspapers and 109 other periodicals, most having only local distributions.[10]

This unprecedented form of communication between Church and laity was soon accompanied by another innovation: the formation of societies—mainly locally based—of devout lay people dedicated to defending the position of the Church in society and to championing Catholic values. In fact, Italy was a laggard in this movement, for such associations of lay people had already been formed in France, Belgium, Germany, and elsewhere. Beginning in 1865, local Catholic associations sprang up throughout Italy, particularly in the North. In 1867, the first association with national ambitions was formed, the *Società della Gioventù Cattolica Italiana*, the Society of Italian Catholic Youth. In 1874, following the further proliferation of Catholic lay

---

[10] Giacomo Martina, 'Sguardo alla stampa cattolica italiana'. Appendix 5 to Aubert, *Il Pontificato di Pio IX (1846–1878)*, p. 832.

groups, a national conference of representatives was called, resulting in the founding of the *Opera dei Congressi*, an association of Catholic lay organizations that would play an influential role in Italy for the rest of the century.

As the first article of its 1883 statutes proclaimed, the *Opera* was intended to 'unite and reorganize Catholics and Catholic associations from all of Italy in a common and coordinated action to defend . . . all of the sacrosanct rights of the Church and of the papacy and the religious and social interests of the Italians, in conformity with the desires and the directives of the Holy Father and under the guidance of the episcopate and the clergy.'[11]

The lay Catholic movement embodied in the *Opera* led, in the final decades of the nineteenth century, to a series of diocesan, regional, and national conferences; pilgrimages were organized to famous sanctuaries and, especially, to St Peter's tomb; petitions were sent to parliament protesting the treatment of the Church; and public meetings were organized to denounce the anti-Catholic policies of the government.

The Catholic movement came to be closely identified with Pope Leo XIII (1810–1903), who was elected to the papacy following Pius IX's death in 1878. Guiding the Church throughout the rest of the century, Leo XIII assumed as intransigent a stand against the new government as his predecessor, but saw the importance of adapting Church tactics and Church organization to the new times. The *Opera*, despite the perceived risk of a lay association that might get out of the hierarchy's control, became a central tool in the Church's efforts to retain its influence in Italy. In 1891, Leo XIII's encyclical, *Rerum novarum*, is credited with first enunciating the modern Church position on social policy, rejecting socialism but calling on Catholics to actively engage in solving the social and economic problems facing society. It was a pronouncement that gave a further boost to the Catholic social movement.

The *Opera* was organized in a capillary manner mirroring that of the Church itself, with both diocesan committees and parish committees. However, at the local level it also had youth sections, as well as local organizations devoted to providing credit for peasants, and

---

[11] Angelo Gambasin, *Gerarchia e laicato in Italia nel secondo Ottocento* (Padova, 1969), p. 4.

others devoted to the problems faced by non-agricultural workers. These peasant and worker associations flourished especially in the last two decades of the century, as the Church faced the threat posed by the growing socialist movement, with its own rapidly expanding rural and urban associations.

The associations that composed the *Opera* were not equally well developed in the different regions of the country, nor did they have precisely the same character everywhere. In Veneto, a stronghold of the Catholic Church, a thick network of Catholic associations blanketed the region. However, the highest levels of the organization there were in the hands of a small lay and Church elite, the former including many aristocrats. While this elite was primarily concerned with ways to battle the liberal state and defend the position of the Church, the mass of members—poor peasants—were more concerned with local activities aimed at helping them feed themselves, and were organized into a series of rural cooperatives.

The *Opera* and the Catholic movement had their greatest strength in the regions of the North; in the South they faced many obstacles. With the loss of their privileged relationship to the state, the clergy of the South tended to build on their earlier relations with local notables, who offered them protection and support. When added to their traditional diffidence towards the power of the Vatican, these circumstances militated against investing much energy in organizing the laity to fight on behalf of the pope's prerogatives and against the new state.

Reflective of these regional differences were the contrasting reactions to the death of King Victor Emanuel II in 1878. The king had long been reviled by the Vatican and the Catholic press for his role in 'usurping' the temporal power of the pope, and his death became an occasion in the North, as in Rome, for further battles between the patriots, who idolized him, and the devout, who spurned him. The higher clergy boycotted the king's funeral, and some of the Catholic press showed satisfaction rather than remorse for his death (as in *Il Veneto Cattolico*'s exclamation: 'The king is dead, the pope is well!'). In Parma, when the bishop, following Vatican orders, refused to allow the cathedral to be used for a mass marking the king's death, a group of radicals organized a violent demonstration in protest. Yet when news of his death reached the southern city of Potenza, for example, the bells of all the churches sounded in mourning for a full hour, and a solemn ceremony was held in the cathedral, at which the bishop himself spoke.[12]

Religious minorities: Jews and Protestants

From the perspective of the Holy See, there was only one true religion. Those who were not of the true religion were either heretics—as in the case of the Protestants—or they were infidels. The concept of religious freedom was firmly rejected by the Church. One of the effects that the Church's fall from political power had in Italy was the erosion of the second-class status of Italians who were not Catholic.

In fact, there were relatively few members of other religions in Italy in the nineteenth century. At mid-century there were about 38,000 Jews and around the same number of Protestants, together accounting for well under 1% of the population.

The Jews were concentrated in a limited number of cities, reflecting the fact that they had been banished from much of Italy (including all of the South) in the sixteenth century. At unification two-thirds of the Jewish population lived in just 11 central and northern Italian cities, with the three largest—Rome, Livorno, and Trieste—having over 2500 Jews each. When the French forces swept into the peninsula in the late eighteenth century, they pronounced the Jews (and Protestants) free and equal citizens, liberated them from the ghettoes into which they had been forced to live, and allowed them to attend all schools, practice all professions, and own land and other property, all rights previously denied them. No longer were they forbidden to have any social contact with Catholics, nor were they required to wear the distinctive sign on their clothes that alerted others to the fact that they were Jews.

Yet with the fall of Napoleon and the advent of the Restoration, the old restrictions were reimposed: Jews were forced back into the ghettoes and attempts were made to strip them of the property they had

[12] 'La morte di Vittorio Emanuele II'. Appendix 8 to Aubert, *Il Pontificato*, pp. 855–6. On Potenza, see Giampaolo D'Andrea, 'Società religiosa e movimento cattolico a Potenza tra XIX e XX secolo'. In Antonio Cestaro (ed.), *Studi di storia sociale e religiosa. Scritti in onore di Gabriele De Rosa* (Naples, 1980), pp. 252–4.

acquired during what came to be called their first emancipation. The laws against the Jews were not, however, everywhere the same, nor were they always fully enforced. In Austrian-ruled or influenced lands (which included not only the north-east but also the Grand Duchy of Tuscany), the Jews enjoyed greater freedoms than they did in the Papal States, where the Inquisition continued to take a great interest in them.

With the granting of a constitution in the Kingdom of Sardinia as a result of popular pressure in 1848, the Jews of Piedmont were largely freed of the old restrictions and became the first Jews of Italy to enjoy modern civil rights. As Piedmont became the backbone of the emerging Italian state in 1859–61, Jews throughout Italy were emancipated. They moved out from the old ghettoes, entered the larger society, and rapidly acquired positions of social, intellectual, and economic influence.

Since the first appearance of the Protestant movement in the sixteenth century, the Catholic Church in Italy had done all it could to prevent the Protestant 'heresy' from spreading to the peninsula. In general it was successful in this effort, the main exception being the Valdese movement, which had its origins in the twelfth century but which in the sixteenth adhered to Protestantism and became heavily influenced by Calvinism. Scattered among the Alpine valleys of north-western Piedmont, the Valdesi had been forced to rely on seminaries outside Italy to train their clergy, and only in the 1850s were they able to open a seminary in Piedmont (transferred to Florence in 1860).

Otherwise, the Protestant movement in Italy was primarily identi-fied with foreigners. When Garibaldi, in one of his first actions upon driving out the old regime in Naples in 1860, authorized the estab-lishment of an Anglican church there, his action was seen as a boon to the foreign merchants living in the city. With unification, Italy became open to Protestant missionaries for the first time, and first Methodists and then Baptists and other denominations sent mission-aries to open churches in the major Italian cities. Most of these churches were very simple affairs, many housed in people's homes, where bible discussions, prayer meetings, and communal singing of hymns were held. These churches were often located in out-of-the-way places due to fear of local hostility.[13]

---

[13] Valdo Vinay, 'Spiritualità delle Chiese evangeliche in Italia fra il 1861 e il 1878'. In *Chiesa e religiosità in Italia dopo l'Unità (1861–1878)*, Vol. 2 (Milan, 1973), pp. 129–53.

Anticlericalism

The fact that Italy was in some sense 99% Catholic does not mean that practically everyone identified as Catholic, much less that they felt bound by Church strictures. The very position of the Church as a centre of power, and the very size of the clergy in the peninsula, helped assure a long-standing tradition of anticlericalism. This anticlericalism both expanded and changed its nature over the course of the nineteenth century.

Dislike of the clergy, accused of hypocrisy and worse, was of ancient origins. This antipathy was fed, following 1859, by anger at the Church's continuing opposition to Italian unification. With the Church seen as the enemy not only of the new state, but also modernity itself, increasing numbers of Italians not only attacked the clergy, but also questioned the Catholic view of the world in general and their own identification as Catholics.

A movement of Free Thinkers developed immediately following unification, and expanded rapidly after the taking of Rome in 1870. Local associations of all kinds were formed, and a wide assortment of newspapers, journals, posters, and 'scientific' studies published. Some activities were intentionally provocative, such as the organization of banquets on holy fast days and the use of anti-religious masks during carnival celebrations. Closely linked to the Free Thinkers were the Freemasons, long a thorn in the side of the Church, and indeed viewed by popes throughout the century as among the greatest sources of evildoing.

The two heroes of unification, Giuseppe Mazzini and Giuseppe Garibaldi, illustrate two different sides of this movement. Mazzini, the theorist of nationalism, remained in many ways an intensely religious person, with a belief that sovereignty was to be found in both 'God and the people', and he maintained a positive view of the teachings of Jesus. For him, the problem was that the Church had become corrupt; in any case, he had little sympathy for an organized church or a priesthood. By contrast, Garibaldi was a fervent anticleric who had only contempt for those who turned to religion. His various novels, widely read, were filled with priests and monks portrayed as evil hypocrites.

Some of the forms that this struggle took can be illustrated from events that occurred in Rome in the 1880s. In July 1881, a solemn Church procession set out from the Vatican to take the mortal remains of Pius IX to the basilica of San Lorenzo. As the procession approached the bridge over the Tiber River, a mob of anticlerics descended on it, pelted the cardinals and others with various missiles, and threatened to push the carriage itself into the river. Only the intervention of Italian police put an end to the mayhem, which in turn triggered a new wave of Church denunciations of the new state. Seven years later, another incident provoked the ire of Catholics. When word reached the government that the mayor of Rome, Duke Leopold Torlonia, had sent the pope the best wishes of the citizens of Rome on the occasion of the 50th anniversary of his ordination, the duke was immediately stripped of his office by Prime Minister Francesco Crispi. And then, in 1889, the Catholics were again enraged when a statue of Giordano Bruno was unveiled on the spot in the Campo dei Fiori, in the middle of Rome, where in 1600 he had been burned as a heretic on orders of the Inquisition. The unveiling had been accompanied by a gleeful demonstration of Free Thinkers and Masons.

To these other currents of anticlericalism, the new movements first of the anarchists and then, by the 1880s, of the socialists added a new dimension, one that helped spread anticlerical ideology from the cities to the countryside, and from the artisans and literate classes to the peasants, the workers, and the illiterate. By the 1890s, proclaiming oneself a socialist would be seen as tantamount to a rejection of the Church.

The Church and religious practice in nineteenth-century Italy

The unification of Italy did not mean the unification of the Italian Catholic Church. Nourished by the Vatican's rejection of the new political status quo, the Church hierarchy continued to reflect the old political divisions. One manifestation of this was the continued practice of having papal nuncios stationed in what had until unification been the capitals of the states of the old regime. Hence, for example, a nuncio continued to be based in Naples, a vestige of the time when it was a Bourbon capital requiring papal representation.

Bishops continued to come from the region, and often the city, where they were based. From 1861 to 1878, for example, every one of Sicily's bishops had been born and largely educated on the island. Continuity also marked the social origin of the high clergy, who continued to come disproportionately from the old aristocracy. Indeed, even at century's end, when a non-nobleman was appointed archbishop of Milan, the local nobility lodged a vigorous protest with Pope Leo XIII.

Although the *ricettizie* churches had been devastated as a result of the statutes of the new Italian state, the southern Church remained distinct in many ways from the Church in the North. Not least important was the continued disparity in organization, with, for example, the northern region of Lombardy having just nine dioceses, containing 3214 parishes, compared to the 32 dioceses and only 259 parishes of the southern region of Puglia.[14]

Finally, while we have been largely concerned here with the life of the Church, and popular participation in its activities, no discussion of the role of religion in the nineteenth century would be complete without recognizing that a great deal of religious expression and religious belief took place either apart from the Church or at least in obeying a dynamic not principally directed by the Church.

There were many forms of popular Catholic religiosity that grew in strength during the century, from the devotion to various cults— such as that of the Sacred Heart, the Madonna, and Saint Anthony of Padua—to assorted pilgrimage sites and the magical use of various sacred objects. The spread of literacy also had an effect, with huge numbers of little pamphlets published instructing the devout in the mysteries of the rosary, and others devoted to catechism, prayers, and providing words to go with holy religious images. In these forms of religious devotion, as in the more traditional setting of attendance at mass and the taking of Communion, it was women who were the most devout.

And even among many of the fiercest anticlerics, there is reason to believe that the rejection of the Church did not mean a full rejection

---

[14] Penco, *Storia della Chiesa*, pp. 381–3.

of Catholic belief and practice. Emblematic of this syncretism was Garibaldi's march through Sicily in 1860. On the battlefield his recruits claimed to have seen the archangel Michael appear over the head of their famously anticlerical leader, whirling a sword aimed at the Bourbon troops opposing him. And through the heavily anti-clerical districts of central Italy—from the Marches through Romagna—the same people who denounced Pius IX and the priests had crucifixes hanging in their homes, with pictures of their deceased parents and likenesses of Garibaldi and Mazzini beside them, in front of which, on special anniversaries, they lit candles.[15] If a new religion was gaining ground at the close of the century, it was not one that even went by the name of religion. Rather it was a mix of Catholicism and anticlericalism, as the cult of the new nation—with its own rites and myths—began to face a new faith, socialism.

The legacy, however, of the long battle between the Church and the forces of Italian unification—which occupied practically the whole of the nineteenth century—would continue to exert a powerful influ-ence into the twentieth. Indeed, that legacy has persisted into the twenty-first. The much lamented weakness of the Italian state—with such manifestations as the Fascist assumption of power for two decades, the disaster of the crumbling of the Italian state during the Second World War, and the continued failure of the Italian govern-ment to be fully legitimated in the eyes of the population—has been to no small degree a product of the previous century during which the Church did all it could to rob the Italian state of its legitimacy. Or, seen from a different perspective, it was the inability of the secular elites of the new Italian state to enlist the support of the Church in its mission to establish its legitimacy that was so costly to their liberal revolution, a revolution that foundered repeatedly from the 1890s to the early 1920s, before succumbing, in Mussolini, to a leader who would finally have the blessings of the Church.

---

[15] Pietro Stella, 'Religiosità vissuta in Italia nell'800'. In Jean Deumeau and Franco Bolgiani (eds), *Storia vissuta del popolo cristiano* (Turin, 1985), pp. 761–2.

Culture and society, 1796–1896

Raymond Grew

The importance of high culture

Concern for culture held a central place in Italian intellectual life. In the eighteenth century, the elites of Sicily and Naples were connected to those of Lombardy, the Veneto, and Piedmont by cultural ties more than by political or economic interests. Learned treatises on the subjects of the day and individual artists and intellectuals moved from city to city more easily than any commerce in material goods. Educated Italians took delight in their common culture: the Latin classics; Dante, and all the Italian poets after him; five centuries of paintings and sculptures recognized as Italian, and music that was admired and imitated across Europe. Culture ranked with geography—Italy's distinctive shape, clear boundaries, and picturesque terrain—as a marker of Italian identity.

The principal participants in this culture (aristocrats, upper clergy, officials, artists, intellectuals, and cultural entrepreneurs like printers and impresarios) shared an urban lifestyle that was associated with regal and ducal courts, aristocratic salons, academies, institutes, and opera houses scattered across the country. Even towns of modest size participated as best they could in this cultural life, much as on a more informal level they welcomed itinerant street entertainers on market days. Multiple sites and local roots made room for spontaneity and colourful variety within fairly static cultural forms. This shared style and content, together with the ubiquitous presence of the Catholic Church, inconsistent but extensive censorship, and dependence on petty rulers and unreliable patrons, shaped public discourse. Discussions of culture easily slid into talk of political reform.

The French presence in Italy from 1796 to 1815 had a profound effect on Italian culture as well as institutions, and it is worth considering why a culture already so well established should have been so open to revolutionary influence. Of course, living in a hierarchical society and the experience of multiple, often foreign, rulers provided some training in adaptability. In poetry remarkable for its skilful use of classical myth and descriptive beauty, Vincenzo Monti denounced French republicans before their armies arrived, wrote in unremitting praise of Napoleon throughout French rule, and then hailed the Austrians on their return in 1815. But the public engagement of Italian intellectuals after 1796 reflects important aspects of Italian culture as well as French rule.

Intellectual life had remained in touch with major European trends throughout the seventeenth and eighteenth centuries. The famous works of the French and English Enlightenment were well known; and some Italian contributions, like those of Antonio Genovesi on economics and Cesare Beccaria on crime and punishment, were widely cited abroad. Some Italian scientists and mathematicians had founded the National Society of the Sciences as an academy to exchange publications with the leading academies of Europe and to report on their own research.[1] Gazettes of *letterati* published in Venice, Modena, and Rome had circulated among a small elite across the peninsula, carrying word of the latest ideas and discoveries gaining attention throughout Europe. In the decades before the French Revolution, *Il Caffè* of Milan featured detailed discussions of reform, and the *Gazzetta Universale* of Florence reported on the revolution in France. Preoccupation with politics would become as characteristic of Italian culture as references to Dante.

Vittorio Alfieri illustrates how that came about. He was born in 1749 into the Piedmontese nobility and given an education customary for his class, which introduced him to the classics and prepared him for a military career he did not want. He spent the next half-dozen years travelling across Europe, combating boredom with love affairs and racehorses. Only after that did he begin to write tragedies in verse. French had been the language of his home, and so he went to

---

[1] Giuseppe Penso, *Scienziati italiani e unità d'Italia: Academia dei XL* (Rome, 1978).

Tuscany (taking an impressive array of horses and servants with him) to perfect his Italian. He wrote with focused passion and poetic language of heroic-sized figures in tragic situations taken from classical Greek, the Bible, and modern history. In many respects his plays, like his personal life, belonged to the old regime. In Paris at the time of the French Revolution, which he initially supported, he had turned bitterly against it by the time he escaped to Italy in 1792. As the lover of the woman married to the Stuart claimant to the English throne (he styled himself Charles III; she was called Queen), Alfieri continued to move in aristocratic circles.

His political writings, however, were arguments for change. His essay, *Della Tirannide*, denounced absolute power and was dedicated to liberty as a universal right. In *Del Principe e delle Lettere*, he declared poets to be the heralds of freedom and human dignity and the natural enemies of tyrants. He wrote a collection of odes published as *L'America libera* and dedicated a play about the ancient Romans to George Washington. He vented his hatred of revolutionaries and his resentment of French cultural dominance in a group of pieces called *Il Misogallo*. When the French arrived in Italy, they honoured him, nevertheless. Napoleon himself attended a performance of Alfieri's *Virginia*, a play set in ancient Rome in which the people cry liberty or death and rise to overthrow a tyrant.

Alfieri considered literature to have a pedagogic, civilizing function. Although he offered no concrete political programme, the last chapter of his essay, *Del Principe*, was provocatively titled, 'An exhortation to free Italy from the Barbarians'. His lack of specificity, like his use of history and his moral concern for Italian liberty, set a tone that would resonate throughout the *Risorgimento*. A noble who decried autocracy and wrote paeans to liberty but distanced himself from politics, Alfieri died in Florence under Napoleonic rule in 1803, having in his contradictions as well as in his art given voice to a new era.

To an extent, then, the increased activity after 1796 was an expansion of what had gone before; in part it represented the coincidence of general ideas of reason and reform with French policies and interests. From 1796 to 1799 some 40 journals were founded in Milan, 20 in Genoa, and at least 10 in such cities as Venice, Rome, and Naples. These included the first real daily papers, and most were short-lived. Not all were radical, and most were as candidly political as the

Milanese paper that described itself as 'the impartial defender of property, the rich, notables, and the clergy', and that lasted only two months. Nearly all disappeared with the return of the Austrians, to be reborn more cautious and under heavier tutelage after Napoleon's return. Among their editors were many who were or would soon be among Italy's most prominent authors, including Ugo Foscolo and Alessandro Manzoni.[2]

Noted figures flocked to Milan from all over Italy. Vincenzo Cuoco went there from Naples after the overthrow of the Neapolitan republic, established in 1799. He had played a part in that revolution, and his analysis of its failure remains an important contribution to Italian historiography. His major activity during the years of French rule, however, was as editor of the semi-official *Giornale Italiano*, which proclaimed that its purpose was 'to form the public spirit of a nation'. Even such sober documents as proposed constitutions stressed the importance of education and of having theatres accessible to all. Italian culture now included high civic purpose.

The years of French dominance brought new energy to Italian culture in other ways as well. New roads and urban streets, new monuments, and great public projects—like a handsome building to close off St Mark's Square in Venice or completion of the façade of Milan's gothic cathedral—tied progress to tradition. Governments reorganized museums, granted subsidies to scientific projects, commissioned paintings and monuments, and established schools, universities, and conservatories. Previous regimes had done similar things, but there were now more such projects in more fields, done more rapidly, and conducted more openly. More important, they were all undertaken in the name of civic culture. Band concerts, parades, ceremonies around liberty trees, patriotic plays, and slogans on official stationery proclaimed that concern. Over the years, political reality eroded that revolutionary vision, and the grandiose representations of Napoleon were closer to an older tradition of cultural patronage. For the hundreds of local committees working on cultural projects, however, even disillusionment reinforced attention to the national themes that were part of French propaganda.

The French regimes struck a cultural chord in other ways as well. They adopted the symbols of ancient Rome, used Roman-sounding

[2] Paolo Murialdi, *Storia del giornalismo italiano* (Turin, 1986), pp. 25–30.

names for officials and regions, and fostered neoclassical styles in art, furnishings, dress, and architecture. All that could easily be made to seem at home in Italy, and it was fitting that the period's greatest sculptor, Antonio Canova, should be an Italian. His appointment as director of the Academy of San Luca in Rome gave him considerable influence; and his famous reclining sculpture of Napoleon's sister, Paolina Borghese, as Venus Victrix was one of many commissions he received from the Bonapartes. When Alfieri died in 1803, the government commissioned Canova to design an appropriate monument. He sculpted the figure of Italy standing over Alfieri's tomb, weeping at the country's loss. The monument was placed in Florence in the church of Santa Croce, its renown as a national shrine confirmed in Ugo Foscolo's most famous single work, his long ode, *I Sepolcri*.

Foscolo's writings capture the ambiguity of the Napoleonic experience. He grew up in Venice, where he received a classical education and studied Italian literature. He welcomed the arrival of Napoleon, fought in the French army, and moved to Milan when Venice was lost to Austria. From then until Napoleon's final defeat in 1815, he held a number of prominent positions in Milan and was sent on missions that took him to the cities of northern Italy and to France. His *Ultime Lettere di Jacopo Ortis*, often called Italy's first modern novel, was written in the epistolary form fashionable in eighteenth-century French and English novels. The letters are those of a young Venetian, heartsick at having to leave his city when Napoleon ceded the Venetian republic to Austria. It describes his travels in northern Italy, the beauty and diversity of Italian landscapes, and a visit to Santa Croce, where the tombs of Galileo, Machiavelli, and Michelangelo stimulate reflection on Italy's past greatness. His ode takes up that theme again. Written in opposition to a new French law that required cemeteries to be located outside cities, in the interests of hygiene, and to have tombstones of uniform size, in the name of equality, his tightly structured poem insists on the importance of tombs as the focus of memories to be cherished, and which honour cultural achievement and national glory. After Napoleon's fall Foscolo lived in England where, until his death in 1827, he wrote extensively on Italian literature. When Italy was united a generation later, Foscolo's body was placed in Santa Croce, and *I Sepolcri* became required reading in Italian schools.

Italian culture and the making of a nation

Foscolo bridged eighteenth-century classicism and the newer romantic movement in European literature and art which opened a debate that reverberated through Italy's intellectual journals. Recognized as both foreign and new, its appeal and popularity raised a series of issues for intellectuals self-consciously seeking to shape a modern Italian culture. The debate was stimulated by an article published in 1816 and written by Madame de Staël, the prominent French figure as famous for her admiration of German romanticism as for her opposition to Napoleon. Her article called for the translation into Italian of current European literature and suggested that Italian culture had suffered from isolation. The subsequent flood of responses opened far-reaching debates about what the Italian language should be, whether Italian culture was and should be fundamentally classical, the moral purpose of literature, and the centrality of history to understanding the present.

Defenders of classical forms charged romanticism with encouraging looseness in style and content, contrasted classical high culture with a corrosive aim for popularity, and associated the proud maintenance of a distinctive, purer, Italian culture with resistance to foreign importations. Defenders of romanticism heralded the dawn of a new era and the role of untrammelled genius. Controversial social and political issues underlay these emotional exchanges. Concern for Italian culture's place in the European mainstream led to questions about what social changes were possible and desirable. Hope for an intellectual revival clashed with fear for social order. Because the Italian culture in dispute was an elite culture, separate from daily life and ordinary language, debates about language (whether Tuscan should be the model and whether, even so, it should be restricted to a formal vocabulary closer to Dante's or to current usage) had practical and immediate import. Debates over literary form were about what was distinctive in Italian culture and how a culture associated with the aristocracy and autocratic courts could adapt to the contemporary world.

Romanticism encouraged the growing artistic attention to family ties, religious experience, history, and the nation, but did not constitute the decisive shift in Italy that it brought to the literature and art of Germany and England. Rather, the combination of romantic effects and themes with classical forms and restraint (reinforced in literature by the question of language) continued in all the arts. Among the hundreds of visual artists, Francesco Hayez was one of the most talented. Close to the circle of Canova, yet influenced by Delacroix's use of line and colour, he employed a rich palette in rather theatrical historical paintings and in skilful portraits of leading Italian writers and statesmen.

Although Italian musicians and composers were in demand throughout Europe, Paris and Vienna were more important musical centres than any Italian city; but a new generation of great opera composers emerged in Italy. Gioacchino Rossini became famous at the age of 21 following the success of his operas in Venice and Milan. After a decade of further triumphs, he moved to Paris; but after Italy became a national state, his body, too, was ceremoniously entombed in Santa Croce. Rossini's operas preserved much that was classical (he greatly admired Mozart) and also opened the way to innovation. He obscured the sharp distinction between 'serious' and comic opera, and his use of musical ornamentation pointed to the flowering of the *bel canto* style. His orchestrations echoed the Napoleonic years in their evocation of the military band and employment of the newly popular clarinet. His use of librettos with exotic settings and based on biblical stories, Shakespeare, and Sir Walter Scott became a characteristic of romantic opera. Much of Rossini's career was closely associated with the conservative governments that replaced Napoleon in Italy and France; yet his last opera, *William Tell*, was about the patriotic defence of liberty in a medieval Swiss commune.

That example greatly influenced Vincenzo Bellini's *I Puritani*, about the conflict between Calvinist Scots and English Stuarts. Bellini raised the *bel canto* style to new heights; and his extraordinary lyricism, use of a conversational tone, and ability to create distinctive, romantic moods were recognized everywhere as particularly Italian gifts. A Sicilian trained in Naples, he came from the opposite end of the peninsula from his contemporary and rival in the 1830s and 1840s, Gaetano Donizetti, who was from Bergamo, near Milan. The works of both composers, performed across Italy and abroad from St Petersburg to London and the Americas, were received as representative of Italian rather than regional culture.

Opera was a nexus of cultural connections within Italy itself. These prolific composers often wrote several operas in a single year, and reports of new performances spread quickly from city to city. Companies of singers, stage managers, set designers, and impresarios moved from theatre to theatre. Opera stars were enthusiastically welcomed everywhere, and performances were gala events, attracting audiences that included aristocrats and local notables but also many of the urban poor. Nervous Restoration regimes often censored plots and banned outspoken lyrics (the soprano who sang 'Cara Italia' in Rossini's *Tancredi* was afraid she would be arrested in Naples). Nevertheless, the appeal of melody, vocal pyrotechnics, and dramatic sets could not be denied. No government, not even the papacy, dared ban these festive occasions, despite fears of large, mixed crowds likely to cheer references to liberty or to *Italia*, finding parallels to their own circumstances in historical, biblical, and mythical references.

Some of the hope, much of the doubt, and all of the ambivalent angst of the era found expression in the work of Giacomo Leopardi. He came to the attention of the literary world in 1816 when he entered the debates between classicists and romantics and disputed the need to translate recent writing from other European languages. Leopardi wrote passionately in defence of the Greek, Latin, and Italian classics. In doing so, he reflected his own formation and patriotism. Born and raised in an isolated small town in the Marches in the Papal States, his education had come primarily from pouring over the works in his father's extensive library. By his teens he had acquired extraordinary erudition and knowledge of a great many languages. His first major poem, *All'Italia*, followed by another on the erection of a monument to Dante, proclaimed an intense love for the scenes and culture of Italy but denounced Napoleonic tyranny and Italy's decadence.

From his precocious beginning to his death in 1837, his works stood out for their deft use of language, compelling beauty, and originality, paradoxically romantic in their sense of loneliness and despair. Admiration for Italy's great past led to disillusionment with a tawdry present; joy at the wonders of nature concluded by stressing nature's indifference to the fate of man; delight in pictures of daily life and ordinary pleasures emphasized their transience. He also wrote on immediate social issues, with acid disdain on Italian public mores, and with informed clarity on science, noting the errors of the ancients. His love of Italy persisted, enlarged by years spent in Rome,

Bologna, Florence, and Naples; but he remained sceptical of promises that life held any larger meaning or that Italy had a brighter future. Restoration censors, sensing the radical implications in Leopardi's work, banned much of it. Contemporaries managed to find a call to patriotism in it and recognized him as a truly great poet.

At the time, however, Alessandro Manzoni was Italy's most honoured writer. From the moment *I Promessi Sposi* was published, the novel was admired in France, Germany, and England; yet it has never had the following abroad that it had in Italy, where it quickly became the most admired work of the nineteenth century. Set in seventeenth-century Lombardy, it is a love story on an epic scale, filled with psychologically subtle depictions of peasants, aristocrats, and princes of the Church, and with penetrating descriptions of Spanish rule, a predatory social structure, and a hypocritical Catholic hierarchy.

Beyond its descriptive richness (including unforgettable scenes of famine and plague), the novel's use of language, religion, and history give it a unique place in Italian culture. Manzoni first circulated the manuscript among his friends and then allowed its limited publication in 1827 before completely rewriting it in exemplary Italian. To do so, he moved with his family from Milan to Florence so that he might absorb the presumably purer language spoken there. The novel published in 1840–42, intended as a model of what the national language should be, went far to settle the debate on language. Manzoni's strong ties to a Catholic tradition of religious reform and his austere religious faith enabled him to invoke the moral power of religion while probing cynical corruption within the Church. The novel thus implied that Catholicism and progressive change were compatible. Manzoni used his own historical research to construct a story that shows the connection between oppressive social relations and bad government. Sympathy for the downtrodden (a romantic trope) could then lead to a view of history progressing toward greater liberty, justice, and economic growth.

Manzoni's achievement was philosophical as well as literary, and it reflected a particular intellectual milieu. The grandson of Beccaria, he had connections to most of the major Lombard intellectuals. He lived for a number of years in Napoleonic Paris, where he was in touch with leading French liberals. Strongly attracted to romanticism, he read French translations of the leading German authors and of Sir Walter Scott yet remained attached to a kind of classical restraint in tone and form. Even his poems were often reflections on historical events in which, as in his historical essays, he sought moral meaning and historical purpose. Manzoni's carefully restrained writings pushed against conventional limitations of form and genre; and in his network of personal connections and his multiple interests, he embodied the intellectual programme of the *Risorgimento*.

The restoration of Italy's former rulers following Napoleon's final defeat had lowered the volume of this rising chorus. Many leading thinkers went into exile, others lost influential positions, and the most influential newspapers closed. The restored regimes had their own traditions of cultural patronage and recognized the value of supporting high culture so long as it did not challenge them politically. Opera flourished, and cautious periodicals closely read by Italy's elites were published in Milan, Modena, Florence, and Naples. Milan's Austrian rulers subsidized the *Biblioteca Italiana*, which (although Foscolo, Monti, and Manzoni among others refused to take part) attracted hundreds of contributors from throughout Italy. It defended Italy's traditional culture, attacking romanticism long after the battle over classicism had ceased to be exciting.

The most vigorous intellectual life, however, took place in informal salons that functioned as schools and discussion groups, sponsored short-lived journals, and despite censorship remained aware through correspondence and publications of similar activities across the peninsula. These small circles of intellectuals influenced a whole generation.

Gian Domenico Romagnosi was central to such a group in Lombardy. Known for his work in legal theory, he held a post in the Austrian administration, drew up plans for restructuring the educational and judicial systems under the Cisalpine republic, and was appointed to professorships at Parma and Pavia in the Napoleonic period. Proscribed by the Austrians on their return, he was eventually permitted to teach privately; and a great many prominent young Milanese studied with him.

Il Conciliatore was one of several periodicals that reflected his influence. Calling itself a 'scientific–literary' journal, it campaigned for roads and schools while embracing the new trends in literature. It gained a notable following before the Austrian authorities closed it in 1819, to be succeeded a few years later by the *Annali Universale di Viaggi, Geografia, Storia, Economia Pubblica e Statistica*, its very title a programme for modernization. The government's fear of *Il Concilia-tore* was not without foundation. In 1821 several of its sponsors were implicated in the revolt in Piedmont and in Charles Albert's quixotic effort to annex Lombardy (Manzoni wrote a fiercely patriotic poem rejecting the artificial boundary between Piedmont and Lombardy). The Lombard conspirators were sentenced to prison in an Austrian fortress, and in 1832 one of them, Silvio Pellico, an aspiring poet and dramatist, wrote a memoir of his ordeal that was translated into all the major European languages. The message of *I Miei Prigioni* was one of Christian resignation that revolutionaries disdained, but Pellico's touching account became one of the most effective works of *Risorgimento* propaganda.

It was Carlo Cattaneo who most directly carried on Romagnosi's legacy. In 1839 he founded *Il Politecnico*, a journal influential across Italy for its analysis of public policies and economic development and for its use of statistics. Little moved by myths of Italy's past grandeur, Cattaneo assessed the present with passionate rationality and remained prominent after the government closed *Il Politecnico* in 1844. During the Milanese revolution of 1848, he established himself as one of Italy's leading republicans, opposing Piedmont's annex-ation of Lombardy and arguing instead for a federated Italy. Forced into exile when the revolution failed, he held to his position through-out his life, even after he returned to Milan once the Austrians were driven out in 1859 and re-established *Il Politecnico*. Committed to democracy, he combined Italy's strong legal tradition and literary culture to lay the foundations for a progressive social science.

In other cities, too, newly formed intellectual circles established lasting influence. In Tuscany, *L'Antologia*, founded in 1821 as a 'jour-nal of science, letters, and the arts', reported evidence of the progress 'more or less general in civilized Europe'. It described developments in England and France, praised the public schools of Boston, and reviewed German literature and philosophy. The journal's founder, G. P. Vieusseux, also opened a reading room that became a gathering place for the city's intellectuals and reformers; and when the govern-ment shut down *L'Antologia* in 1833, Vieusseux readily produced other publications to bring news of improvements in education, agri-culture, and historical research. Comparable circles published similar journals in Naples but were even more important as private schools where students learned law and literature and formed ties that would be important in the Neapolitan revolutions of 1821 and 1830. Throughout Italy, groups like these gave local reform a national meaning, prospering in the artificial environment of inefficient repression.

Italian scientists, too, maintained periodicals and networks of correspondence. Some did work of distinction (Alessandro Volta died in 1827), most were erudite amateurs. When in 1839 a congress of scientists from all over the peninsula met in Pisa, 400 attended. Governments watched warily as these congresses became an annual, and national, event. Some of the talk at these meetings was learned; much of it was about Italy's needs in order to attain the level of scientific achievement in France, England, and Germany. Although each host city brightened up its laboratories and museums for these meetings, concern that Italy was backward acquired a lasting place in Italian national discourse.

Catholicism could also serve the national cause in the view of Vincenzo Gioberti. A Piedmontese priest exiled in 1853 because of his association with revolutionaries, he spent a dozen years in Paris, and it was there that he wrote *Il Primato morale e civile degli italiani*, which was published in 1842–43. His prolix, impassioned essay argued that Catholicism was one of Italy's contributions to European civilization and that Italy would contribute yet more once renewed in a federation led by a liberal papacy. The effect was electric, and it seemed prescient in 1846 with the election of Pius IX, a pope who was unusually young, thought to be liberal, and known to have read Gioberti. High culture and religion had come together.

Gioberti's dreams were quickly overturned by events. With revolution defeated and the papacy again an outspoken opponent of Italian nationalism and liberalism, Gioberti took up his pen once more. *Il Rinnovamento civile d'Italia* bitterly attacked the Jesuits, Italy's reactionary clergy, and Piedmont's timid monarchy. The work of a disillusioned democrat, it had little of the effect of his earlier book. Yet something of Gioberti's early optimism lived on among the liberal aristocrats and intellectuals who had been advisers to the liberal Pius IX and afterwards turned to support the national aspirations of Piedmont's liberal monarchy. There were even theologians, like Father Rosmini Serbati, eager to reconcile liberty, a national culture, and the Church. A more systematic thinker than Gioberti, Rosmini built on German philosophy and a very spiritual piety in influential writings on reform of the Church, on its social role, and on constitutional government.

Thus, on the eve of the revolutions of 1848 there was a *Risorgimento* culture that claimed to embrace all that was most vibrant in Italy's high culture, that was insistently if vaguely liberal, allowed room for religion, emphasized the importance of education and science, and was attentive to economic growth. No one embodied that combination of values more dramatically than Massimo d'Azeglio. Born into a noble Piedmontese family, he spent his boyhood in Florence, received the expected training to be an officer in Piedmont's army, then lived in Rome as bohemian and socialite. He first gained recognition as an able and serious painter, whose historical canvases with their patriotic themes and romantic landscapes won praise in Turin and Milan. Two successful historical novels consolidated his fame (and cost a dull-minded Austrian censor his job for having permitted publication). D'Azeglio, who lived for years in Milan and travelled to Naples and Sicily, had an intimate knowledge of Italy.

In 1844, after a tour in the Papal States, he wrote a searing indictment of papal rule that circulated widely despite efforts to ban it and was much cited in England and France. D'Azeglio knew Alfieri and married Manzoni's daughter; he was acquainted with Charles Albert and everyone who mattered in Turin, and the artists and intellectuals of Florence, Rome, and Milan. He mingled easily with influential foreign diplomats, had a private audience with Pius IX in 1847, and was the affectionate brother of the Jesuit priest who would become a founder of *Civiltà Cattolica*, the Vatican's voice of militant opposition to everything D'Azeglio stood for. After the failure of the revolutions of 1848 and Piedmont's defeat by Austrian armies, D'Azeglio became prime minister of Piedmont, dealing for three years with the defeated country's inexperience in parliamentary government, heavy debts, and rancorous relations with the Church, until giving way to the firmer hand of Camillo Cavour. An anticlerical from a religious family, a liberal who disliked political deals, a Marchese who took pride in knowing the people but distrusted democracy, and an artist who never found a truly distinctive voice, his independence was personal. He flourished in a moment of transition, and his failures measured the limitations of ideas loosely held.

The place of high culture in Italian affairs was changing. The newspapers that had burst forth in all the cities of Italy, exuberant declarations of how much ideas mattered, were largely silenced by 1849 outside Piedmont. Executions, prison sentences, and exile cramped intellectual life, especially in the Kingdom of Naples and the Papal States. Many prominent scholars, writers, and journalists left for Turin, making Piedmont's capital more intellectually alive than it had ever been. Cultural engagement had been a principal stimulus to patriotism, overcoming political repression and fragmentation. Ideas of regeneration had achieved a dominant consensus. That was a remarkable accomplishment, but after the disillusionment and military defeats of 1848–49, the focus turned to practical politics and to Piedmont.

That shift had begun earlier in Piedmont. Cesare Balbo, a Piedmontese noble who had written a life of Dante and was D'Azeglio's best friend, had published *Le Speranze d'Italia* in 1844, shortly after Gioberti's *Primato* and partly inspired by it. The hopes for Italy that Balbo had in mind began with the removal of foreign domination. This was not a work about cultural identity or the inevitability of modern progress, although it assumed all that, but rather a book about the power politics necessary to win Austria's withdrawal from Italy and in effect a rebuttal to the dreams of Gioberti and Giuseppe Mazzini.

Mazzini (see also Chapter 3), the radical democrat who spent most of his life in exile and who opposed the liberals who would become Italy's new leaders, was nevertheless just as much a carrier of Italian culture. As a student in Genoa, he had wanted to be a literary critic and philosopher; he became instead a revolutionary conspirator feared by the governments of Europe. In 1831 he founded Young Italy, its name an expression of romantic generational optimism. His publications and private letters were smuggled across the Italian borders he sought to remove, and they inspired a generation of potential leaders. Mazzini extended that universalism recurrent in *Risorgimento* thought to envision a Europe of democracies living in harmony. His confidence in God's providence was close to that of the people in whose potential righteousness he so deeply believed, and it enabled him to write as a prophet, one of the great propagandists of the age. Perhaps more than any *Risorgimento* figure, he bequeathed the nation he would find so disappointing a tradition of idealism and social criticism.

The bridge most travelled between Italy's high culture and daily life was built on the music of Giuseppe Verdi. His operas used biblical themes, historical subjects, and the plays of Shakespeare and contemporary French authors; and they provided the occasion for staging scenes familiar to every Italian of crowded piazzas, village bands, and evening prayers. His melodies were repeated on street organs and whistled by draymen; yet no other opera composer has written so often about politics and power, the evils of tyranny, and fatal conspiracies. The opera that first made him famous, *Nabucco*, used the Old Testament story of Jews taken captive by the Babylonian king, Nebuchadnezzar. At its opening at La Scala in Milan in 1842, when the Hebrews sang in pulsing chorus about their homeland 'so beautiful and so lost', the response was thunderous. The chorus had to be sung again (as it has been ever since), despite police orders against such encores because of the demonstrations against Austrian officials they were likely to provoke. When Verdi died in 1901, the crowd at his grave softly and spontaneously sang it, and so did a chorus of 800 at official ceremonies a month later.

Verdi found the material of tragedy in bourgeois concerns as well as royal conflicts, and his operas have moments of striking intimacy, of family love, and of the bond between fathers and daughters. He led Italian opera in new directions with a richer and more complex use of the orchestra and an unparalleled musical probing of psychological tension. World famous by the 1850s, he continued to compose successful operas throughout his long life, a revered symbol of Italian culture. When Manzoni died in 1873, the new nation went into mourning; and Verdi, calling Manzoni 'the greatest of our glories', responded by writing a requiem that expressed the sadness of that death and also, perhaps, the passing of an era.

Extending the cultural base

This formal, humanistic, rhetorical, high culture—devoted to the language of Dante, immersed in classical literature, committed to established forms in every genre, ethically concerned yet tolerant, and permeated with political purpose—was in effect the official culture of united Italy, taught in *liceo*, disseminated on the cultural page of nearly every daily paper, and shared by members of the professions and politicians. This was the culture of a tiny proportion of the nation it was supposed to express. Only a quarter of the population was literate; only one person in ten comfortably spoke Italian in daily life; the tiny number of habitual Italian speakers was about the same as the tiny number of those who could vote. Most of Italy's leading figures literally knew each other, an advantage in a country not yet a nation, a troubling limitation once the national state had been created. The grave problem of Italian culture was not communication within the elite but beyond it, and Italy's new leaders were right to worry about making their language and culture penetrate the larger society. The less obvious risk was that language and culture might wither in stuffy isolation.

One person, one cultural form, and one institution in particular demonstrated the ability to reach deep into Italian society. Giuseppe Garibaldi may well have been the most popular figure of the nineteenth century, the hero of two continents, admired by aristocrats (especially in England) and adored by Italian artisans and peasants. He was not a product of Italy's rarefied high culture; yet he sat easily with those who were, and in his way he shared their belief in its importance. Largely self-taught, he had much more than the usual sailor's knowledge of astronomy, mathematics, and several languages. As he sailed back from the Americas to fight for Italy in 1848, he had his soldiers taught to read so they could appreciate Italian literature. He wrote poetry all his life and, near the end of it, three romantic novels which included descriptions of battles he had fought in, of lecherous priests, and of heroes who were artists. Intellectuals saw in Garibaldi proof that the modern world had room for heroes of mythic proportions; and Victor Hugo, Alexander Dumas, and George Sand wrote about him, as did dozens of Italian authors.

For ordinary people, he represented a set of values and a kind of personal connection to great events. His leonine beard and the red shirt became symbols of valour, integrity, and independence. His image circulated on medals, amulets, calendars, and postcards. Woodcuts of Garibaldi sold on the streets and hung in huts: Garibaldi holding the dying Anita although pursued by Austrian troops, Garibaldi riding out in front of his troops to shake hands with Victor Emmanuel and hand the king all of southern Italy, Garibaldi humbly sailing away from fame and glory to his lonely island. Patriotic altars were built to him, and people held up their babies for him to touch. After unification, he continued to evoke democracy in a nation far from democratic. He lent an aura of patriotic legitimacy to innumerable workers' associations by accepting honorary presidencies and speaking at their banquets. His presence on behalf of any cause seemed a continuation of the great demonstrations of the *Risorgimento* in which the people had a part.

Opera remained the cultural experience in which the nation most broadly shared; yet with unification it lost its role as the carrier of covert, patriotic messages. Verdi's later works, which became musically more complex, continued to fill opera houses, but in a world of free speech, metaphors of freedom sung to audiences from different social classes lost their explosive potential. Loved as an art form and important as a social bond, opera retained its emotive power. In terms of the patriotic, pedagogic function it had once had, nothing else replaced it.

The one institution that touched the lives of nearly all Italians was the Roman Catholic Church. It had long been a chief patron of the arts and learning, and many of Italy's leading scientists, philosophers, and poets had been priests. This cultural role, which declined during the nineteenth century, was in any case overshadowed by the Church's attacks on liberalism and the *Risorgimento*. Catholic publications and Sunday sermons angrily denounced every aspect of the new society, including its professors and poets, theatre productions, and philosophic treatises. Anti-Catholic sentiment was general in the social sciences but less so in the humanities. Nevertheless, many academics were practising Catholics, and Catholics sent their children to public secondary schools and universities. Overall, the conflict remained more political than cultural. The novels of Antonio Fogazzaro, Italy's most distinguished Catholic novelist since Manzoni, explored the complex intersection of faith and modernity in provincial society, and they are a reminder that Catholicism was strongest at the parish level, where high culture hardly reached. Conflicts among elites may have mattered less than the gap between national elites and local affairs.

With unification, some groups did gain a greater chance to participate in a national culture. Many Jews could now have distinguished careers in science, scholarship, and the arts. Opportunities for women evolved more slowly. Interest in women's past achievements and future opportunities was a minor thread of the *Risorgimento*, and several books had appeared listing notable women of the past and present and advocating greater freedom for women. Within traditional roles, women were influential as hostesses in intellectual circles, as governesses (Emilia Luti, governess in the D'Azeglio household, helped Manzoni rewrite his novel in Tuscan Italian), and as organizers of women's committees that raised funds and made bandages during the *Risorgimento*. The women best known for public activities were likely to belong to noble families or to be foreigners, like Princess Christina Belgioioso, or Jessie White Mario, the English-born friend of Mazzini.

Still, there were signs of change. The Princess Belgioioso, who had financed some of Mazzini's activities and founded a journal for peasants, called in 1866 for an expansion of women's opportunities as a natural fulfilment of the *Risorgimento*. The journal, *La Donna*, founded in Venice in 1868, would in the next decades publish a number of articles by Anna Maria Mozzoni, who demanded legal equality for women; and several other women who had been prominent in *Risorgimento* politics established women's journals. From the girls who improvised poetry on stage and in cafes to popular novelists, literature was more open to women than most fields. Anna Zuccari, know as Neera, wrote stories that described the lives of middle-class married women with sad candour; yet she opposed feminist arguments. Secondary schools for girls from the upper classes were growing, and a few young women sat in on university courses. A law of 1876 formally declared that women could matriculate in universities (opponents argued the law was not needed because Italian universities had admitted women and appointed women professors in the past). Soon two women took medical degrees, and in 1879 a woman received a degree in letters for the first time, from the University of Naples. A decade later, Anna Kuliscioff, one of the founders of the socialist party and a doctor, won the right to practise in hospitals in Milan after a well-publicized battle against the medical establishment. The fact remains that the Italian women with careers outside the home were primarily those in religious orders or among the tens of thousands, uneducated and poorly paid, who had gone to work in the textile mills of northern Italy and the factories of Turin and Milan.

Although a majority of Italians were peasants, Italian nationalism had been remarkably inattentive to the peasantry.[3] There was little inclination to romanticize peasants as the carriers of quintessential Italian qualities in an ideology that emphasized universal values and modern progress and no possibility, given Italy's history, of claiming that Italians shared a common ethnic origin. Culture was thought of as urban, and villages and towns imitated urban life. Even when fond of the dialect they spoke at home, educated Italians tended to consider dialect a provincial marker of ignorance; and liberals fearful of the Church's influence in the countryside were not drawn to a communal life that revolved around the religious calendar.

Interest in studying the peasantry increased somewhat after unification; and by the 1870s a few intellectuals called for more attention to Italian folklore. Stimulated by German scholars and by the development of anthropology as a discipline (the first chair of anthropology was established in Florence in 1871), Italy's anthropologists tended to write, however, about peasant superstitions and primitiveness. By the 1890s, a national society for Italian popular tradition enjoyed the queen's patronage, but it was more attentive to artisans, peddlers, and street performers than peasants. Folklorists were particularly attracted to collecting folk songs, in which they believed that the richness of regional diversity culminated in something distinctively Italian.[4] As Italy's leaders, who knew little about peasant culture and were not skilled at connecting with it, became more aware of the disappointing realities of southern Italy, they easily attributed violence, corruption, and even poverty to backwardness. Belief in the power of culture, which had contributed so much to making a nation, also fostered harmful stereotyping.

Education was the panacea. In the first years of the new nation, remarkably able ministers of education devoted themselves to that cause, despite inadequate budgets, schools, and teachers. Progress was slow and every step controversial; policies proudly announced often changed before they could be carried out. Although enrolments

---

[3] Pietro Clemente, 'Alcuni momenti della demologia storicistica in Italia'. In Pietro Clemente et al., L'Antrolopogia italiana: un secolo di storia (Bari, 1985), pp. 18–19.

[4] Luisa Rubini, 'Della 'traducibilità' del folklore: figure e aspetti della mediazione culturale tra Italia e Germania nell'ottocento'. In Giorgio Cusatelli, et al., Romantici in Europa: tradizioni popolare e letteratura (Brescia, 1996), pp. 51–7. Giuseppe Cocchiara, L'Anima del popolo italiano nei suoi canti (Milan, 1929). Angelo De Gubernatis's address of 20 November 1893, cited in Sandra Puccini (ed.), L'Uomo e gli uomini: scritti di antropologi italiani dell'ottocento (Rome, 1991), pp. 175–81.

doubled in the nation's primary and secondary schools and in its 23 universities in the two decades following 1861, the limitations were more dramatic: large areas with no elementary schools at all, primary instruction that for most students lasted only two or three years, poorly qualified teachers, secondary schooling largely restricted to children of the upper classes, and universities with poor libraries and laboratories.

Against this stood the achievement of a semi-official, humane national culture. Francesco De Sanctis was central to that. Exiled for his part in the Neapolitan revolution of 1848, he had become the era's most important literary historian and critic. He was twice minister of education and both a strong supporter of the government and a critic of its caution and bureaucratic centralization. His history of Italian literature, first published in 1870, quickly became a standard in the schools. It celebrated the moral passion of *Risorgimento* radicals, combining critical insight and romantic nationalism. De Sanctis presented Italian literature as a coherent whole, the voice of a people evolving toward national consciousness and freedom. Betrando Spaventa accomplished something similar with his history of Italian philosophy. He, too, reflected Neapolitan intellectual traditions in his use of Hegel's ideas of history and his emphasis on the importance of law and the state. More than most patriotic thinkers, Spaventa included much taken from Catholic thinkers like Gioberti and Rosmini in his version of Italy's intellectual development.

Intellectuals of this sort succeeded in establishing the canon of Italian high culture that, along with Latin and Greek, would for generations to come remain at the core of Italian education, especially in the demanding *liceo*, the secondary school that was a mark of bourgeois status. In Giosue Carducci, the most important poet of the post-unification period and Italy's first Nobel laureate in literature, this patriotic culture had a powerful voice. His crisp, controlled verse addressed contemporary life but honoured classical forms, harking back to Italy's great tradition of poetry. An admired essayist and orator, Carducci reminded his countrymen of the *Risorgimento*'s unfulfilled promise (Mazzini stood first in his patriotic pantheon). His oration on the death of Garibaldi, in 1882, moved the nation, confirmed the hero's mythic stature, and became another classic to be thrust on every student.

That culture was unabashedly bourgeois, generally secular, moralistic, and committed to progress. New schools, museums of crafts and industry, theatres, and opera houses even in the smaller cities disseminated its values. Professors presented it to workers' societies in lectures that mentioned proletarian leaders from the Gracchi of ancient Rome to those of the *Risorgimento*, and that assimilated artisans to famous artists. In most Italian towns Dante Alighieri societies helped organize ceremonies renaming streets after *Risorgimento* heroes and the unveiling of monuments to great figures from the past. On such occasions local pharmacists, doctors, and politicians could feel themselves to be part of national culture. Marble inscriptions and obelisks in stiff, eclectic, late nineteenth-century styles were declarations of cultural continuity; and these commemorations which invited rhetorical excess and grandiose architecture (as in the neoclassical monument to Victor Emmanuel in the centre of Rome), could also add dignity to ordinary lives as in some of Carducci's poems, statues of figures in bourgeois dress, and the paintings of the Tuscan artists called Macchiaioli.

The paintings and drawings of the Macchiaioli rank among the outstanding achievements in nineteenth-century Italian art. As young men, many of these artists had taken part in the revolutions of 1848, and they were in touch with Florentine intellectuals and reformers. Giovanni Fattori, today the most admired of the Macchiaioli, first achieved fame with his painting of a *Risorgimento* battle, which won the prize for a patriotic work established in 1859 by the new government of Tuscany. The group's name referred to one of their distinctive techniques, the use of blotches of dark pigment (*macchia*, or spots) to emphasize the play of light and shadow and to give objects three-dimensional weight. In this and in their preference for landscapes and scenes of peasants and everyday life, they consciously broke with Italian academic painting and expressed their own democratic inclinations. Even their battle scenes had featured stalwart soldiers more than heroes or villains. Although the group soon drifted apart, individually many of them continued doing strong work into the 1890s. In their disillusionment with the results of the *Risorgimento* and their increased international (especially Parisian) connections, as in their technique and their shift from history painting to landscapes (influenced by foreign artist's visions of Italy) to portraits of great psychological power to paintings that now seem precursors of twentieth-century proletarian art, the Macchiaioli recapitulated much of post-unification Italian culture.

By the end of the century the great majority of Italians were at least minimally literate: four-fifths of them said they could speak Italian,[5] and newspapers had established a tradition of devoting at least a page each day to culture, printing discussions of art, literature, and science. At the same time, a growing professionalism reduced the role of intellectuals as public sages. The great majority of university students studied law, medicine, or engineering and expected appropriate careers.[6] As the number of serial publications steadily increased, they were more likely to have a topical focus or be ideological and, in the case of Catholic and socialist papers, sharply critical of the dominant consensus.

Although most journalists continued to write in an allusive style clearly not aimed at the masses, there were significant signs that a common Italian culture was reaching across classes and regions. In the larger cities, some papers began to print more easily accessible human-interest stories. Every city featured places where the general public mingled, as in Milan's new gallery, which was completed in 1878 and quickly became the city's living room. Popular theatre flourished, in Italian and dialect, and so did cafes. Such places of relaxation remained very different in working-class districts from the ones with a middle-class clientele, but the same songs were likely to be sung in both. The 1880s began a golden age of Neapolitan popular music, with songs, enjoyed today as folk music but new then, like *Funiculì, Funiculà*, about young, urban lovers and the funicular railroad on Vesuvius inaugurated in 1880.

Pellegrino Artusi taught Italians that they had a national cuisine. *The Science of Cooking, the Art of Eating Well, a Practical Handbook for the Family* was first published in 1891. Aimed at those who could afford to vary their diet and cared about appearances, the book was intended for a middle and lower-middle class that believed in science, admired art, and was devoted to the family. A self-made man and 71-year-old bachelor living in Florence, Artusi begins his cookbook with a good-humoured account of his difficulty in finding a publisher, an

[5] Tullio De Mauro, 'La questione della lingua'. In Corrado Stajano (ed.), *La cultura italiana dell novecento* (Bari, 1996), pp. 428–9.

[6] Maria Malatesta (ed.), *Society and the Professions in Italy, 1860–1914* (Cambridge, 1995).

account that also announces his cultural connections. A friend and noted scholar invited to Florence to take part in planning the monument to Foscolo to be erected in Santa Croce (Artusi had published an essay on Foscolo) looks at the manuscript and declares it will have few readers. Three different publishers, all friends who enjoy having dinner at Artusi's home, decide they cannot afford to print it. So Artusi printed his 800 recipes at his own expense. Then Paolo Mantegazza, the first person to hold the new chair in anthropology and a famous physician, pronounces Artusi's cookbook valuable and important; and it began to sell out in ever-larger editions.

The book is needed, Artusi explains, because although Italian cuisine can match the French, it is often improperly prepared or altered to meet the tastes of foreign tourists. He carefully included recipes from every region of Italy, assigning each to one course in the larger meal, so that all become part of a single national cuisine. Little stories accompanied most recipes, and in them Artusi tells of his first encounter with that food or gives its history. Ice cream, for example, although associated with the French court, really comes from Italy, and Artusi gives an account of how that happened, adding some citations to suggest that the ancient Romans enjoyed it, too. Filled with interesting erudition, quotations from poets ancient and modern, recommendations on hygiene, and advice on how to serve graciously and make food attractive, his cookbook was a cultural guide.

By the end of the nineteenth century two other best-selling books also furthered the post-*Risorgimento* effort to make good Italian citizens. Both were children's books, a middle-class genre with an expanding market thanks to public schooling. Carlo Lorenzetti (he used Collodi as a pen name) was a journalist interested in children's literature who had written several moralizing books for schoolroom use before publishing *The Adventures of Pinocchio* in 1883. Written for a new children's magazine and intended to illustrate the value of honesty and good citizenship in a harsh world, the charm of its fantasy has carried beyond its purpose and era. Edmondo De Amicis wrote *Il Cuore* for similar reasons three years later. A former army officer, who fought in the war in 1866, he had written about army life and then published a series of successful travel books. Like Lorenzetti, he had experience at writing for popular audiences and believed moral instruction crucial to the nation. The novel reflects its author's patriotic socialism. Cast as a schoolboy's diary, it includes letters from the boy's friends describing other regions of Italy as well as his touching accounts of events in the classroom, his lower-class neighbourhood, and his family. The pathos of poverty is mitigated by the hero's simple descriptions, the strength of his character, and a community in which virtue is rewarded by a grandmother's smile or children's cheers when the mayor awards a medal to a classmate who saved someone from drowning. *Il Cuore*, soon the most widely read book in Italy, was quickly translated into all the major languages and, for seventy years, assigned to every school child. Italy's literate culture had learned to make a mass appeal.

Challenges to cultural consensus

Even as this national culture achieved what Antonio Gramsci would later label cultural hegemony, the consensus on which it rested began to break up. Public life broadened to include groups with pressing problems, new schools of thought engaged social issues more directly, and creativity burst traditional frameworks. A new generation pushed in new directions, and new challenges came especially from Marxism, Catholic Action, and positivism.

The working-class movement of the 1870s and 1880s continued to grow, invigorated, particularly in Naples, by the anarchist ideas of Michael Bakunin. Despite failed plots and repression, the revolutionary Left coalesced into a political party with strong union ties, and its formal embrace of socialism in 1892 marked an important turning point. The transition from its Mazzinian roots had come slowly. The weekly *La Plebe* (which was founded in 1868 and enjoyed Garibaldi's support) published some of Marx's writings; in 1891 Filippo Turati, already well known as a Milanese poet and democrat, joined with Anna Kuliscioff in founding *La Critica Sociale*. While seeking to unite the social concerns of earlier radicals with a strengthened workers' movement, the magazine gave increasing attention to Marxist theory; and Turati, a key figure in founding the socialist party, would be elected to parliament in 1896. In that same year Arturo Labriola published his most important work on historical materialism. A professor of philosophy at Rome, who had studied with Spaventa and absorbed some of latter's interest in Hegel and

German philosophy, Labriola shocked many intellectuals with his conversion to Marxism and his rejections of Turati's tactical compromises, a criticism that electrified the Left. Labriola's own sophisticated version of Marxism would in turn be criticized for being more concerned with ideas (and culture) than revolution, but it had a profound influence on the coming generation of Italian intellectuals.

Whereas socialism provided a new challenge to the cultural consensus, the Catholic Church sustained a well-established one. Vatican policies and the Catholic press kept the political conflict alive, although many priests and bishops maintained good relations with civil authorities. The aura of crisis fed by the conflict between Church and state extended beyond politics to cultural issues as well. Catholics, appalled that Italian society appeared ever more secular, responded organizationally and intellectually. A Catholic youth movement and the activities of the *Opera dei Congressi*, which included 24 daily newspapers and more than 150 other periodicals, maintained a fusillade of cultural criticism. Catholic social thinkers, of whom the most prominent was Giuseppe Toniolo, professor of economics at the University of Pisa, developed a programme for what they called an ethical, Christian economy (citing the ideas of Rosmini). Opposed to socialism, they were critical of capitalism, insistent on social justice, sympathetic to corporatism, and willing to concede the potential merits of democracy; but they found little to admire in contemporary Italy.

The cultural and political values of the *Risorgimento* were also challenged by positivism, a loose term that implied confidence that scientific methods, using objective observation and cold reason, constituted the only source of reliable knowledge. In Italy that credo created a kind of cultural shock, often associated with explicit philosophical materialism and strident anticlericalism. Many Italian positivists were physicians eager to apply scientific knowledge to social problems. Their campaigns to improve the diet, hygiene, and conduct of peasants stressed education and the need for systematic programmes but gained attention by exposing the underside of social life. Most of the founders of Italian anthropology were positivists who associated wife beating, vendettas, and distrust of civil authorities with local superstitions. Newspapers and official reports published sensational accounts of rural violence, cruelty, filthy living conditions, and ignorance; and the field of criminal anthropology was all but invented in Italy.

Cesare Lombroso was its most famous figure. Like most positivists, a committed reformer and something of a socialist, he hoped to solve the glaring social problems of Italy's industrial slums and backward South. He studied the social environment that conditioned crime, but his fame came with his focus on the individual criminal as a physiological and psychological type. Lombroso's ideas seemed applicable everywhere, an impression furthered by his own loose and contradictory writings. By measuring skulls and cataloguing behaviours, he claimed to identify the typologies of anarchists, backward southerners, and the excessively devout. Although he sometimes contrasted northern European and Mediterranean physical types, race was not a central category. Rather, Lombroso made his conception of the European middle-class male the norm; those who behaved differently were thus deviants to be classified, isolated, and corrected. He confirmed the intellectual inferiority of women and in the name of science provided ammunition for the racial theories and repressive practices of others. Such tough-mindedness continued in Italian social science with the work of Vilfredo Pareto and Gaetano Mosca, who in the 1890s were just becoming well known for their theories that political systems were inevitably dominated by elite minorities.

These Marxist, Catholic, and positivist movements all analysed, and amplified, critical social divisions—of class, religion, and region—in Italian society. They also divided other groups seeking change. Labour movements split over ties to socialism; and feminists divided, between those like Mozzoni, who pressed for women's suffrage and believed women's concerns applied to all classes, and those like Kuliscioff, who argued that issues of class were decisive and campaigned for equal pay and for legislation limiting the conditions of women's work. The exhibition of women's crafts, held in Florence in 1889, and the women's society for science, letters, and the arts (under the patronage of the queen) were already beginning to look a bit old fashioned. Newer directions were foreshadowed by Maria Montessori, who had started her career as an educational pioneer, and Grazia Deledda, journalist and novelist, who had begun to write in biting detail of political careerism in Rome and about the life of the lower classes in Naples in novels for which she was awarded the Nobel prize in literature in 1925.

Social realism in literature greatly increased public awareness of social issues and did so with particular power in the work of Giovanni Verga. A Sicilian who lived for years in Florence and became active in the cultural life of Milan, Verga was a prolific writer. His early stories dissected the artificiality of bourgeois life, but in the 1870s and 1880s he turned to Sicilian subjects. Much like the positivists, he adopted a coldly objective tone; and the Sicilian fishermen and peasants in his novels speak with crude directness in phrases that echo the rhythms and dialects of Sicilian speech. No match for market forces, arbitrary authorities, and bad luck, they fall victim in the end to their own ignorance, cruelty, and avarice, their efforts to preserve family or acquire status overwhelmed by disaster.

These competing approaches to literature marked a break from the more homogeneous culture of earlier generations. In subject matter and tone, Verga opened one avenue away from the traditions of Italian high culture, one that many would follow in the next century. At the same time those traditions would continue to thrive, often enlarged and enriched as in the moving, pastoral poetry of Giovanni Pascoli, another in that long line of Italian poets who used Latinate forms to convey the beauty of nature and the stability of humble virtues. Gabriele D'Annunzio staked out still another course. He rose to stardom as poet and novelist. His brilliant, lush writing was close to that of the symbolists and to the so-called decadents of northern Europe, a kinship he acted out in striking dress and lurid love affairs (accounts of his life with Eleonora Duse, one of the most famous actresses of the day, filled the newspapers). In Milan a group called themselves *scapigliati*, a term suggesting disorder, and wrote of the alienation of modern life; and artists experimented with new styles that broke with the canons of realism. Satirical wit, provocative daring, D'Annunzio's pyrotechnics, and Verga's fatalism all rejected the moral seriousness and pedagogical purpose that had characterized Italy's high culture earlier in the century.

Even opera changed. Popular as ever, with young composers and new opera houses to keep the offerings fresh, performances were no longer the occasion for political demonstrations. Verdi's last opera, *Falstaff*, had no one singing of patriotism and, in an important break with his own past, no separable arias but instead a continuous musical flow. The compact libretto used less of the flowery, arcane language that once had seemed a requisite of high style. The opera's premiere in Milan in 1893, Verdi's eightieth year, was a gala event attended by scores of famous people, among them Duse and a number of younger composers, including Giacomo Puccini and Pietro Mascagni. The occasion emphasized continuity with an admired past, but these composers' operas embraced a new style of realism (known as *verismo*). Mascagni was in that distinguished audience because just three years before, in 1890, the performance in Rome of his first opera, *Cavalleria Rusticana* had created a sensation, when he was said to have taken 40 curtain calls. Within the next two years it had been performed across Europe and in New York, and Mascagni had been heaped with honours, from medals and parades in Italy to George Bernard Shaw's declaration that the successor to Verdi had been found.

Cavalleria Rusticana was already a landmark in two other genres. It began as a short story by Verga in which even a love story turned into a relentlessly harsh look at peasant life. The story was soon made into a play, and its performance in 1884, with Duse in the lead, is often taken to mark the beginning of modern Italian drama. Here was a play set in a Sicilian village in which jealousy, obsession with female honour, intolerance, and violence are unrelieved by noble language. Mascagni wrote his opera based on the play. Its lovely music was less innovative than the realistic plot and staging, and the operatic version muffled the starkness of the original story. But peasants had made it to centre stage even in the opera house, and operatic *verismo* would become an established form.

Inspired by Mascagni's success, Ruggiero Leoncavallo wrote *Pagliacci*, performed in Milan in 1892 and also an immediate success. Here, the love triangle and violent death unfolds through a play within a play. On a feast day in a southern village, a small travelling troupe performs a play about a jealous lover, but off stage the actors have parallel relationships; and the curtain falls when the staged murder on stage proves to be real. Leoncavallo used events from his own experience as the basis for his plot; and there is a touch of positivist realism in the staging, a gesture to Neapolitan folk music in the singing, and a modern touch to the theme of confused identities. Both short operas, *Cavalleria Rusticana* and *Pagliacci*, are almost always performed together. Both strive for emotive musical effects and provide attractive vehicles for famous singers, confirming, despite the *verismo* of their plots, the continuing appeal of traditional

Italian opera. In his *verismo* opera, *La Bohème*, first performed in 1896, Puccini developed a distinctive musical style in which singing voices come close to conversational speech and the orchestra provides a kind of musical commentary. Puccini's later compositions would continue in this direction, although few would have the *verismo* setting of *La Bohème* about starving young artists in a Parisian garret. Italian opera after Verdi was opening to a new era; and the conductor of the first performances of both *Pagliacci* and *La Bohème* was Arturo Toscanini, who over the next decades would become arguably the most famous orchestral conductor of the twentieth century.

The vigorous cultural life of the new Italian nation continued to have a place in the European mainstream and remained preoccupied, as it had been a century earlier, with politics. By the end of the nineteenth century, it reached more effectively across regional and social divisions than ever before and attended with greater candour and creativity to the lives of ordinary people. As it broke away from the old rhetorical and formal constraints, the old cultural consensus was blown apart, but Italian thought gained greater resonance in the rest of Europe. Still, efforts to work outside the coherent culture codified in the *Risorgimento* seemed especially radical and divisive in Italy because its formal culture had achieved such hegemony. In the next century the new forms and ideas to which Italian culture had begun to turn would lead to far more explosive experiments.

Economy, society, and the state

John A. Davis

Introduction

Economists were among the first to extol the advantages of Italy's political independence, yet at the time of unification Italy had little economic unity. Every Italian state depended primarily on agriculture (which remained the largest source of employment down to the First World War) although the forms of agriculture and the organization of rural society varied enormously from region to region and from state to state. Separated by geography and customs barriers, the foreign trade of the Italian states was mainly with non-Italian partners: the Habsburg Empire in the case of Lombardy and Venetia; Britain and France in the cases of Piedmont and Tuscany; Britain, France, Austria, and Russia in the case of Naples and Sicily.

Political unification was not in any sense, therefore, the result of economic convergence: on the contrary, political unification was no more than the premise on which to start building national markets, a process that was far from complete by the end of the nineteenth century. Yet economic forces did have a direct bearing on the struggles for political change in the first half of the century. Economic liberalism played a critical role in rallying the Italian propertied classes to the Piedmontese monarchy in the 1850s, while the social unrest provoked by the disruptive impact of economic change in the countryside contributed directly to the collapse of the legitimist autocracies.

For most of this period, Italy was more exposed to the disruptive than to the constructive forces of economic change. None of the Italian economies would be contenders in the early industrial revolutions. Italy had no deposits of carbon fuel, and few mineral resources—some iron ore in the Alpine valleys and on the island of Elba and important supplies of sulphur in Sicily, which by the beginning of the nineteenth century were largely controlled by British merchants. New textile industries appeared in the first half of the nineteenth century, but expansion was difficult. Low productivity in agriculture meant that domestic markets were weak and inelastic outside the towns and cities, while competition from the more powerful European economies threatened to reduce the Italian states to supplying raw materials in exchange for imports of manufactured goods.

The Italian states nevertheless felt the impact of economic change in other parts of Europe from an early date. Increased demand for Mediterranean products placed new incentives on commercial farming in the eighteenth century that had far-reaching consequences for rural society. It brought both new opportunities of wealth for landowners and unprecedented insecurity for the vast majority of the rural population. The consolidation of the new industrial economies in north-western Europe in the first half of the nineteenth century also faced the Italian rulers with stark choices. The Restoration rulers had set their face against progress in any form, yet without economic growth their dynastic independence could not be sustained. Every autocratic ruler faced the same dilemma, but it was only in the Kingdom of Sardinia that a political formula emerged in which dynastic ambition and economic growth could be reconciled. That formula established a new political context for Italy's subsequent economic development.

The agrarian economies

At the end of the eighteenth century the vast majority of Italians were engaged in agriculture as labourers or peasant farmers. Levels of agricultural productivity were low and most rural communities hovered precariously on the margins of subsistence under constant assault from crop failures, natural disasters, and disease. But it was in the countryside that the impact of economic change was felt first and most forcefully. As foreign demand for Mediterranean staples such as grain, silk, olive oil, citrus fruits, spices, and wine increased, land-owners attempted to increase production with consequences that varied according to the forms of agriculture practised.

In regions like the upper Po Valley where intensive farming methods were well established, large farms grew at the expense of smaller, independent peasant farms, while the number of landless labourers rose. The insecurity of the rural population increased, caus-ing unemployment, vagrancy, crime, and banditry to grow in ways that greatly alarmed contemporaries. In the South, where agrarian feudalism was still a reality and where agriculture and transhumant sheep-grazing were still interdependent, the expansion of enclosures and private land threatened the survival of entire rural communities. Seasonal access to feudal estates, the right to graze and farm on the village commons and to exercise customary rights such as gleaning, collecting firewood, or hunting on the open land and woodlands were critical to the economy of the rural population. The situation was aggravated by unprecedented rates of population growth that brought further pressure on land and resources that were already inadequate to support an increasingly impoverished rural population.

These changes were driven not only by market forces but also by the state, and in the second half of the eighteenth century Italian rulers actively sought to promote the expansion of private property and commercial farming. The lands of many religious orders were sold, feudal and customary limits on enclosures were removed, efforts were made to increase foreign trade. During the brief period of French rule (1800–14) these initiatives were consolidated and Napoleon's satellite rulers introduced the package of reforms that had been honed through the experience of the revolution in France. The abolition of feudalism was the juridical basis of a new political and economic order. The private jurisdictions of the *ancien régime* disappeared, to be replaced by a centralized, bureaucratic state. Stripped of the multiple use-rights and constraints that were insepar-able from feudal tenure, land was transformed into private property and became the corner-stone of the new state. Citizenship was defined by the ownership of land, which now became the principal source of direct taxation. Sales of vast tracts of land belonging to religious houses and the former rulers also provided the capital needed to liquidate the debts of the *ancien régime* and establish state and public finances on a new and more solid basis.

Some peasants benefited from these changes, but for most they brought insecurity and threatened ruin. Tensions and violence spread through the countryside as rural communities attempted to defend customary rights that were threatened by the incursions of private property and market economies. But both liberals and democrats were committed to the advancement of a market economy, and saw in the rural protests only a doomed and reactionary struggle against progress.

In the first half of the nineteenth century the pace of rural change accelerated, particularly after the 1830s. In the Po Valley landlords imposed increasingly onerous leases on their tenants to increase production for the market, causing the peasants to seek additional work or seasonal migration to supplement their meagre incomes. The Habsburg administration also actively promoted the privatization of village commons and woodlands, thereby removing the resources on which the poorest rural communities depended. In the South, the Bourbon government in 1816 extended the abolition of feudalism and the French administrative reforms to Sicily, which lost its centuries-old autonomy in a new centralized monarchy: the Kingdom of the Two Sicilies. On the mainland, the Bourbons also pushed ahead with the privatization of former feudal lands and the division of village common lands that had begun in the Napoleonic period. Throughout Sicily and the Mezzogiorno the destruction of the collective rights on which the rural communities had depended down to the end of the eighteenth century was the principal cause of social unrest and rural conflicts, whose targets were the landowners who had profited most from these changes.

Rural unrest did not end with unification, although the new state was able to marshal greater fire-power to maintain public order than its predecessors. The civil war that swept through the southern mainland in the wake of Garibaldi's expedition of 1860 marked the penultimate explosion of anger against a landowning class whose power had been consolidated by the liberal revolution of 1860. The final collective cry of protest would come thirty years later when the peasant farmers of the Sicilian interior organized collectively in what were known as *Fasci* to force the landowners to renegotiate leases that were widely acknowledged to be ruinous. In defence of the landowners the government mobilized a full-scale military occupation of the island, and in the wake of the defeat of the *Fasci* the first waves of emigration from Sicily across the Atlantic began, soon to be followed by the peasants of the Mezzogiorno. Between 1890 and the outbreak of the First World War some 11 million Italians would emigrate, the majority from an impoverished and hopeless South.

Rural unrest in the South was finally crushed by force and emigration, but in the North began to take new and less easily controlled forms. The reintroduction of a deeply resented tax on grist (the *macinato*) in the former papal provinces of Emilia and Romagna provoked widespread unrest in the late 1860s. In the 1880s collective protest and demonstrations swept through the Po Valley when farm prices fell as a result of the arrival of cheap North American grain and meat on European markets. In Italy the landowners passed the burden on to the tenant farmers, causing many wealthier peasants in Piedmont, Liguria, and Lombardy to sell up and seek their fortune on the expanding wheat frontiers of Argentina. The impoverished communities of the rural Veneto followed a harder path and emigrated to replace the recently emancipated slave labourers on the coffee plantations of Sâo Paolo province in Brazil.

In other parts of the Po Valley the peasants and tenant farmers attempted collective resistance, to which the authorities reacted with a customary excess of force. The peasant farmers were defeated, but the principle of collective resistance was not and it was in these years that the landless farm hands (*braccianti*) began to organize leagues and cooperatives in the Romagna. It was here too that socialism first found a rural following, which quickly spread throughout the Po Valley to become the most distinctive feature of the Italian labour movement by the end of the century. The clergy responded to the incursion of socialist ideas by promoting Catholic cooperatives and 'white' leagues amongst the peasant farmers of Lombardy and the Veneto. These conflicts also began to spread even to the hitherto tranquil share-cropping regions of Tuscany and central Italy so that by the end of the century Italy's most advanced agricultural regions had become the theatre for violent confrontations between the landowners and the militant leagues of the landless *braccianti*, while the Catholic cooperatives were often caught in the cross-fire.

In the South, by contrast, the landowners reacted aggressively against any attempts by the peasant farmers or labourers to establish collective bargaining. When at the end of the century emigration reduced the surplus labour supply and potentially gave the labourers new bargaining opportunities, the landowners responded with force and, with the tacit approval of the authorities, armed private militias where necessary to break collective resistance. Such responses propped up an agrarian social order still dominated by the power and influence of the landowning classes, which continued to be founded on the terrible poverty of the vast mass of the rural population. Emigration could reduce the pressures of over-population in the South but not remove the causes of poverty or the backwardness of much of southern agriculture. As a result, the older agrarian order that was being widely challenged throughout northern and central Italy by the turn of the century remained firmly in place throughout much of the Mezzogiorno, Sicily, and Sardinia.

Urban Italy

The contrast between rural Italy and urban Italy was perhaps the most visible legacy of Italy's past. Despite the predominance of agriculture, a high proportion of Italy's inhabitants lived in towns and cities. Naples had until the seventeenth century been one of the most populous cities in Europe, and continued to be the largest city in Italy until the end of the nineteenth century. At the start of the nineteenth century it still had nearly half a million inhabitants and was much larger than any of the other major Italian cities. These included the principal administrative capitals (Palermo, Rome, Florence, Turin, Milan, and Venice) and the larger ports (Messina, Catania, Civitavecchia, Livorno, Genoa, Venice, Ancona, and Bari). Milan was Italy's wealthiest commercial city but at the time of the Restoration did not exceed 120,000 inhabitants, and it was not until the final decades of the century that it became an industrial city. The same decades saw the development of important new industrial sectors in Genoa (shipbuilding), Florence (engineering), and Turin (engineering, although its industrial expansion came mainly after 1900). The majority of nineteenth-century Italian town-dwellers lived, however, in the lesser provincial centres where the rent-rolls of rural estates were spent in ways that sustained a range of urban services, trades, and professions.

Although the cities would be the principal theatres of political unrest and the epicentres of the revolutions of 1820, 1831, and 1848, the impact of economic change was less disruptive for urban than for rural society. The primary agent of change was the expansion of commerce, which strengthened rather than threatened the urban social order. This was well illustrated by Milan, whose wealth came from agriculture and trade, and especially from the silk-worms produced in the surrounding rural areas and from the trade in silk yarn. The profits from these activities provided work for an endless array of builders, carriage-makers, tailors, seamstresses, domestic servants, cab-drivers, and victuallers. Despite the city's growing wealth its social fabric remained cohesive and the different social classes continued to live side by side as in most other Italian cities. It was only with the development of new industrial suburbs at the end of the century that this integrated urban structure began to change and break down.

The new industries that came to Italy in the first half of the century were in any case overwhelmingly rural. The principal sector was the production of textile fibres (wool, silk, and cotton) and the introduction of new industrial technologies took their manufacture out of the cities where they had previously been located to rural areas closer to the sources of water power needed to drive new machinery and where rural poverty provided an abundant and cheap supply of labour.

Earlier in the century the largest concentrations of workers were to be found in the port cities of Genoa, Livorno, Venice, Naples, Messina, and Palermo, and in a smaller number of manufacturing enterprises such as the state-run tobacco factories. These workers were part of the established urban communities, although in periods of major economic recession such as the 1840s they could become a dangerous source of disorder. The decision to build a new coast road in Genoa provoked militant protests amongst the powerful corporation of lightermen in 1847, for example, while the relaxation of protective tariffs in numerous Italian states in the same decade gave rise to demonstrations and protests by printers, typesetters, and other highly skilled urban tradesmen whose livelihood was threatened by foreign imports.

The mobilization of protest in all the major Italian cities that gave rise to the revolutions of 1848–49 indicated that urban society was not immune to the impact of economic crisis, and it was the more dangerous for the rulers because popular urban unrest was compounded by the discontents of the urban middle classes amongst whom under-employment was severe.

Other and less visible changes were also taking place in urban society during the century that concluded with unification. Everywhere the corporate organization that typified the *ancien régime* cities was being dismantled, albeit in most cases slowly and hesitantly. The French reforms at the start of the century had in this respect also consolidated earlier attempts to reduce the power of corporate organizations that had been one of the principal features of the *ancien régime* cities. The French pulled down the remaining city walls that had symbolized the former autonomy of the cities, and replaced municipal self-government with new forms of bureaucratic administration. The urban craft guilds and lay confraternities were finally abolished.

These changes had important consequences, and the removal of corporate monopolies and regulations exposed citizens to market forces. Access to urban trades became more open, but the loss of the charitable functions formerly provided by the guilds and confraternities meant that responsibility for welfare now fell more heavily on the parishes, the remaining religious orders, and above all on the family and household. The reorganization of public charitable institutions was designed to exclude all but the most desperate and deserving of the poor and indigent.

These changes went hand-in-hand with new measures to regulate and police every aspect of urban life. Details of every family and household were meticulously recorded in new municipal registers (the *Anagrafe*) that governed the daily lives and even identities of every citizen: without complete and up-dated records no one could obtain the permits and licences which were necessary for everything from selling goods to running a business, having a job, or obtaining papers to travel outside the city. An adverse police report on the register was sufficient to make all these things unattainable, but to be registered was the condition of citizenship. Those who were not might easily fall foul of the police regulations that had made vagrancy and homelessness criminal offences, with the aim of forcing families to take care of the destitute and deterring a potentially inexhaustible influx of impoverished migrants from the countryside.

Characteristically the Restoration rulers looked to soften the impact of these changes. Except in the Austrian territories, guilds and lay confraternities were at first restored but then subsequently abolished again in Naples after the revolutions of 1820–21 and in the Kingdom of Sardinia in 1844. In the meantime even voluntary charitable organizations remained technically illegal, and it was only once the Piedmontese constitution of 1848 had made public gatherings legal that the first workers' mutual aid societies were founded in Turin. These did not spread to the rest of Italy until after 1860, but as late as the 1880s lay confraternities were still the main providers of welfare for most sections of society in Naples.

The relatively homogeneous social fabric of the pre-unification cities was reflected in the strong sense of municipal identity evident in the revolutions of 1848, which tended to set cities and towns against one another, rather than divide them internally. The fierce rivalries between neighbouring cities, and the revolt of the provincial towns against the capital cities, would be a dominant feature of the revolutions of 1848–49.

Urban political unrest was a major factor in the crisis that overwhelmed the pre-unification states, but after unification new social tensions began to make themselves felt within urban Italy. In Rome, the armies of workers who were recruited from the surrounding rural areas to rebuild the capital of the new state in the 1870s had little contact with the rest of the city and lived in isolated and impoverished shanty towns where they became early but enthusiastic converts to revolutionary anarchist ideas. Much the same occurred in the cities where the first engineering, iron making, and chemical and electrical industries were established in the 1880s and 1890s. In Milan and Genoa, and to a lesser extent Florence and Turin, a new industrial working class took shape that had few links with the older, established urban craft workers. The new industrial workers were typically immigrants from surrounding rural areas, who had to make do with inadequate, insanitary, and exorbitantly expensive housing in the new jerry-built suburbs that sprang up outside the old city centres. They had no access to the craft organizations, lay confraternities, and mutual aid societies of the artisan communities, and although trade unions of any sort were illegal they quickly began to organize collectively.

In the South there were no comparable developments, and in the larger cities corporate organization remained intact and, if anything, expanded. One important example was the Neapolitan *camorra*, a corporate organization with deep roots in Neapolitan subculture that had existed for centuries and effectively controlled key sectors of the urban economy. Originating amongst the communities that had a monopoly over work in the city's port, *camorra* also controlled the city's principal food markets. *Camorra* developed into an autonomous form of corporate government that used its power to enforce monopolies and a variety of illegal activities (smuggling in particular), but also to enforce community regulations, punish those that transgressed, and take care of the unfortunate. The relatively static character of the city's economy ensured the survival of these corporate structures, while the introduction of elected municipal governments after unification enabled *camorra* to assume new political power through organizing and brokering municipal votes. In Sicily, the *mafia* developed in very similar ways, although its origins were more recent. It had originated in the rural hinterland of western Sicily, where *mafia* factions acquired monopolist controls over the scarce supplies of water and pasture, without which Sicily's arid land could not be farmed. By the early nineteenth century *mafia* also controlled the provisioning of Palermo, enabling it to gain control over the richer markets and political opportunities offered by the city. The *mafia* associations established deep roots in the popular culture of Palermo and other western Sicilian towns, and the advent of the vote gave them new powers as brokers and managers of the local and parliamentary electorate. Both *mafia* and *camorra* were also deeply involved in protection-racketeering, extortion, prostitution, and organized crime, and their presence was a barrier to the development of more independent forms of social or political organization.

The interdependence of industry and agriculture

If the urban and rural experiences of change differed in many important ways, the two were also closely interdependent. Even at the close of the century the majority of Italian industries were located in the countryside and not in cities, and the majority of industrial workers were young peasant women, not men. This was especially true of the textile industries that continued to be Italy's largest industrial sector down to the First World War. Their rural setting was not a sign of backwardness, however, but the result of entrepreneurial strategies designed to maximize Italy's scant comparative economic advantages. The principal constraint for the manufacturers of consumer goods was the small and inelastic domestic consumer market, which made Italian industries heavily dependent on exports. Rural sites enabled manufacturers like Alessandro Rossi, whose wool mills at Schio (in the upper Veneto) made him the largest single employer in Italy in the 1880s, to adopt modern technologies and methods of production while at the same time taking advantage of a cheap but flexible and skilled labour force. Rossi's mills were organized as a utopian rural community that was regulated along strictly paternalist and Catholic lines. The mills were worked by women and girls from the surrounding rural villages who lived under close supervision in dormitories run by the company but maintained close contact with their peasant families. This freed the employers of the problems posed by a fixed urban labour force, and in times of recession or falling demand the workers could return to their families and be reabsorbed back into the farming economy. At the same time, the wages earned from these rural industries went back into the peasant households in ways that helped maintain the older structures of rural society.

Foreign observers noted that the relative cheapness of Italian labour, its high levels of skill, and the flexibility of the labour market constituted the critical comparative advantages of northern Italian entrepreneurs operating on competitive foreign markets. But agriculture and industry were linked in other ways, too, and throughout Piedmont, Lombardy, the Veneto, Emilia, and the Romagna agriculture had by the 1880s also become an important consumer of a wide range of industrial products, from farm machinery to chemicals and fertilizers. Profits from agriculture were also reinvested in trade, banking, insurance, and in industrial ventures in ways that helped propel autonomous forms of economic growth.

Outside those regions there was nothing comparable. In the South, until the end of the nineteenth century there were virtually no successful new industrial initiatives, one reason being that agriculture—with very few exceptions—remained unproductive and impoverished, continuing to rely primarily on the cheapness and abundance of rural labour. Even the most advanced sectors of southern agriculture were dependent on highly unstable and unpredictable foreign markets, creating permanent uncertainty that inhibited long-term investment and more solid forms of growth. As a result, agriculture failed to generate significant new demand for industrial products and the conditions for the inter-dependence between agriculture and industry that developed in the North were not repeated.

The state and the economy before unification

Well before unification the state had been an important agent in economic growth. From the reform initiatives undertaken with varying degrees of success in the second half of the eighteenth century by Joseph II in Lombardy, Victor Amadeus III in Piedmont, Peter Leopold in Tuscany, and Ferdinand IV in Naples to those of the Restoration rulers, the driving logic was that dynastic independence and economic growth were inseparable. This made the political and ideological premise of the Restoration all the more contradictory, however, since unbending opposition to any form of economic and cultural change threatened the rulers' own dynastic self-interest.

The Bourbon rulers of Naples were the first to discover this awkward truth. The revolutions of 1820–21 left the Neapolitan monarchy virtually bankrupt, and the collapse of the kingdom's finances was only averted when the Rothschild bank purchased and successfully refloated the entire national debt in 1822. The Neapolitan finance minister, Luigi de' Medici, then experimented with a strategy designed to ensure the kingdom's future economic and commercial independence. In 1823 Naples adopted one of the highest protective tariffs in Italy, with the aim of promoting strategic industries that would enable the Bourbon kingdom to modernize its merchant fleet and build a modern navy.

De' Medici's strategy was quite explicitly aimed at escaping British commercial domination by expanding the Neapolitan merchant fleet and developing a native textile industry capable of meeting domestic demand. But the strategy failed because it incurred fierce opposition from two sources. Most immediately it attracted fierce opposition from the Kingdom's principal trading partner, Great Britain, which retaliated with punitive duties on Neapolitan trade. In 1840, on the pretext of a commercial dispute, Lord Palmerston sent a squadron of British gunships to the Bay of Naples and forced the Neapolitan government to abandon its protective tariffs. The increase in unemployment caused by the flood of British manufactures that entered the kingdom in the following years was a major cause of the social unrest that exploded in the revolutions of 1848–49.

Although the Bourbon protectionist strategy collapsed in the face of powerful foreign resistance, domestic opposition was equally strong. The landowners argued that the cost of the protectionist tariffs was borne by agriculture, which was also exposed to reprisals against Neapolitan exports. At the same time the protectionist strategy made it impossible for southern agriculture to benefit from the expansion in European markets, and pressures for freer commercial regulations mounted. But these were not granted because the government feared that freedom to export might cause domestic prices to rise and provoke dangerous social unrest. Following the collapse of the revolutions of 1848–49 new restrictions on agricultural exports were imposed, aggravating the tensions between the monarchy and the southern landowners who now looked with growing enthusiasm to the free trade programme championed by Cavour and Piedmont.

The rulers of the Kingdom of Sardinia faced a similar dilemma, but adopted different solutions. Measures to promote economic growth in Piedmont came late, and started only well after Charles Albert came to the throne in 1832. Although deeply conservative, Charles Albert understood that his kingdom could not become a modern military power without economic and commercial expansion. Dynastic self-interest was again the main incentive, but in Piedmont this resulted in a loose alliance between the monarchy and the progressive landowners and liberals whose spokesman was Cavour.

Their interests were always parallel rather than convergent, but were sufficient to enable Cavour to carry through the reforms that made Piedmont the most dynamic economy in Italy in the 1850s. The alliance that took shape around the Piedmontese constitution of 1848 was precarious, but proved a sufficient sign of political stability and progress to enable Piedmont to attract the foreign capital investment to finance the infrastructures needed for commercial expansion (improved roads, canals, railways, tunnels through the Alps to link Piedmont with the European markets of the Rhine–Rhone corridor). In the South, by contrast, the Rothschild bank was considering winding up its affairs in the 1850s because neither investment prospects nor those of the Bourbon monarchy looked promising.

There were other alternatives, and the Tuscan Grand Duchy offered a quite different example of the imprint of the visible hand on economic growth. Although early converts to reciprocal trade, the Grand-Ducal governments and the Tuscan landowners were wary of economic change that might upset Tuscany's proverbial social tranquillity. This was generally identified with the Tuscan share-cropping system (the *mezzadria*) that was considered to be a model of harmonious economic interests. The estates of the Tuscan landowners were divided into smaller farmsteads that were leased to peasant families who worked the land and at the end of each harvest divided the produce of the farms with the landowners. The system met the subsistence needs of the peasant households, while the remainder of the farm produce (normally considerably more than the 50% implied in the name of the lease) was available for the market. Its critics argued strenuously in the 1830s, however, that *mezzadria* leases prevented the adoption of more specialized commercial farming. But the majority of Tuscan landowners and economists continued to believe that the *mezzadria* contract was the foundation of a deferential agrarian order, and hence a social asset greater in value than the increased profits that more intensive farming might bring. Although there were a number of manufacturing centres in Tuscany, the landed classes generally avoided forms of economic innovation that might bring unwanted social tensions. Instead they invested in international trade and in banking, so that at the time of unification Florence was the principal financial centre in Italy and held that place until eclipsed by Milan in the 1880s.

Austrian Lombardy was the most prosperous region in pre-unification Italy, thanks to high levels of productivity in the irrigated plain, and especially the cultivation of silk-worms and silk fibre, which remained Italy's single most valuable export commodity down to the First World War. But although the Austrian administration was probably more enlightened than that of any other Italian state, subordination to imperial priorities and preferences aroused deep resentment. It was widely, but wrongly, believed that Lombardy paid a disproportionate tax bill, but the main cause of discontent was Vienna's policy of favouring the port of Trieste at the expense of Venice, and preventing the Lombards from trading outside the empire. After the failure of the revolutions of 1848–49 those resentments grew stronger, as did the appeal of the free trade policies adopted in neighbouring Piedmont.

The one pre-unification state that could afford the luxury of not having an economic or commercial policy was the temporal dominion of the Roman pontiff. Papal government was notorious for its inattention to economic matters, and it was not by chance that the landed elites of Bologna, Ferrara, and Ancona were amongst the most enthusiastic converts to Cavour's economic liberalism, and in 1859 among the first to opt for annexation to the new Kingdom of Italy.

The revolutions of 1848–49, therefore, marked a critical turning point in the economic as well as the political history of the peninsula. Only in the Kingdom of Sardinia had a political formula been reached in which economic growth and dynastic self-interest proved compatible.

Unification: a new context of economic growth

Few had expected the Italian struggles for independence from Austria to bring about the political unification of the Italian states, but economic unification proved more difficult to achieve. The first parliamentary inquiry into the state of agriculture reported in the early 1880s that Italy had no single, but a hundred different agricultural economies. Not only types of farming but also the relations between landowners, tenant farmers, and labourers varied enormously from region to region, forming quite distinct agrarian systems. The small peasant farmsteads of the pre-Alpine foothills and the share-cropping farms of the hill country of Tuscany and central Italy contrasted with the big capitalist estates of the irrigated Po Valley. In the South, landowners compensated for the poverty of the soil through the formation of vast estates known as *latifundi*, which depended on the labour of an impoverished peasantry. But there were also pockets of more fertile land in the Neapolitan Campania, in Apulia, and in Sicily where more specialized crops (olive oil, citrus fruit, almonds, wine) were produced for export.

One feature common to all these different types of farming was the poverty of the rural population. Despite the great beauty of the Italian countryside, the lives of the rural population of both sexes passed in unrelenting hardship. They lived under constant threat of debt, disease, and disaster. The fate of their crops and animals was determined by the unpredictable forces of nature, as vulnerable to summer hail or drought as to winter storms. Disease blighted the peasants' crops and killed their livestock and was their daily companion. In the Veneto and in parts of Lombardy the rural population was afflicted by pellagra, a debilitating disease caused by a diet based exclusively on maize meal (polenta) that attacked the central nervous system causing insanity and premature death. The vast coastal swamps caused by centuries of deforestation made malaria endemic in many parts of central and southern Italy. To escape this, agricultural labourers and peasants in the South crowded together in large, impoverished rural cities built on higher ground. But here they were exposed to more typically urban diseases—most dramatically cholera, but also tuberculosis and typhoid fevers. These were commonplaces of life in the larger cities, too, and even by the 1880s only a third of Italian cities had underground water mains and only half any form of sewage disposal.

Political unification did not bring dramatic remedies to these evils. The two decades after unification saw a steady expansion in Italy's foreign trade, but this followed patterns established before unification. The rapid construction of railway lines enabled domestic trade to increase and gave cereal growers in Apulia, for example, access to markets in Rome and northern Italy. But otherwise the pre-unification commercial networks persisted, and southern Italy continued to trade with France, Great Britain, and North America rather than other parts of Italy.

The free trade regime after 1860 did not favour industry. The northern textile industries showed little capacity for expansion, while in the South the loss of the shipbuilding, engineering, and textile industries that had depended on Bourbon protectionism caused widespread unemployment. The loss was the greater because there was little sign of progress in agriculture either, and even those sectors that did succeed in establishing export markets proved vulnerable to fluctuations in the international economy. Exposed to unpredictable markets, southern entrepreneurs looked to minimize risks by investment in a wide range of different activities, and wherever possible to create monopolies. Profits from land were rarely ploughed back into agriculture, but went instead to maintain genteel urban lifestyles or were reinvested in urban property and government stock.

Room for state investment was also tightly constrained. The new state was weighed down by the huge debts resulting from the wars of independence. In 1866 the convertibility of the currency was suspended (*corso forzoso*), and vast tracts of land belonging to religious houses were sold off at knock-down prices. A high percentage of these sales were in the South, but rather than increase productivity the land sales transferred capital from the pockets of southern landowners into the coffers of the state, whose expenditures were focused overwhelmingly in northern Italy.

Free trade was at first considered an almost sacred achievement of the liberal revolution, but in the 1880s began to come under attack from a variety of quarters. Appeals from the northern textile manufacturers for protection received scant attention, however, until the first public inquiries into the state of the army and navy revealed that Italy's newly won independence could not be sustained without strategic new industries. For that reason the government acted as guarantor for Italy's first steel foundry, which was built at Terni in 1884 and backed by a package of government subsidies designed to modernize the merchant fleet and the navy.

When the collapse of European farm prices in the mid-1880s began to devastate Italian agriculture, demands for protection broadened to include agriculture as well. In 1887 the Italian government as a result adopted one of the highest rates of protection in Europe for both industry and agriculture. Historians, like contemporaries, have hotly debated the consequences of Italy's move to protectionism. While it is clear that Italy had little option since every other European state (except Great Britain) abandoned free trade for the same reasons, the debate has focused on whether the Italian tariffs were unnecessarily high and were aimed at the right sectors of the economy. The high protection given to the cotton industry and to agriculture has often been seen as the product of interest lobbying that gave rise to a powerful new political alliance between Italy's nascent industrial sector and traditional agriculture.

The realities were more untidy. Tariff protection divided both industry and agriculture into rival camps, and had contradictory effects. The heavily protected cotton industry did well, although it later ran into serious problems of overproduction. The engineering industries, on the other hand, were not protected but although disadvantaged by the increased cost of the steel produced by heavily protected national foundries they thrived nonetheless. For agriculture, the audit of protectionism was no more straightforward. The principal victims were small peasant farms and the more advanced sectors of southern agriculture, whose products (especially olive oil and wine) were easy targets of retaliatory foreign tariffs. High duties on foreign wheat imports sheltered the most backward landowners in the South, and removed incentives for increasing productivity. But in the Po Valley the same tariffs had the opposite effect and encouraged the adoption of more capital intensive forms of farming. They also forged new links between agriculture and industry, particularly the introduction of sugar beet cultivation on newly reclaimed lands along the south bank of the Po to supply Italy's heavily protected sugar-refining industries in Genoa.

The balance sheet is also complicated by the fact that the new tariffs were quickly followed by a trade war with France in 1889. The consequences were disastrous, and were the immediate cause of the rural unrest in Sicily in 1893 that marked the start of the political crisis that came close to overwhelming parliamentary government in Italy. The economic crisis was the greater because the trade war with France coincided with the collapse of a massive speculative boom in urban development that had grown in scale throughout the 1880s. Italy's leading banks were heavily (and in many cases fraudulently) over-exposed in these investments, and when the speculative bubble burst in 1890 it threatened to bring down the entire banking system.

Yet it was right in the middle of this decade that Italy's new industrial sectors began to expand rapidly, and between 1896 and 1907 the base of Italy's new industrial economy took shape and was consolidated. The new protective tariffs were too recent to have been the main cause of this expansion and many of the most successful new ventures were in high risk sectors, such as the automobile industry, that lacked protection or government subsidies.

The cycle of expansion after 1896 was driven by a revival of international trade, new confidence, and easier access to long-term investment capital. The founding of the Bank of Italy in 1893 to reorganize and regulate the banking system after its near collapse played an important part in restoring confidence. The creation of two new industrial investment banks, the Banca Commerciale Italiano (Comit) and the Credito Italiano, modelled on the German 'mixed' bank also made available the long-term investment capital demanded by the capital intensive and high technology industries of the 'Second' Industrial Revolution. The two mixed banks were closely involved in the development of new sectors such as steel, chemicals, engineering, shipbuilding, and electricity, which played the key role in establishing a modern industrial economy. The first electro-generating plant opened in Milan in 1888, and the expansion of the electro-generating industry also finally emancipated Italy from some of the constraints imposed by the lack of carbon fuel deposits and made it possible to harness Italy's abundant supplies of hydroelectric power.

The new industries were concentrated in northern Italy in the 'industrial triangle' formed by Milan, Genoa, and Turin that extended outwards along the industrial pre-Alpine valleys of northern Piedmont, Lombardy, and the Veneto. But these new developments contrasted with the bleak conditions in the South. Here the decade of Italy's industrial 'take-off' coincided with the beginning of the mass transatlantic emigration, which revealed that the Italian economy was still far from unified: the southern emigrants were drawn not to Italy's industrial cities but to the rapidly expanding cities of the North American seaboard.

The debate on the causes of the 'Southern Question' grew more urgent as evidence of the growing disparity between North and South increased. Some accepted the fatalistic conclusions of the southern landowner Giustino Fortunato, who argued that the natural poverty of agricultural resources—poor soil, low rainfall, lack of irrigation—made it impossible to adopt more intensive forms of agriculture. Many northerners, on the other hand, blamed the corruption and indolence of the southern ruling classes. At the turn of the century another southern landowner turned economist, Francesco Saverio Nitti, challenged Fortunato's pessimistic conclusions, arguing that the fiscal policies of the Italian state had consistently discriminated against the South since unification and starved it of capital. To reverse this, Nitti called for government intervention to create the infrastructures needed to revitalize southern agriculture and at the same time encourage the development of new industries in the South. Nitti fervently believed that hydroelectric power and electricity would open a new industrial vocation for the South. But while many groups in the South responded enthusiastically to Nitti's proposals, they also met with strong opposition from influential local interests who feared that competition from northern concerns backed by powerful banks like the Banca Commerciale would undermine their own economic influence. Despite this opposition, however, Nitti was the architect of the first measures to promote economic development in the South taken by Giolitti's government after the turn of the century.

The growth in Italy's economy by the end of the century had been achieved at the cost of great human hardship and was accompanied by serious internal disparities and dualisms. Protectionism tended to further restrict the domestic consumer market, so that Italy's principal consumer goods industries continued to rely heavily on exports and its heavy industries on demand generated by the state. Although this was by no means an uncommon pattern in late nineteenth-century Europe, it reflected Italy's relatively subordinate position on international markets. The limits of Italy's economic independence were also demonstrated by continuing dependence on foreign capital, and on imports of industrial raw materials and capital goods. Another sign of the underlying poverty of the Italian economy was the growing importance after 1900 of the meagre remittances sent home by the Italians overseas as a source of foreign exchange.

However, the role of the state had been important. That role cannot be limited to the narrower perspective of protectionism after 1887 and has to be seen in broader terms. The policies followed by successive Italian governments had brought political and monetary stability that made Italy attractive for foreign investors. Its fiscal policies had transferred resources from the South to promote the development of modern infrastructures. State intervention had also brought about improved regulation of financial institutions and the promotion of institutional and juridical modernization. State contracts, military procurement, and the preferential terms given to the shipbuilding and railway locomotive industries had also played a key role in promoting major new industrial sectors.

Italian society 1870–1900

By the close of the nineteenth century Italy was the only Mediterranean country to have acquired an industrial base, but it was still far from an industrial society. Nearly 40% of the active population was still engaged in agriculture, which contributed more than 50% of gross national product. These proportions were not far out of line with Italy's wealthiest Continental neighbours, however, and disguised important changes. As in the rest of Europe, Italy's population had expanded at unprecedented rates: from around 18 million in 1800 to 25 million at the time of unification, nearly 30 million by 1887, and over 32 million by 1900. The population was young at the time of unification, but life expectancy was short. Women died earlier than men (the average female life expectancy was 34 years in 1881) and although infant mortality rates had fallen from around 22% in 1860 to 19.5% twenty years later, they remained amongst the highest in Western Europe.

These 'averages' revealed the continuing poverty of Italians, but they also concealed widely different realities. At the time of unification 74% of Italians were illiterate, for example, but even within the North illiteracy rates had varied between 53% in Lombardy and 83% in Umbria in 1865, whereas in the Mezzogiorno they were rarely below 80% and in Sicily and Sardinia even exceeded 90%. Forty years later, the rates for Piedmont and Lombardy had fallen to 17% and 21%, respectively, but remained at 70% and higher in the rural South. While the number of offspring per couple remained constant in the South, reproduction rates were beginning to fall amongst the northern urban population in the second half of the century.[1]

These statistics reveal the two great divides in Italian society: the first between North and South, the second between the urban and the rural populations. For all classes, the towns were the principal theatres of social and cultural change and it was in the towns that new bourgeois lifestyles took shape. Although the Restoration rulers had qualms about exposing urban society to the unmediated force of the market, they made no attempt to restore the eighteenth-century society of orders. The demise of the aristocracy was recorded in the new civic registers introduced during the French period. The aristocracies did not disappear in the nineteenth century, but became instead a subgroup of the broader category of 'property owners' with no special juridical privilege. The Piedmontese constitution of 1848, for example, omitted any reference to the nobility and established a senate nominated by the king rather than the British model of a hereditary House of Lords.

In economic terms the aristocracy had lost more from the abolition of entails than from the abolition of feudalism. Entails had formerly enabled noble families to transmit their patrimonies intact from one generation to another, and were the key to their independence. No one understood this better than Napoleon, who in 1806 instructed his brother Joseph to introduce the new Civil Code as soon as he reached Naples because 'all wealth that is dependent on entails will vanish, so there will be no powerful families except those whom you choose to create as your vassals'.[2]

Half a century later the Marchese Alfieri explained why the great noble palaces of eighteenth century Turin had been abandoned or divided:

Fortunes then were large and permanent since they were entailed and in fact the younger branches of the family never married. The head of the household maintained them: they filled the army and the high offices of the

---

[1] The statistical data are taken from G. Sabbatucci and V. Vidotto (eds.), Vol. 2, *Il nuovo stato e la società civile* (Bari, Laterza, 1995), pp. 571–970.

[2] Cited in P. Ungari, *Storia del Diritto della Famiglia in Italia* (Bologna, 1974), p. 103.

Church and formed a large society who having nothing else to do studied the art of pleasing ... Now since we have adopted with some modifications the French system of equal partition, our houses have become too large for us.[3]

Even wealthy families now had to think about finding careers for their sons. But this was not easy because, as another Piedmontese nobleman explained, the upper bourgeoisie could not enter the Church, except at the very highest levels, nor could they become physicians since this was looked on 'as a sort of trade'. They could be judges, but not lawyers whose 'social position is not high'. That left just 'the army and the higher branches of civil administration'. Only what he referred to as the 'middle-classes' might 'fill the medical professions and swarm in the employment of the government'.[4]

Occupation and social status were inseparable and a Neapolitan nobleman recalled that before unification a family needed an income of about 2000 ducats a year to rent accommodation in a fashionable part of the city, employ servants and own a carriage. However:

The son of such a family had to adopt the norms of polite society and so could follow no career other than that of a lawyer or public employee. And why? Because the career of a doctor or a surgeon or an architect or notary conferred no status in society. It would have been beneath their station, and so the son of a property owner normally became either a civil servant or else a magistrate. Only provincials who came to Naples to study sought the other professions.[5]

The ownership of land was the only guarantee of social status and Stefano Jacini proudly claimed in 1857 that nowhere in Europe was the middle class more numerous or influential than in Lombardy, but qualified this by adding: 'the middle class to which I refer is in no way comparable to the bourgeoisie on which was based the system of government that has recently collapsed in France [i.e. the July Monarchy] and which was purely commercial and civic.' The Lombard middle class encompassed 'a great variety of trades and professions,

---

[3] Marchese Alfieri to William Nassau Senior, cited in W. Nassau Snr, *Journals Kept in France and Italy 1848–52* (New York, 1973), pp. 308–9.

[4] Count Sclopis to W. Nassau Snr, *Journals*, Vol. 1, pp. 312–13.

[5] Giacomo Saverese, cited in Davis, *Conflict and Control* (London, 1988), p. 309.

as well as men of learning and wealth, yet its economic base lies above all in the possession of land.'[6]

For those on the lower tiers of middle-class respectability, or who depended on a profession to make a living, career opportunities were meagre. Throughout the century the principal obstacle to the development of a broader professional middle class was the relatively slow pace of economic growth. In the private sector, the numbers of trained lawyers, physicians, surgeons, agronomists, and veterinarians increased much more rapidly than jobs. Expansion of public administration before 1860 was also very limited, although it did create new opportunities for lawyers, civil engineers, architects, surveyors, clerks, and administrators, while local and municipal administrations were also now obliged to employ qualified professionals such as physicians (*medici condotti*) and primary school teachers.

Opportunities for employment fell far short of demand, however, and most of these were notoriously badly paid jobs. The situation was also aggravated by the measures adopted by Restoration rulers to limit the expansion of bureaucracy for reasons that were both financial and ideological. In Naples, for example, although the French system of administration was retained after the Restoration, large numbers of public employees were retired or retained part-time to reduce costs. After the revolutions of 1820–21 the purges and cuts were even deeper. In Lombardy, the Austrian government gave preference to non-Italian employees and made access to public employment more costly by extending and so making more expensive the university courses needed to qualify.

Other careers that had formerly been dominated by the propertied classes were also shrinking. The armies of the pre-unification rulers were small and officers were recruited mainly from families of proven royalist loyalty, although the military provided important opportunities for gaining technical skills. Fewer religious orders also meant fewer opportunities for placing surplus sons in monasteries, and by the mid-century women religious outnumbered men for first time. A career in the secular clergy was always more exacting, and while the sons of elite families continued to provide bishops and prelates, the lower ranks of the secular clergy were staffed primarily by the sons of the poor and peasants for whom the seminary was

---

[6] Count S. Jacini, *La Proprietà Fondiaria* (Milan, 1857), p. 169.

one of the very few ways of escaping a life of unceasing toil and hardship.

Middle class under-employment was a major source of political discontent in all the Restoration states, and explains why during the revolutions of 1820–21 and 1848–49 crowds of place-seekers overwhelmed the provisional governments. After unification many contemporaries believed that there had been a disproportionate increase in the state bureaucracy to accommodate the demand for professional employment, but the evidence for this is weak. Between 1870 and 1915 public and professional employment kept pace with the rate of population increase, but no more. Lawyers and public employees were the largest professional groups, while the numbers in the technical and scientific professions were much smaller and down to the end of the century a remarkably high proportion of those with professional qualifications emigrated.

The focus of cultural and professional life remained strongly localized and municipal. The middle classes tended to marry amongst their own and to conduct their professional and social life within the city of their birth, although there were exceptions particularly amongst the more lowly professions. High school teachers were, for example, overwhelmingly southerners while rural primary schools offered one of the few acceptable, although extremely testing, career opportunities open to unmarried women.

Professional associations were invariably local rather than national, and bourgeois lifestyles varied noticeably from one region to another. Cultural innovations such as the limitation of family size, the adoption of new forms of leisure and sporting activities, and the changing status and independence of women, also followed a hierarchy that descended chronologically from North to South.

Despite these regional and local differences, however, bourgeois Italy adopted the norms of bourgeois Europe. It adopted the distinctions between the domestic arena of the family and household and the public world of urban sociability in theatres, clubs, and cafes. Middle-class wives and daughters became both the embodiment and the vessels of respectability and reputation, trapped in narrow worlds whose only ends were marriage, childbearing, and marriage brokering. Except to attend school, respectable women rarely if ever left the house unaccompanied. Amongst the middle classes schooling for girls was rudimentary and primarily devotional, and by the end of the century even in professional families very few women entered higher education and even fewer the professions. Childhood for women was essentially a matter of waiting and preparing for marriage, and for those whose families could not afford or did not care to find marriage partners, the destiny was either the nunnery or the female religious institutions (*conservatori, educande, convitti, asili*) that with varying degrees of comfort and discomfort offered the only protection of female honour available outside the family.

The daughters of the working classes and the peasants were equally prisoners of their virginity, although their lives were very different from those of middle-class women, above all because they worked. But although women made up the majority of the industrial labour force, their work was strictly gendered. They worked in separate shops from the men, normally under a regime of silence strictly overseen by nuns who controlled every aspect of their lives. This was one of the reasons why peasant families were prepared to allow their daughters to work in mills, where they knew that both the workplace and the dormitories where the girls slept were under the vigilant eyes of the overseeing nuns to whom the girls' honour was entrusted.

Amongst the urban working classes the sense of female propriety was also high. But the rapid increase in the number of abandoned infants in the industrial townships that alarmed contemporaries was not a sign of promiscuity, since most of the children left at the doors of religious institutions for foundlings were legitimate. The great majority were children of urban mothers who without the support networks of an extended family were unable to work outside the home and care for an infant at the same time. In most cases, once the children were old enough to take care of themselves the mothers expected to recover them. The horrific mortality rates in the foundling institutions sadly ensured that this rarely happened.

This was just one example of the strategies of adaptation and change that were taking place at all levels of Italian society. Although the founding of the Socialist Party in 1892 has often been interpreted as the beginning of political confrontation demarcated along explicit class lines, the realities of working-class Italy remained very heterogeneous. This was evident in the mixture of different constituencies from which the Socialist Party drew its votes, which reached over 200,000 in the elections of 1900. Although the party had established close links with the principal workers' unions, the narrow suffrage for parliamentary elections ensured that its leadership remained almost exclusively middle class, while it also had broad electoral support amongst the professional middle classes. As well as peasants and rural labourers, its popular constituencies included both industrial and more traditional craft workers, and large sections of the urban petite bourgeoisie.

The nature and interests of these constituencies were varied and illustrated the different ways in which working people had responded to the challenges of modernization. The poorest took the path of seasonal and permanent emigration, either overseas or to the new industrial centres. Those able to organize collectively to strengthen their bargaining position did so, like the industrial workers and the landless *braccianti* of the lower Po Valley. But there were other variants, too, and in other parts of northern Italy the integration of agricultural and industrial activities gave peasant households an alternative to emigration that reinforced an older patriarchal style of life. But continuity was only possible through adaptation and change.

The most important changes were occurring in the cities, however. Here, too, the occupational structures of the poor were varied, and the vast majority of urban working families formed part of a cohesive urban fabric tied to the older craft trades and the myriad of urban service industries. Even in the industrializing towns, the inner cities retained their integrated social topographies in which the street and district remained the principal focus of life. But the introduction of universal male suffrage for municipal elections in 1888 marked the beginning of wider popular participation in civic and public affairs, and gave rise to new forms of political and civic organizations whose principal aim was the improvement of municipal services.

Once again Italy was divided, and the initiatives came from the North. The first municipal Chamber of Labour was founded in Milan in 1890 on the model of the French Bourses de Travail to help the unemployed find work, and the model spread to other Italian cities. In 1893 the Milan Humanitarian Society was founded as a private charity dedicated to improving the conditions of working people, with a programme of educational initiatives that included the establishment of a popular university, technical training schools for workers, people's libraries, and a social museum.

Other forms of working-class recreational, cultural, and sporting associations were also expanding. The *Casa del Popolo*, a recreational and leisure centre for working people, was established in rural townships in northern and central Italy as well as in the cities. New sporting associations began to attract a wide following amongst the urban working classes and the petite bourgeoisie, and cycling proved particularly popular even though the Church strenuously denounced the use of bicycles by women.

This was only one illustration of the Church's opposition to the new forms of political and cultural association that signalled the growing autonomy of civil society at all levels. Pope Leo XIII's encyclical, *Rerum Novarum* (1891), had committed the Church to winning back the imperilled souls of the European working classes, and under the direction of the lay organization known as the *Opera dei Congressi* the Church became a prime mover in founding rural cooperatives and savings banks, organizing Catholic workers' unions, and in promoting a range of lay cultural and sporting associations. (See also pp. 196–8.)

These initiatives went hand-in-hand with the revival of Marian cults and devotional associations, and the strengthening of Catholic charitable institutions. The aim was to counter the expansion of socialism, but in Italy as elsewhere in Europe this often had the reverse effect and encouraged the formation of new forms of associations that were free of clerical influence. Socialism was a beneficiary of this reaction and many working-class associations adopted socialist affiliations to assert their independence from the influence of the local parish priest, and the resistance to clerical interference reinforced the appeal of socialism in working class subcultures. In the South independent forms of association amongst the working classes were much weaker, although here, too, Catholic associations increased rapidly.

The rapid expansion of new forms of political and recreational associations amongst the working classes and the petite bourgeoisie in northern and central Italy at the end of the century were indications of the emergence of a more open and pluralistic society. In all these respects Italian society by the end of the nineteenth century looked remarkably similar to its Catholic neighbours, and especially to France and Belgium. Where Italy differed was in the high vulnerability of its economy to the unpredictable swings in the international economy. The underlying poverty of large swathes of the population gave them a common platform in the demands for work and food in times of severe economic crisis. During the severe crisis of the 1890s, and again in the recession after 1907, popular protest and unrest took on an appearance of solidarity that in other times it lacked. But the violent political confrontations of those two periods also imposed crude class demarcations that masked the more complex realities of a society that had been reshaped by the same forces that were recasting all European societies in the same period.

Editor's Conclusion

Italy's long nineteenth century ended with a political crisis that came close to overwhelming the liberal parliamentary regime that had been shaped in the *Risorgimento*. Following Crispi's departure in 1896 the political crisis worsened. The new prime minister Di Rudinì responded to renewed strikes and protests against unemployment, high taxes, and bread prices with force, culminating in the decision to use the army against striking Milanese factory workers in May 1898. The spectacle of armed infantry bivouacked in front of the cathedral of Italy's wealthiest and most modern city encaptured only too vividly the dark and menacing political atmosphere of the decade. In the months that followed hundreds of labour leaders, socialist and clerical opponents of the government were sentenced to draconian prison sentences by military courts. Di Rudinì's successor, General Pelloux, attempted to circumvent parliamentary opposition by governing by decree and introduced emergency laws that effectively outlawed the opposition political parties. There were calls for revision of the constitution to give the monarchy and the executive greater powers, and even rumours of a military coup.

When in 1900 King Umberto I was assassinated by an anarchist, Italy's parliamentary regime seemed on the point of collapse. But in fact the crisis had peaked, and in February 1901 a new government committed to replacing the politics of repression with those of consensus and reconciliation came to power, headed by Giuseppe Zanardelli and Giovanni Giolitti.

The significance of that change of political direction will be explored in the next volume in this series. But the crisis of the 1890s brought the age of the *Risorgimento* to an ambivalent close. Although the reactionary and repressive policies of the 1890s had proved unsustainable, the crisis left many unanswered questions. Would the revival of the international economics that marked the opening of the new century lessen social and political tensions in Italy? Would Italy's new industrial vocation reduce or intensify the pains of modernity? Would mass migration and government intervention bring solutions to the poverty of the South? Would more effective ways be found to accommodate the demands of an emergent mass society?

As the new century opened, many foreign observers believed that with the passing of the crisis of the 1890s Italy could look forward to a more stable future.[1] If their optimism would prove misplaced, this was not because the future was already pre-ordained. The nineteenth century had revealed why Italy had experienced the challenges of modernization on difficult and disadvantaged terms. The new century did not promise easier terms. Industrialization was unlikely to reverse Italy's subordinate position in an increasingly competitive international economy, while it threatened to bring new sources of domestic discord. Nor could it quickly redress the precariousness of Italy's status as an independent nation. But this did not mean that history had foreclosed either on the forms these challenges might take in the future, or on how the next generations of Italians would respond to them.

[1] e.g. Bolton King and Thomas Okey, *Italy Today* (London, 1901).

Glossary

Adelfia: a secret society of the Restoration period.

Amalgame: the term used to describe Napoleon's strategy of winning support from individuals who had been associated with different political tendencies in the course of the Revolution, including former political opponents.

Armistice of Villafranca (11 July 1859): instrument by which Napoleon III terminated the war against Austria, without consultation with his ally King Victor Emmanuel.

Asse Ecclesiastica: the lands of religious houses and the former rulers that were put on sale in 1866 to reduce the national debt and finance government expenditure: the majority of these lands were in the South.

Beni nazionali: the lands of religious houses and the former rulers that were put up for sale to finance the reforms of the French period. (See also *Asse Ecclesiatica*.)

Braccianti: farm hands; used specifically to refer to the landless farm labourers in the Po Valley and to distinguish them from peasants (*contadini*) who by contrast either leased or owned plots of land.

Camorra: name for the popular-based criminal associations that had existed from the early modern period in the city of Naples. Comparable in some respects to the Sicilian *mafia*, *camorra* were not only much older but also specifically urban in origin.

Carboneria: name (literally meaning charcoal-burners) taken by one of the principal networks of secret societies, which originated in the South during the period of French rule but later spread to other parts of Italy. Like Freemasons in the eighteenth century, the secret societies were organized in 'lodges'. The organization was probably imported to southern Italy by Jacobin sympathizers in the French army and administration.

Casati Law (1859): legislation regulating the provision of primary education (supplemented by the Coppino Law of 1877).

Central Duchies: collective term for the independent principalities in central Italy: the Duchy of Parma and Piacenza, the Duchy of Modena and Reggio Emilia, the Duchy of Massa Carrara (joined to Modena in 1829), and the Duchy of Lucca (joined to the Grand Duchy of Tuscany in 1847).

Centurioni: militias raised by the papal government to restore order after the insurrections of 1831.

Chamber of Deputies: title of the Piedmontese (and after 1861 the Italian) elected chamber of the parliament. Membership of the Senate was by royal nomination.

Code Napoleon: the code of civil laws introduced in France in 1804, and then extended to all the territories subject to French rule, including the mainland Italian states.

Comuni: the term for towns and villages that formed the initial level of local administration in Italy (in the South the term *università* was also used).

Connubio: meaning 'marriage', the term referred to the parliamentary majority constructed by Cavour in 1852 that included deputies from the groups of the centre-left and centre-right in the Piedmontese parliament.

Corso forzoso: the suspension of convertibility of banknotes; it was introduced in 1866 to protect the exchange value of the lira and remained in force until 1883.

Destra: (Right) name of the political coalitions that identified with Cavour's policies and were in power from 1861 to 1877.

Dominante: term used to describe Venice's authority over the territories and cities of the Venetian *terraferma* (after 1814 termed Venetia).

Estrema: name taken by a group of about 20 radical democrats in the Italian parliament in the 1870s who in the 1880s were the principal opponents of the politics of *trasformismo*. The group played a key role in blocking attempts by Pelloux to limit constitutional and parliamentary rights during the crisis of 1898–99.

Fasci: literally meaning 'a bundle', e.g. of flowers, the word was frequently used at the end of the nineteenth century for associations and clubs: in that sense it was adopted by the Sicilian peasants who tried to negotiate improved collective leases in the early 1890s. This provoked military intervention by the government in 1894.

Fidecommessi: feudal entails designed to prevent the fragmentation of noble patrimonies; where they had survived these were abolished during the period of French rule after 1800, but were selectively reintroduced in some states after the Restoration.

Five Days of Milan: the popular rising of 18–22 March 1848 that forced the Austrians to abandon Milan.

Garibaldini: the volunteers who joined Garibaldi in the expedition to Sicily in May 1860.

Grand Duchy of Tuscany: formerly ruled by descendants of the Medici family; in 1737 Francis of Lorraine (the future husband of Maria Teresa of Austria) became grand duke.

Kingdom of Sardinia: the title acquired by the House of Savoy in 1718, following the acquisition of the island of Sardinia. In addition to Sardinia, the kingdom consisted of the hereditary lands of the House of Savoy (the Duchies of Savoy and Piedmont, and Nice) and its capital was Turin. The Congress of Vienna joined the former Republic of Genoa to the Kingdom in 1815.

Kingdom of the Two Sicilies: since the early fifteenth century the Kingdoms of Naples and Sicily had been part of the Spanish empire, ruled by viceroys in Naples and Palermo. After a brief interlude of Austrian rule, the two crowns became independent dynastic kingdoms in 1734 following the accession of Charles III (the son of Philip V of Spain and Elizabeth Farnese). In 1759 Charles became king of Spain and was succeeded by his infant son Ferdinand IV (who married Maria Carolina of Austria, the daughter of the Empress Maria Teresa, sister of the Emperor Joseph II, of the Grand Duke Peter Leopold of Tuscany, and of Marie Antoinette, queen of France). Following the revolution of 1799 Ferdinand and Maria Carolina fled to Palermo under the protection of Admiral Nelson: they were restored later in the same year, but in December 1805 were deposed by Napoleon and again fled to Sicily. Napoleon made his brother, Joseph, king of Naples in 1806, but in 1808 he was appointed king of Spain and succeeded in Naples by the emperor's brother-in-law, Joachim Murat (husband of Caroline Bonaparte). After the fall of Murat in 1815 the Congress of Vienna restored Ferdinand IV to the throne of Naples, and in 1816 the crowns of Naples and Sicily were unified to form the Kingdom of the Two Sicilies (the king changed his title to Ferdinand I). In 1825 Ferdinand was succeeded by Francis I (1825–30), and then by Ferdinand II (1830–59). The final Bourbon ruler, Francis II, went into exile following the collapse of the kingdom in 1860.

Latifundi: the Latin term used to describe the vast estates that had developed from the early middle ages in the southern Papal States (Lazio), in Calabria and central and western Sicily; following the abolition of feudalism, new *latifundi* were also created in Apulia. Farming on the *latifundist* estates relied on primitive rotations of cereal growing and livestock grazing, with long periods of fallow. The estates were leased to peasant farmers, who were amongst the poorest section of the Italian rural population. (See also **Transhumance**.)

Law of Guarantees (1871): legislation by the Italian parliament recognizing the independent status of the pope and relinquishing civil controls on the clergy.

Letterati: the world of letters.

Mezzadria: the share-cropping system that in different forms was the dominant agrarian system throughout the hill country of central Italy, especially in Tuscany, Emilia, and Umbria. Share-cropping also existed in parts of northern Italy and in the South.

Mezzogiorno: term used to describe the mainland provinces of the Kingdom of the Two Sicilies.

Monarchia amministrativa: term used to describe the autocratic bureaucracies established at the Restoration of 1814–15.

Muratists: those that had served under Joachim Murat in Naples and retained their office after the Bourbon Restoration of 1815: the term was used again in the 1850s for those who supported the replacement of the Bourbon rulers by one of Murat's descendants.

National Guards: civilian militias raised to maintain order during the revolutions of 1848–49. After the revolutions royalists militias were organized, but when the war against Austria started in 1859 the wealthier supporters of the Piedmontese monarchy in central Italy and in the South established their own militias to protect property and take over local administration.

Neo-Guelphs: the term had originally described the medieval supporters of the papacy against the Holy Roman Emperor (whose supporters were *ghibellines*)—in the 1840s it was used for those who supported Vincenzo Gioberti's appeal to the papacy to lead the movement for independence from Austria.

Non-expedit: papal instruction (1868) prohibiting Catholics from standing for election or voting in parliamentary elections.

Opera dei Congressi: lay Catholic organization founded in 1874.

Opere Pie: charitable foundations (hospitals, hospices, homes for unmarried women and foundlings), many of them religious, which were placed under public control in 1890.

Papal States: title of the temporal dominions ruled by the popes. In 1815 these included the provinces of Emilia, Romagna, the Marche, Umbria, and Lazio. The northern border extended to the Po River and to the south bordered the Kingdom of the Two Sicilies along the mountainous frontiers of the Abruzzi and the Terra di Lavoro. Further south Benevento was also a papal possession, while the tiny Republic of San Marino was independent of papal rule. Bologna, Ferrara, Ravenna, and Forlì had special status as Legation cities and were governed by cardinal legates on behalf of the pope.

Party of Action: founded by Mazzini in 1853 to unite the opponents of Cavour's policies.

Porta Pia: the section of the city wall of Rome breached by Italian *bersaglieri* on 20 September 1870 at the start of the occupation of the city.

Quadrilateral: the four fortresses of Verona, Peschiera, Mantua, and Legnano that gave Austria military control of the Po Valley, and hence the whole of Italy.

Rerum Novarum (1891): encyclical of Leo XIII that set out the Church's position on social policy and denounced socialism.

Restoration: the restoration of the legitimist rulers by the Congress of Vienna (1814–15); the term is also used to refer to the period down to the revolutions of 1848–49.

Risorgimento: the term (meaning 'rebirth') adopted by writers in the 1840s to describe Italy's cultural and political revival.

Salasco Armistice (7 August 1848): instrument by which Charles Albert abandoned his claims to Lombardy and Venetia following the Austrian victory at Custoza (23 July 1848).

Sbirri: a popular term used throughout Italy for the *ancien régime* police.

Scrutin de liste: An electoral system based on multi-member colleges, in which electors cast several votes, choosing from lists of candidates presented by each party.

Siccardi Laws: legislation in Piedmont in 1851 reducing and abolishing ecclesiastical jurisdictions in civil affairs.

Sinistra: (Left) name of political coalition led by Agostino Depretis that came to power in 1877.

'**Southern Question**': the debates and inquiries that began in the decade after unification over the reasons for the economic, social, and cultural disparities between the North and the South which have continued, although in varying terms, down to the present.

Statuto: the constitution conceded by Charles Albert of Piedmont in March 1848, which formed the basis of the Italian constitution of 1861 and remained in force until Mussolini's *coup d'état* of January 1925.

Syllabus of Errors (1864): part of the papal encyclical *Quanta cura* that listed the political ideas deemed unacceptable by the papacy.

Terre irredente (or *irredenta*): the Italian-speaking territories that remained under Austrian control after 1870 (south Tyrol and Trieste).

Toppau Protocol (November 1820): the agreement between the Austrian government and the Italian rulers that sanctioned Austrian armed intervention in the Italian states.

Transhumance: the system of migrant livestock (primarily sheep) grazing to be found throughout the Mediterranean, involving seasonal movement of huge numbers of sheep to mountain pastures in the spring and to coastal pasture in the winter. Modelled on the Spanish Mesta, feudal law guaranteed the migrant flocks right of passage across private land along defined routes. Transhumant grazing was the dominant form of agrarian activity in southern Tuscany (the Maremma), the southern Papal States, and throughout the Mezzogiorno and Sicily. The traditional migrations moved backwards and forwards across political frontiers, but were threatened by enclosures and the abolition of feudalism in the eighteenth and nineteenth centuries.

Trasformismo: term for the construction of cross-bench parliamentary majorities on the basis of political favours and patronage. The system developed most fully under Depretis (leader of the Sinistra, and prime minister between 1876 and 1887).

Triple Alliance (1882): diplomatic alliance between Italy, Prussia, and Austria–Hungary.

Vatican I (1870): the first Vatican council convened in Rome, which endorsed the doctrine of papal infallibility.

Verismo: Italian term for realism in art.

Zelanti: ('zealots'): name given to the ultra-conservative cardinals in Rome after the Restoration who opposed Cardinal Consalvi's attempts at reform.

Further reading

General

The principal English-language bibliographies for each chapter are listed below. Recent general studies of the period include: S. J. Woolf, *A History of Italy 1700–1860: The Social Constraints of Political Change* (2nd edn, London, 1988); H. Hearder, *Italy in the Age of the Risorgimento* (London, 1983); D. Mack Smith, *Modern Italy: A Political History* (New Haven and London, 1997); C. Seton Watson, *Italy from Liberalisn to Fascism 1870–1925* (London, 1967); M. Clark, *Modern Italy 1871–1995* (London, 1996).

Short but up-to-date overviews can also be found in the essays in G. Holmes (ed.), *The Oxford Illustrated History of Italy* (Oxford, 1997), while L. J. Riall *The Italian Risorgimento: State, Society and National Unification* (London, 1994) reviews recent interpretations of the nineteenth century. There are now also two journals dedicated specifically to modern Italian history that carry a wide range of articles and book reviews: *The Journal of Modern Italian Studies* and *Modern Italy*.

Chapter 1

For the Napoleonic period, see S. J. Woolf, *A History of Italy 1700–1860: The Social Constraints of Political Change* (2nd edn, London, 1988); R. Palmer, *The Age of the Democratic Revolution*, Vol. II (Princeton, NJ, 1964), provides useful information on the revolutionary triennium. On the Republic and Kingdom of Italy, see articles by A. Grab, 'Army, state and society: Conscription and desertion in Napoleonic Italy (1802–1814)', in *The Journal of Modern History*, 67 (1995); 'The politics of finance in Napoleonic Italy (1802–1814)', in *The Journal of Modern Italian Studies* 3 (2) (1998). On the army of the Kingdom of Italy, F. Della Peruta, 'War and society in Napoleonic Italy: The armies of the Kingdom of Italy at home and abroad', in J. Davis and P. Ginsborg (eds), *Society and Politics in the Age of the Risorgimento: Essays in Honour of Denis Mack Smith*, (Cambridge, 1991). On the end of the Kingdom of Italy, see J. Rath, *The Fall of the Kingdom of Italy (1814)* (New York, 1941). On southern Italy, see works by J. Davis: '1799: The Santafede and the crisis of the *ancien regime* in southern Italy', in Davis and Ginsborg (eds), *Society and Politics in the Age of the Risorgimento*; 'The Napoleonic era in southern Italy: An ambiguous legacy?', in *Proceedings of the British Academy*, Vol. 80: *1991 Lectures and Memoirs*. On the Kingdom of Sardinia under Napoleon, M. Broers, *Napoleonic Imperialism and the Savoyard Monarchy, 1773–1821: State Building in Piedmont* (Lewiston, NY, 1997). Also by Broers, see 'Policing Piedmont:

"The well ordered police state" in the age of revolution, 1794–1821', *Criminal Justice History*, xv (1994); 'Revolution as vendetta: Patriotism in Piedmont, 1794–1821', *Historical Journal*, 33 (1990). On law and order throughout Italy, J. Davis, *Conflict and Control: Law and Order in Nineteenth Century Italy* (London, 1988).

Chapter 2

In Italian, the fullest survey of the Restoration era and the revolutions is to be found in Volumes 2 and 3, respectively, of G. Candeloro, *Storia d'Italia Moderna* (Milan, 1958 and 1960), which should be read in conjunction with M. Meriggi, 'Società, istituzioni e ceti diregenti', in R. P. Coppini, A. De Francesco, M. Meriggi, G. Pescosolido, *Storia d'Italia. 1. Le premesse dell' unità: Dalla fine del settecento al 1861* (Rome–Bari, 1994). On the Austrian hegemony in Italy established by the Congress of Vienna, see D. Laven, 'Austria's Italian Policy reconsidered: Revolution and reform in Restoration Italy', *Modern Italy*, 2 (1997). For the Habsburg Kingdom of Lombardy–Venetia, see R. J. Rath, *The Provisional Austrian Regime in Lombardy–Venetia 1814–1815* (Austin, Texas, 1969), and M. Meriggi's important *Amministrazione e classi sociali nel Lombardo-Veneto (1814–1848)* (Bologna, 1983). K. R. Greenfield, *Economics and Liberalism in the Risorgimento: A Study of Nationalism in Lombardy 1815–1848* (Baltimore, 1934) is still an important account of the development of moderate opposition in Lombardy. On the Napoleonic legacy in Piedmont, see M. Broers (1997). For the reign of Charles Albert see *Dallo stato assoluto allo stato costituzionale: Storia del regno di Carlo Alberto dal 1831 al 1848* (Turin, 1980). There is a wider available literature on the Papal States: E. E. Y. Hales, *Revolution and the Papacy 1769–1846* (London, 1960) gives a slightly old-fashioned, but clear and perceptive account of papal politics in the Restoration era. More detailed and demanding is A. J. Reinerman, *Austria and the Papacy in the Age of Metternich*, 2 vols (Washington, DC, 1979 and 1989). S. C. Hughes, *Crime, Disorder and the Risorgimento: The Politics of Policing in Bologna* (Cambridge, 1994) is excellent on the ambivalent nature of the papal authorities towards reform. For the Kingdom of the Two Sicilies little is available in English beyond J. A. Davis's detailed study of Bourbon economic policies, *Merchants, Monopolists and Contractors: A Study of Economic activity and Society in Bourbon Naples, 1815–60* (New York, 1981). In Italian, see P. Villani, *Mezzogiorno tra riforme e rivoluzione* (Rome–Bari, 1974); C. Cingari, *Mezzogiorno e risorgimento: La restaurazione a Napoli dal 1821 al 1830* (Bari, 1970), and R. Moscati, *Ferdinando II di Borbone nei documenti diplomatici austriaci* (Naples, 1947). For the smaller states there is even less available in English. In Italian, B. Montale, *Parma nel Risorgimento* (Milan, 1993) is a useful collection of articles most of which have appeared elsewhere. For Tuscany, E. Sestan, *La Firenze di Vieusseux e di Capponi*

(Florence, 1986) gives a good insight into Restoration Florence, especially as an intellectual centre.

Until recently much of the literature on opponents and critics of the Restoration order tended to place a strong, and rather uncritical, emphasis on patriotic struggle. Consequently most pre-1970 material needs to be read with caution, as does some more recent work. Useful studies include F. Della Peruta, *Mazzini e i rivoluzionari italiani: Il partito d'azione, 1830–1845* (Milan, 1974) and C. M. Lovett, *The Democratic Movement in Italy 1830–1876* (Cambridge, Mass., 1982). The same author's *Carlo Cattaneo and the Politics of the Risorgimento* (The Hague, 1972) provides a useful introduction to the ideas of the Milanese polymath. R. Marshall, *Massimo d'Azeglio: An Artist in Politics 1798–1866* (Oxford, 1966) is an enjoyable biography of an important moderate thinker. On the 1848–49 revolutions, by far the best book in English is P. Ginsborg, *Daniele Manin and the Venetian Revolution of 1848–9* (Cambridge, 1979), which deals with issues that go far beyond the Venetian provinces. Adopting a radically different perspective is A. Sked, *The Survival of the Habsburg Empire: Radetzy, the Imperial Army and the Class War, 1848* (London, 1979), a stimulating study of the Austrian response to the Lombard rising. Also useful is H. Hearder, 'The making of the Roman Republic, 1848–9', *History*, **60** (1975). For a lively account of the revolution in Sicily, see D. Mack Smith, *A History of Sicily: Modern Sicily after 1713* (New York, 1968). For the south in general during the revolutionary period, see E. Di Ciommo, *La nazione possibile. Mezzogiorno e questione nazionale nel 1848* (Milan, 1993).

Chapter 3

Anglophone readers are well served by the literature on Mazzini in English. While the *Edizione Nazionale* of Mazzini's *Scritti editi ed inediti* (Imola, 1906–90), 106 vols, is the indispensable source for any scholarly study of Mazzini, there are several useful English-language collections of his writings. The most comprehensive, though couched in archaic-sounding English, is the *Life and Writings of Joseph Mazzini* (London, 1890–91), 6 vols. Slenderer compilations include N. Gangulee (ed.), *Giuseppe Mazzini, Selected Writings* (London, 1945); B. King (ed.), *Mazzini's Letters* (London, 1930); T. Okey (ed.), *Essays by Joseph Mazzini* (London, 1894); and I. Silone's *The Living Thoughts of Mazzini* (New York, 1939). Another important source is Mazzini's *Letters to an English Family* (London, 1920–22), 3 vols.

Major biographies of Mazzini in English include S. Barr, *Mazzini: Portrait of an Exile* (New York, 1935); G. O. Griffith, *Mazzini: Prophet of Modern Europe* (London, 1932); B. King, *The Life of Mazzini* (London, 1902); D. Mack Smith, *Mazzini* (New Haven, 1994), and R. Sarti, *Mazzini: A Life for the Religion of Politics* (Westport, CT, 1997). For an overview of Mazzini's nationalist ideology, see the chapter on Mazzini in H. Kohn, *Prophets and peoples: Studies in Nineteenth-Century Nationalism* (New York, 1946). G. Salvemini's *Mazzini* (London, 1956) is better at capturing the multifaceted nature of Mazzinian thought.

Other studies look at specific aspects or moments of Mazzini's life. His youth and conspiratorial activities before his arrival in England are the topic of E. E. Y. Hales, *Mazzini and the Secret Societies* (New York, 1956). The English stay is covered in W. Roberts, *Prophet in Exile: Joseph Mazzini in England, 1837–1868* (New York, 1989). On the same subject, see also E. Morelli, *Mazzini in Inghilterra* (Florence, 1938). For a neglected but important topic, see F. Gunther Eyck, 'Mazzini's Young Europe', *Journal of Central European Affairs*, XVII (1958). For Young Italy, see S. Mastellone, *Mazzini e la Giovine Italia, 1831–1834* (Pisa, 1960). Mazzini features prominently in G. M. Trevelyan's marvellously readable *Garibaldi's Defence of the Roman Republic, 1848–49* (London, 1914). For Mazzini's dealings with other Italian patriots and currents, see R. Grew, *A Sterner Plan for Italian Unity: The Italian National Society in the Risorgimento* (Princeton, 1963), and C. M. Lovett, *The Democratic Movement in Italy, 1830–1876* (Cambridge, MA, 1982).

Chapter 4

While there is an enormous body of literature on the contributions of Cavour and Piedmont to Italian unification, little new scholarly work has appeared on the subject since the late 1970s. The most recent general accounts in English that examine the Piedmontese role in the *Risorgimento* include D. Beales, *The Risorgimento and the Unification of Italy* (London, 1971), S. J. Woolf (1988); H. Hearder, *Italy in the Age of the (1983)*; F. Coppa, *The Italian Wars of Independence* (London–New York, 1992); A. Lyttelton, 'The national question in Italy', in M. Teich and R. Porter (eds), *The National Question in Europe in Historical Perspective* (Cambridge, 1993); and L. J. Riall (1994). For an updated survey of the latest interpretations and scholarship in Italian on the subject, readers should consult G. Candeloro, *Storia dell'Italia moderna*, Vol. IV, *Dalla rivoluzione nazionale all'unità, 1849–1861* (Milan, 1990); N. Nada and P. Notario, *Il Piemonte sabaudo: Dal periodo napoleonico al Risorgimento* in G. Galasso (ed.), *Storia d'Italia*, Vol. VIII (Turin, 1993), and R. P. Coppini, 'Il Piemonte sabaudo e l'unificazione (1849–1861)', in G. Sabbatucci and V. Vidotto (eds), *Storia d'Italia*, Vol. I, *Le premesse dell'Unità* (Bari, 1994).

D. Mack Smith, *Cavour* (London, 1985) provides a useful, albeit critical, introduction to the life of Camillo Benso di Cavour. Other recent biographies in English include F. Coppa, *Camillo Benso di Cavour* (New York, 1973) and H. Hearder, *Cavour* (London, 1994). For the most deeply researched and richest treatments of the Piedmontese statesman and his role in Italian unification, the work of R. Romeo remains without a parallel; see, in particular, *Dal Piemonte sabaudo all'Italia liberale* (Turin, 1963), *Cavour e il suo tempo*, 3 vols (Bari, 1969–84), and *Vita di Cavour* (Bari, 1984).

Romeo's multi-volume study also offers a thorough examination of economic developments in Piedmont in the nineteenth century, while in English P. Howell, *Capitalism in the Risorgimento* (Berkeley, 1983) and V. Zamagni, *The Economic History of Italy 1860–1990* (Oxford, 1993) survey changes in the decades preceding unification. For different perspectives on Church–state conflicts in Piedmont, see E. E. Y. Hales, *Pio Nono* (New York, 1954) and F. Coppa, *Pope Pius IX: Crusader in a Secular Age* (Boston, 1979). On the dramatic events of 1859 and 1860, readers should consult A. Blumberg, *A Carefully Planned Accident: The Italian War of 1859* (London, 1990) and D. Mack Smith's classic, *Cavour and Garibaldi: A Study in Political Conflict* (2nd edn, Cambridge, 1985).

Chapter 5

There is no single book in English which covers the whole period 1848 to 1876 in southern Italy. For an introduction to Sicilian history, readers should consult the relevant chapters of D. Mack Smith, *A History of Sicily: Vol II, Modern Sicily after 1713* (London, 1968). L. Riall, *Sicily and the Unification of Italy: Liberal Policy and Local Power, 1859–66* (Oxford, 1998) is a detailed study which focuses on the years of national unification. In Italian, R. Romeo, *Il Risorgimento in Sicilia* (Bari, 1950) is the fundamental starting point. The mainland south is even less well served in the English-language literature, although the main events and protagonists are discussed in S. J. Woolf (1988) and there is a chapter on the Kingdom of the Two Sicilies in H. Hearder, *Italy in the Age of the Risorgimento* (London, 1983). A. Spagnoletti, *Storia del Regno delle Due Sicilie* (Bari–Rome, 1997) is the most useful, and up-to-date, textbook in Italian. For the social history of the *Mezzogiorno*, the most important general study is J. A. Davis (1988); D. Mack Smith analyses the land problem in 'The Latifundia in modern Sicilian history', *Proceedings of the British Academy*, 51 (1965), an issue examined from a different, more favourable perspective in M. Petrusewicz, *Latifundium: Moral Economy and Material Life in a European Periphery* (Ann Arbor, 1996). There are detailed analyses of elites and community conflict in G. Fiume, 'Bandits, violence and the organization of power in Sicily in the early nineteenth century', in J. A. Davis and P. Ginsborg (eds), *Society and Politics in the Age of the Risorgimento: Essays in Honour of Denis Mack Smith* (Cambridge, 1991), and P. Pezzino, 'Local power in southern Italy', in R. Lumley and J. Morris (eds), *The New History of the Italian South: the Mezzogiorno Revisited* (Exeter, 1997).

The events of 1848–49 in southern Italy and their aftermath are discussed in specific sections of C. M. Lovett's biographical study, *The Democratic*

Movement in Italy: 1830–1876 (Cambridge, MA, 1982); the decline and fall of the Bourbon kingdom is described in vivid, anecdotal terms by H. Action in *The Last Bourbons of Naples, 1825–61* (London, 1961). For the events leading up to the overthrow of the Bourbons by Garibaldi and Garibaldi's government, see Riall (1998). D. Mack Smith's classic analysis of the relationship between Cavour and Garibaldi, and of the conflicts which led to the unification of north and south, is in *Cavour and Garibaldi: A Study in Political Conflict* (2nd edn, Cambridge, 1985). Also of crucial importance is his description of social conflict in 1860, 'The peasants' revolt in Sicily: 1860', in D. Mack Smith, *Victor Emmanuel, Cavour and the Risorgimento* (London, 1971). For a similar in-depth analysis of political conflict on the southern mainland, only Italian-language literature is available: see, in particular, A. Scirocco, *Il Mezzogiorno nella crisi dell'unificazione 1860–1* (Naples, 1981).

The brigands' war after 1860 is described in Davis, *Conflict and Control*, and there is an interesting commentary in J. Dickie, 'A world at war: the Italian Army and brigandage', *History Workshop Journal*, 33 (1992). On the problems of law and order and the military campaigns in Sicily, see Riall (1998). The debate on the origins and character of the 'southern question' has generated a substantial and impressive literature, but it is mostly in Italian. For contributions in English, see in particular J. A. Davis, 'Casting off the 'Southern Problem': or the peculiarities of the South reconsidered', in J. Schneider (ed.), *Italy's 'Southern Question': Orientalism in One Country* (Oxford, 1998) and the same author's earlier essay, 'The south, the Risorgimento and the origins of the "southern problem"', in J. A. Davis (ed.), *Gramsci and Italy's Passive Revolution* (London, 1979). For a critical analysis of revisionist literature see J. Morris, 'Challenging *meridionalismo*: constructing a new history for southern Italy', in Lumley and Morris (eds) (1997).

Chapter 6

This period has in general been less well studied, certainly in English, than the periods that both precede and follow it. Useful introductions—from varying standpoints—can be found in: B. Croce, *A History of Italy 1871–1915* (Oxford, 1929); D. Mack Smith, *Modern Italy: A Political History* (New Haven and London, 1997); C. Seton-Watson, *Italy from Liberalism to Fascism* (London 1967); M. Clark, *Modern Italy 1871–1995* (London, 1996); G. Candeloro, *Storia d'Italia, Vol. VI 1870–1914* (Milan, 1970); R. Romanelli, *L'Italia liberale (1861–1900)* (Bologna, 1979); G. Sabbatucci and V. Vidotto (eds), *Storia d'Italia*, Vol. 2, *Il nuovo Stato e la società civile* (Rome–Bari, 1995), and Vol. 3, *Liberalismo e democrazia* (Rome–Bari, 1994). F. Chabod, *Storia della politica estera italiana dal 1870 al 1896*. Vol. 1, *Le premesse* (Bari, 1951), now available in F. Chabod, *Italian Foreign Policy: The Statecraft of the Founders* (Princeton, NJ, 1996), is a classic study of the political landscape and culture of the period and one of the great works of post-war European historiography. Church–state relations have not been adequately explored, but A. C. Jemolo, *Church and State in Italy 1850–1950* (Oxford, 1960) is a useful starting point. For the southern question, see the relevant chapters in J. A. Davis, *Conflict and Control: Law and Order in nineteenth century Italy* (London, 1988). In Italian, the best introduction to the southern question is the anthology assembled by R. Villari, *Il Sud nella storia d'Italia* (Rome–Bari, 1978). For economic issues relating to the southern question, see V. Zamagni, *The Economic History of Italy 1860–1990* (Oxford, 1993). On anarchism and early socialism there are several fine studies in English: R. Hostetter, *The Italian Socialist Movement: Origins 1860–1882* (Princeton, 1958); M. G. Gonzalez, *Andrea Costa and the Rise of Socialism in the Romagna* (Washington, DC, 1980); N. Pernicone, *Italian Anarchism 1864–1892* (Princeton, 1993). A good study of local working-class politics is D. H. Bell, *Sesto San Giovanni: Workers, Culture and Politics in an Italian town, 1880–1922* (Rutgers, 1986). Milan has been looked at by L. Tilly, *Politics and Class in Milan 1881–1991* (New York, 1992), and from a more specific perspective by J. Morris, *The Political Economy of Shopkeeping in Milan 1886–1922* (Cambridge, 1993); Naples by F. M. Snowden, *Naples in the Time of Cholera 1884–1911* (Cambridge, 1995). A lively introduction to the culture of disillusionment in this period is R. Drake, *Byzantium for Rome: The Politics of Nostalgia in Umbertian Italy, 1878–1900* (Chapel Hill, 1980). For the intellectual debates over the shortcomings of parliament and parliamentary government see L. Mangoni, *Una crisi fine secolo: La cultura italiana e la Francia fra Otto e Novecento* (Turin, 1985). The dilemmas and contradictions surrounding the implementation of liberalism by the state in these years have been well explored by R. Romanelli in various important works. See, for example, *Il comando impossibile: Stato e società nell'Italia liberale* (new edn, Bologna, 1995). The best study of Depretis and 'transformism' remains that of G. Carocci, *Agostino Depretis e la politica interna italiana dal 1876 al 1887* (Turin, 1956). Despite his importance and interest Crispi has been ill-served in both English and Italian. His private papers were edited and published in various volumes after his death by his nephew. A selection appeared in English as, F. Crispi, *The Memoirs of Francesco Crispi*, 3 vols (London, 1922). There is a short biography by S. Romano, *Crispi: Progetto per una dittatura* (Milan, 1973), and a longer one by M. Grillandi, *Francesco Crispi* (Turin, 1969). Neither is very illuminating. For Crispi's foreign policy, see the fine study by R. Mori, *La politica estera di Francesco Crispi (1887–1891)* (Rome, 1973). For foreign policy generally in this period, there is in English, C. J. Lowe and F. Marzari, *Italian Foreign Policy 1870–1940* (London, 1975). For the African campaigns of the 1880s and 1890s, the best general work is that of A. Del Boca, *Gli italiani in Africa orientale: dall'unità alla marcia su Roma* (Bari, 1976). An excellent more recent study is N. Labanca, *In marcia verso Adua*

(Turin, 1993). In English the African campaigns and the politics of the Italian army in these years are explored by J. Gooch, *Army, State and Society in Italy 1870–1915* (London, 1989), and J. Whittam, *The Politics of the Italian Army 1861–1918* (London, 1976). An extremely acute analysis of the political and economic crisis of the 1890s is G. Manacorda, *Dalla crisi alla crescita: Crisi economica e lotta politica in Italia 1892–1896* (Rome, 1993). The important, and at times decisive, role of the monarchy in Italian politics in this period can be studied from D. Mack Smith, *Italy and its Monarchy* (New Haven and London, 1989). For an extraordinary contemporary picture of the malevolence and intrigue of Italian politics in the 1890s by a well-placed insider, see D. Farini, *Diario di fine secolo* (ed. E. Morelli) (Rome, 1961).

Chapter 7

English-language scholarly works on religion in Italy in the nineteenth century are few. Only where Church history interacts with political history are many sources to be found, for any general history of Italy in this period must deal with the fraught relations between the Church and the state. For the years from the French occupation to the founding of the Italian Republic, see S. J. Woolf, *A History of Italy 1700–1860: The Social Constraints of Political Change* (2nd edn, London, 1988); for the later decades of the nineteenth century see the new edition of D. Mack Smith's *Modern Italy: A Political History* (New Haven and London, 1997). F. Coppa has written biographical studies both of Pius IX— *Pope Pius IX: Crusader in a Secular Age* (Boston, 1979), and his secretary of state— *Cardinal Giacomo Antonelli and Papal Politics in European Affairs* (Albany, 1990). On church–state relations, see also E. E. Y. Hales, *Italy and the Vatican at War* (New York, 1968) and, more generally for Europe, O. Chadwick's *The Popes and the European Revolution* (Oxford, 1981). On Mazzini's religious ideology, see R. Sarti, *Mazzini: A Life for the Religion of Politics* (Westport, CT, 1997) and D. Mack Smith, *Mazzini* (New Haven, 1994). For insight into the role of the Church in enforcing public morality under the Papal States, see D. I. Kertzer, *Sacrificed for Honor: Italian Infant Abandonment and the Politics of Reproductive Control* (Boston, 1993). For a look at popular religious practices over the centuries, see M. P. Carroll's books, *Madonnas That Maim—Popular Catholicism in Italy since the Fifteenth Century* (Baltimore, 1992), and *Veiled Threats—The Logic of Popular Catholicism in Italy* (Baltimore, 1996). On the history of the Jews in Italy, see the classic work by C. Roth, *The History of the Jews of Italy* (Philadelphia, 1946); on the history of the Jews of Rome, see S. Waagenaar, *The Pope's Jews* (La Salle, Illinois, 1964). The history of the Church's relations with the Jews through 1870 may also be gleaned from a dramatic case of forced baptism in D. I. Kertzer, *The Kidnapping of Edgardo Mortara* (New York, 1997).

Chapter 8

Although the literature in Italian on nineteenth-century Italian culture is extensive, the number of works available in English is limited. There are, however, valuable biographies and critical studies for nearly every figure mentioned in this chapter.

A good introduction to the writers can be found in the essays treating this period in L. Pertile and P. Brand (eds), *The Cambridge History of Italian Literature* (Cambridge, 1996). Two older and briefer general works remain useful: E. H. Wilkins, *A History of Italian Literature* (Cambridge, MA, 1954); and C. Cairns, *Italian Literature: The Dominant Themes, Comparative Literature* (New York, 1977). For women writers, see L. Kroha, *The Woman Writer in Late-Nineteenth-Century Italy: Gender and the Formation of Literary Identity* (Lewiston, NY, 1992); S. Wood, *Italian Women's Writing 1860–1994* (London, 1995). On the importance of conceptions of history: C. Della Coletta, *Plotting the Past: Metamorphoses of Historical Narrative in Modern Italian Fiction* (West Lafayette, IN, 1996).

There are a number of valuable essays for the period since unification in *Modern Italy: Images and History of a National Identity*, Vol. I, *From Unification to the New Century* (Milan, 1982); and M. Malatesta (ed.), *Society and the Professions in Italy, 1860–1914* (Cambridge, 1995) analyses elite formation.

C. L. V. Meeks, *Italian Architecture, 1750–1914* (New Haven, 1966) covers the topic well; general histories of music (especially opera) and art in the nineteenth century provide useful background.

Chapter 9

There are two excellent recent economic histories of Italy in this period: G. Toniolo, *An Economic History of Liberal Italy* (London, 1990); V. Zamagni, *The Economic History of Italy 1860–1990: Recovery after Decline* (Oxford, 1993). Shorter accounts can be found in L. Cafagna, 'The industrial revolution in Italy 1830–1914', in C. Cipolla (ed.), *Fontana Economic History of Europe*, Vol. 4 (London, 1973); and G. Mori, 'The process of industrialization in general and in Italy', *Journal of European Economic History* 8 (1979). K. R. Greenfield, *Economics and Liberalism in the Risorgimento* (Baltimore 1934/ 1964), remains an outstanding study of the relationship between economics and politics in the *Risorgimento*, and this has been addressed more recently in S. Patriaca, *Numbers and Nationhood: Writing Statistics in Nineteenth Century Italy* (Cambridge, 1996).

On more specific aspects of economic history, see A. Gerschenkron, *Economic Backwardness in Historical Perspective* (Cambridge, MA, 1962); S. Feonaltea, 'The growth of the Italian silk industry (1861–1913), *Rivista di Storia Economica* ns 5 (1988); S. Feonaltea, 'Italy', in P. O'Brien (ed.), *Railways and the Economic Development of Western Europe 1830–1914* (London, 1983);

J. S. Cohen, 'Italy 1861–1914', in R. Cameron (ed.), *Banking and Development: Some Lessons of History* (London, 1972).

On agriculture, see P. Corner, 'Italy—the eternal late-comer?', in P. Mathias and J. A. Davis (eds), *Agriculture and Industrialization from the Eighteenth Century to the Present Day* (Oxford, 1996). On technology and labour see: J. A. Davis, 'Innovation in an industrial late-comer: Italy in the nineteenth century', in P. Mathias and J. A. Davis (eds), *Innovation and Technology in Europe* (Oxford, 1991); J. A. Davis, 'Entrepreneurs and economic growth: the case of Italy', in P. Mathias and J. A. Davis (eds), *Enterprise and Labour from the Eighteenth Century to the Present* (Oxford, 1996).

On social history, see J. A. Davis, *Conflict and Control: Law and Order in Nineteenth Century Italy* (London, 1988); J. A. Davis and P. Ginsborg (eds), *Society and Politics in the Age of the Risorgimento* (Cambridge, 1991); J. A. Davis (ed.), *Gramsci and Italy's Passive Revolution* (London, 1979). For the debates on social class see A. Lyttelton, 'The middle classes in Liberal Italy', in Davis and Ginsborg (eds), *Society and Politics in the Age of the Risorgimento*; M. Malatesta (ed.), *Society and the Professions in Italy 1860–1914* (Cambridge, 1995); A. L. Cardoza, *Aristocrats in Bourgeois Italy: The Piedmontese Nobility 1861–1930* (Cambridge, 1997).

On more specific aspects of social history see: S. C. Hughes, *Crime, Disorder and the Risorgimento: The Politics of Policing in Bologna* (Cambridge, 1994); S. J. Woolf 'The poor and how to relieve them: the Restoration debate on poverty in Italy and Europe', in Davis and Ginsborg (eds), *Society and Politics in the Age of the Risorgimento*; M. Barbagli, 'Marriage and family in Italy in the early nineteenth century', in Davis and Ginsborg (eds), *Society and Politics in the Age of the Risorgimento*; D. Kertzer, *Sacrificed for Honor: Italian Infant Abandonment and the Politics of Reproductive Control* (Boston, 1993). On urban society before unification see P. Ginsborg, *Daniele Manin and the Venetian Revolution of 1848–9* (Cambridge, 1979) and O. Fallon, *La ville des destins croisés: Recherches sur la société milanaise du xixe siècle* (Rome, 1997). The anglophone bibliography on the urban working classes after unification is vast: for an overview see J. A. Davis, 'Socialism and the working classes in Italy before 1914', in D. Geary (ed.), *Labour and Socialist Movements in Europe before 1914* (London, New York, 1989). On the urban petite bourgeoisie see J. Morris, *The Political Economy of Shopkeeping in Milan 1886–1922* (Cambridge, 1993).

The most recent guides to the vast Italian bibliographies can be found in the volumes of the *Storia d'Italia* edited by G. Sabbatucci and V. Vidotto: Vol. 1, *Le premesse dell'Unità* (Bari, Laterza, 1994); Vol. 2, *Il nuovo stato e la società civile* (Bari, Laterza, 1995); Vol. 3, *Liberalismo e democrazia 1887–1914* (Bari, Laterza, 1996), which also contain detailed statistical tables. On the state see R. Romanelli (ed.), *Storia dello Stato Italiano* (Rome, 1995) and S. Cessese, *Lo*

Stato Introvafile. Modernità ed arretratezza delle i stituzioni Italiane (Rome, 1998). For the social history of this period and the debate on the Italian middle class, see A. M. Banti, *Storia della Borghesia Italiana: L'Età Liberale* (Rome, 1996), and M. De Giorgio's outstanding *Le Italiane dall'Unità a Oggi* (Laterza, 1992), which finally reconstructs the social experience of Italian women in the nineteenth and twentieth centuries.

Chronology

1796 French armies invade Italy; the era of the Italian Republics
–99

1797 Treaty of Campoformio (18 Oct.)

1799 Popular anti-republican risings (summer–autumn)

1800 Napoleon's victory over the Austrians at Marengo (14 June)

1802 Napoleon proclaimed president of the Italian Republic (26 Jan.); publication of Ugo Foscolo's *Le ultime lettere di Jacopo Ortis*

1804 Napoleon crowned emperor of France (2 Dec.)

1805 Napoleon crowned king of Italy in Milan (26 May); after victory over Austrians at Ulm, edict from Schönbrunn Palace deposes Bourbon rulers of Naples and Sicily (Dec.)

1806 Joseph Bonaparte becomes king of Naples (30 Mar.); Berlin Decrees impose blockade of British trade (21 Nov.)

1807 Foscolo writes *Dei sepolcri*

1808 French troops occupy Rome (2 Feb.); Joseph Bonaparte nominated king of Spain (Mar.), replaced in Naples by Joachim Murat (1 Aug.)

1809 Papal States annexed to France (17 May): Pope Pius VII excommunicates Napoleon, is arrested, and imprisoned at Savona

1810 Napoleon's marriage to Maria Luisa of Austria

1812 Sicilian Constitution (Apr.); Spanish Constitution (8 May); start of the retreat from Moscow (19 Oct.)

1813 Napoleon's defeat at Leipzig (Nov.); defection of Joachim Murat

1814 Lombardy and Venetia annexed to Habsburg Empire; restoration of King Victor Emanuel I (Sardinia), Pope Pius VII, Grand Duke Ferdinand III (Tuscany), Duke Francis IV (Modena); Congress of Vienna (1 Nov.)

1815 Murat's 'Appeal to the Italians' (Rimini, 30 Mar.) and defeat at Tolentino (3 May), Ferdinand IV restored to Naples; closure of Congress of Vienna (9 June); Napoleon's defeat at Waterloo (18 June); Emperor Francis I of Austria, Frederick William of Prussia, and Tsar Alexander I of Russia sign the Holy Alliance (26 Sept.)

1816 Administrative reorganization of the restored states: Pius VII's *motu proprio* in Rome (6 July), Tuscany (6 Sept.); creation of the Kingdom of the Two Sicilies (8 Dec.); first performance of Gioacchino Rossini's *Il barbiere di Siviglia* (Rome)

1818 –19 Circulation of the Milanese cultural journal *Il Conciliatore*

1820 Revolution in Naples begins at Nola (1 May); Ferdinand I of Naples takes oath to the constitution (13 July); Palermo rebels against Naples (15–17 July) and declares independence (Aug.); Neapolitan troops land at Messina (Sept.); Holy Alliance powers sanction intervention against revolution in Italy (Toppau, 23 Oct.); Austrian authorities in Milan claim discovery of a Carbonarist lodge

1821 First issue of Gian Piero Vieusseux's *Antologia* in Florence; Congress of Lubjana authorizes Austrian intervention against the revolutionary government in Naples; Spanish Constitution proclaimed at Alessandria (Piedmont); abdication of King Victor Emanuel I; Charles Albert appointed regent; Austrian troops enter Naples (24 Mar.); royalist army led by Charles Felix enters Turin (10 Apr.)

1825 First performance of Rossini's *Semiramide* (Venice); Alessandro Manzoni writes first version of *I promessi sposi*

1831 Modena rising led by Ciro Menotti (Feb.); Austrian troops enter Duchy of Parma, Modena, and the Papal States (1 Mar.); Giuseppe Mazzini founds Young Italy in Genoa (14 Aug.); first performance of Bellini's *Norma* (Milan); publication of Giacomo Leopardi's *I canti*

1834 Mazzinian insurrection in Piedmont fails; Mazzini founds Young Europe (Berne, 15 Apr.)

1835 Emperor Francis I dies and is succeeded as king of Lombardy by Ferdinand I; cholera outbreaks in Lombardy, Venetia, Ancona, and Naples; Gaetano Donizetti composes *Lucia di Lammermoor* (first performance, Naples)

1839 First issue of Carlo Cattaneo's *Politecnico* (Milan, Jan.); first meeting of the Congress of Italian Men of Science (Pisa, 1 Oct.); opening of first Italian railway (Naples to Portici, 3 Oct.)

1840 –42 Manzoni's second version of *I promessi sposi*, substantially rewritten in Tuscan literary idiom

1842 First performance of Giuseppe Verdi's *Nabucco* (La Scala, Milan)

1843 Publication of Vinceno Gioberti's *Moral and Civil Primacy of the Italians* (Brussels)

1844   Publication of Cesare Balbo's *Hopes of Italy* (Paris, Jan.);
Emilio and Attilio Bandiera captured and executed (Cosenza,
24 July)

1845   Mazzinian rising in Rimini (Sept.); Massimo D'Azeglio publishes
his pamphlet *On Recent Events in the Romagna*

1846   Election of Pius IX (17 June)

1847   Pius IX reforms censorship in the Papal States; Leopold II of
Tuscany establishes a *consulta* (Aug.); Turin enters into a customs
league with Rome and Florence; publication of Cavour's journal
Il Risorgimento (Turin)

1848   Rising in Livorno (6 Jan.); insurrection in Palermo (12 Jan.);
Ferdinand of Naples concedes constitutions (11 Feb.), followed by
Leopold II of Tuscany (17 Feb.), Charles Albert of Sardinia
(4 Mar.), Pius IX (14 Mar.); popular rising against Austrians in
Milan (18–22 Mar.: 'le quattro giornate'), Manin declares the
republic in Venice; Charles Albert declares war on Austria
(23 Mar.) and enters Lombardy; Pius IX denounces war against
Austria (29 Apr.), Ferdinand of Naples suspends parliament and
withdraws from war against Austria; Piedmontese forces defeated
by the Austrians at Custoza (24–5 July); Austrians reoccupy
Lombard, Modena, and Reggio Emilia; Venice continues to resist;
in Tuscany, Giuseppe Montaneili and Dominico Guerrazzi head a
radical government (28 Oct.); in Rome Pellegrino Rossi is
murdered (15 Nov.) and Pius IX and cardinals flee to Gaeta
(24 Nov.)

1849   The Roman Republic is established (5 Feb.); Piedmont resumes
war against Austria (12 Mar.) but is again defeated (Novara,
23 Mar.); Charles Albert abdicates and is succeeded by Victor
Emanuel II, who signs the armistice at Vignale (25 Apr.); French
troops land at Civitavecchia to restore the pope; Rome surrenders
(1 July); Victor Emanuel's 'Moncalieri Proclamation' promises to
maintain the constitution (20 Nov.)

1850   Siccardi Laws approved in Piedmont (Apr.); Cavour appointed
minister of agriculture, commerce, and the navy by Massimo
D'Azeglio

1851   Verdi composes *Rigoletto* (first performance, Venice, Mar.); its
success together with that of *Il trovatore* (first performance,
Rome, Jan. 1953) and *La traviata* (first performance, Venice, Mar.
1853) establishes his international reputation

1852   Cavour becomes prime minister in Piedmont (4 Nov.) following
the resignation of D'Azeglio

1853   Mazzinian rising in Milan (6 Feb.)

1855   Piedmont joins Anglo-French alliance against Russia in the Crimea (10 Feb.); Cavour resigns because of opposition to his bill to abolish religious houses but is reinstated as prime minister (4 May); Cavour and Victor Emanuel visit Paris

1856   Paris Peace Congress (Feb.): Britain and France break diplomatic relations with the Kingdom of the Two Sicilies; Austrian troops withdraw from the Romagna (Oct.), but retain garrisons in Bologna and Ancona

1857   Carlo Pisacane's expedition to Sapri (2 July); founding of the Italian National Society in Turin (1 Aug.)

1858   Felice Orsini attempts to assassinate Napoleon III in Paris; secret meeting between Cavour and Napoleon III at Plombières (20–1 July); Mazzini founds new periodical, *Pensiero e Azione*, in London (1 Sept.)

1859   Secret treaty between Victor Emanuel II and Napoleon III signed in Turin (24 Jan.); Austrian ultimatum to Kingdom of Sardinia (24 April) and Austrian invasion of Piedmont (27 Apr.); flight of Leopold II of Tuscany; Franco-Piedmontese victories at Magenta (4 June), Solferino, and San Martino (24 June); armistices signed with Emperor Francis Joseph (8 July) at Villafranca; elected assemblies in Tuscany, the duchies and Legations vote for annexation to Piedmont (Aug.–Sept.)

1860   Cavour resumes office (21 Jan.); plebiscites in Tuscany and Emilia confirm vote for annexation to Piedmont; first elections for the new parliament; annexation of Nice and Savoy to France (15–22 Apr.); revolution in Palermo (3 Apr.); Garibaldi's expedition sails from Quarto, landing at Marsala (11 May); Bourbon troops defeated at Calatafimi (25 June); Francis II of Naples reintroduces the constitution of 1848; Garibaldi enters Naples (7 Sept.); Piedmontese ultimatum to Rome, Piedmontese troops enter the Papal States (18 Sept.); plebiscites on annexation in Kingdom of Two Sicilies (21 Oct.), Umbria, and the Marches (4 Nov.)

1861   First elections for the new Italian parliament; Victor Emanuel of Savoy II assumes title of king of Italy (17 Mar.); rural insurrections spread throughout the Mezzogiorno; Cavour dies (6 June); General Cialdini given emergency powers in the south

1862   Urbano Rattazzi replaces Ricasoli as prime minister (3 Mar.); Garibaldi's attempt to resume the march on Rome halted by the Italian army in the Aspromonte mountains (29 July); Rattazzi resigns (29 Nov.) as prime minister, succeeded by Luigi Carlo

Farini; the term *scapigliatura* begins to be used in connection with the work of young writers, painters, and sculptors in Milan and Turin

1863   Farini resigns, Marco Minghetti becomes prime minister (24 Mar.); Pica Laws on repression of brigandage

1864   Garibaldi's visit to England; Pius IX publishes the *Syllabus of Errors*

1865   Capital moved from Turin to Florence (3 Feb.)

1866   Italy becomes secret ally of Prussia against Austria (8 Apr.); controvertibility of the currency suspended (*corso forzoso*); Prussia declares war against Austria (17 June), followed by Italy (20 June); Italian army defeated at Custoza (24 June); Prussian victory over Austria at Sadowa (3 July); damage inflicted on Italian fleet at Lissa by the Austrian navy; Vienna cedes Venetia to Napoleon III who concedes it to Italy

1867   Garibaldian invasion of Papal States routed at Mentana (3 Nov.); Vatican I begins (8 Dec.)

1870   Napoleon III defeated at the Battle of Sedan (1 Sept.); Italian troops enter Rome (20 Sept.); Rome and Lazio annexed by plebiscite; Pius IX denounces the occupation of Rome and excommunicates Victor Emanuel II; parliament votes to transfer the capital to Rome (23 Dec.)

1871   Transfer of capital to Rome (July)

1876   Minghetti's government of the right falls and Depretis forms government (Mar.)

1878   Death of Victor Emanuel II and succession of Umberto I (Jan.)

1880   Giosue Carducci begins work on *Odi barbare*

1881   Publication of Giovanni Verga's *I malavoglia*

1882   Electoral reform approved (Jan.); Triple Alliance with Germany and Austria–Hungary (May); death of Garibaldi

1887   Renewal of Triple Alliance (Feb.); new tariff approved and Crispi becomes prime minister (June–July)

1891   Papal Encyclical *Rerum Novarum*

1892   Founding of Italian Socialist Party (Aug.)

1896   First performance of Puccini's *La Bohème* (Turin); Abyssinians defeat Italian army at Adowa (1 Mar.); fall of Crispi

1898   Riots in Milan (May)

1900 King Umberto assassinated, Victor Emanuel III succeeds (July)

1901 Death of Giuseppe Verdi (Jan.); Zanardelli and Giolitti form government (Feb.)

Maps

Map 1 Italy in 1797

Map 2 Napoleonic Italy (1807)

Map 3 Italy in 1815

Map 4 Italy in 1861

Map 5 Italy in 1870

Index